FAVORITE BRAND NAME

ALL-NEW

BEST-LOVED
RECIPES
of all time

Publications International, Ltd.

Favorite Brand Name Recipes at www.fbnr.com

All recipes and photographs that contain specific brand names are copyrighted by those companies and/or associations, unless otherwise specified. All photographs *except* those on pages 19, 23, 29, 37, 39, 45, 69, 79, 87, 93, 113, 119, 121, 131, 167, 183, 189, 201, 219, 225, 241, 253, 271, 285, 305, 309, 319, 331 and 359 copyright © Publications International, Ltd.

BREYERS® is a registered trademark owned and licensed by Unilever, N.V.

DOLE® is a registered trademark of Dole Food Company, Inc.

™/© M&M's, M and the M&M's Characters are trademarks of Mars, Incorporated.
© Mars, Inc. 2003.

Nestlé, Ortega and Toll House are registered trademarks of Nestlé.

TACO BELL® and HOME ORIGINALS® are trademarks owned and licensed by Taco Bell Corp.

Butter Flavor CRISCO® all-vegetable shortening and Butter Flavor CRISCO® No-Stick Cooking Spray are artificially flavored.

Some of the products listed in this publication may be in limited distribution.

Pictured on the back cover *(clockwise from top left):* Grilled Sherry Pork Chop *(page 156),* Chocolate Fudge Pie *(page 288)* and Stir-Fry Vegetables *(page 124).*

ISBN: 0-7853-6123-5

Library of Congress Control Number: 2002110206

Manufactured in China.

8 7 6 5 4 3 2 1

Microwave Cooking: Microwave ovens vary in wattage. Use the cooking times as guidelines and check for doneness before adding more time.

Preparation/Cooking Times: Preparation times are based on the approximate amount of time required to assemble the recipe before cooking, baking, chilling or serving. These times include preparation steps such as measuring, chopping and mixing. The fact that some preparations and cooking can be done simultaneously is taken into account. Preparation of optional ingredients and serving suggestions is not included.

CONTENTS

❧ *Great Starters* ❧

Three Pepper Quesadillas

1 cup *each* thin green, red and yellow
    pepper strips
½ cup thin onion slices
½ teaspoon ground cumin
⅓ cup butter or margarine
1 package (8 ounces) PHILADELPHIA®
    Cream Cheese, softened

1 package (8 ounces) KRAFT® Shredded
    Sharp Cheddar Cheese
10 flour tortillas (6 inch)
    TACO BELL® HOME ORIGINALS®*
    Thick 'N Chunky Salsa

TACO BELL and HOME ORIGINALS are registered trademarks owned and licensed by Taco Bell Corp.

COOK and stir peppers, onion and cumin in butter in large skillet 4 minutes or until vegetables are tender-crisp. Drain, reserving butter.

MIX cream cheese and Cheddar cheese until well blended. Spoon 2 tablespoons cheese mixture onto each tortilla; top with scant ⅓ cup vegetable mixture. Fold tortillas in half; place on cookie sheet. Brush with reserved butter.

BAKE at 425°F for 8 minutes. Cut each tortilla into thirds. Serve warm with salsa.

Makes 30 appetizers

Prep Time: 20 minutes
Bake Time: 8 minutes

Make-Ahead: Prepare as directed except for baking; cover. Refrigerate. When ready to serve, bake, uncovered, at 425°F, 15 to 18 minutes or until thoroughly heated.

Three Pepper Quesadillas

Hawaiian Ribs

1 can (8 ounces) crushed pineapple in
    juice, undrained
1/3 cup apricot jam
3 tablespoons *French's*® Classic Yellow®
    Mustard

1 tablespoon red wine vinegar
2 teaspoons grated peeled fresh ginger
1 clove garlic, minced
3 to 4 pounds pork baby back ribs*

*Or, if baby back ribs are not available, substitute 4 pounds pork spareribs, cut in half lengthwise. Cut spareribs into 3- to 4-rib portions. Cook 20 minutes in enough boiling water to cover. Grill ribs 30 to 40 minutes or until no longer pink near bone, brushing with portion of pineapple mixture during last 10 minutes.

1. Combine crushed pineapple with juice, apricot jam, mustard, vinegar, ginger and garlic in blender or food processor. Cover and process until very smooth.

2. Place ribs on oiled grid. Grill ribs over medium heat 40 minutes or until ribs are no longer pink near bone. Brush ribs with portion of pineapple sauce mixture during last 10 minutes of cooking. Cut into individual ribs to serve. Serve remaining sauce for dipping.

Makes 8 servings (1½ cups sauce)

Vegetable Hummus

2 cloves garlic
2 cans (15 to 19 ounces each) chick peas
    or garbanzo beans, rinsed and drained
1 package KNORR® Recipe Classics™
    Vegetable Soup, Dip and Recipe Mix
1/2 cup water

1/2 cup olive oil
2 tablespoons lemon juice
1/4 teaspoon ground cumin
6 (8-inch) whole wheat or white pita
    breads, cut into wedges

• In food processor, pulse garlic until finely chopped. Add remaining ingredients except pita bread. Process until smooth; chill at least 2 hours.

• Stir hummus before serving. If desired, add 1 to 2 tablespoons additional olive oil, or to taste. Serve with pita wedges.

Makes 3½ cups dip

Prep Time: 10 minutes
Chill Time: 2 hours

Hawaiian Ribs

Italian-Topped Garlic Bread

1 pound BOB EVANS® Italian Roll
    Sausage
1 (1-pound) loaf crusty Italian bread
½ cup butter, melted
2 teaspoons minced garlic

2 cups (8 ounces) shredded mozzarella
    cheese
2 cups diced tomatoes
8 ounces fresh mushrooms, sliced
3 tablespoons grated Parmesan cheese

Preheat oven to 325°F. Crumble and cook sausage in medium skillet until browned. Drain off any drippings. Cut bread into 1-inch slices. Combine butter and garlic in small bowl; brush bread slices with mixture. Arrange on ungreased baking sheet. Combine mozzarella cheese, tomatoes, mushrooms, Parmesan cheese and sausage; spread on bread slices. Bake 10 to 12 minutes or until cheese is melted and golden brown. Serve warm. Refrigerate leftovers.

Makes about 10 appetizer servings

Cheddar Cheese Puffs

Puffs
1 cup water
6 tablespoons butter, cut into pieces
1 teaspoon salt
    Pepper to taste
    Ground nutmeg (optional)
1 cup all-purpose flour
5 large eggs, divided

1 cup plus 3 tablespoons finely shredded
    Cheddar or Swiss cheese, divided

Filling
1 (11-ounce) jar NEWMAN'S OWN® All
    Natural Salsa
12 ounces cream cheese, softened

Preheat oven to 425°F. In heavy 2-quart saucepan, place water, butter, salt, pepper and nutmeg. When butter has melted and water is boiling, remove from heat. With wooden spoon, beat in flour all at once. (If mixture does not form a ball and leave the sides of pan clean, return to medium heat and beat vigorously for 1 to 2 minutes.) Remove from heat and beat in 4 eggs, 1 at a time, until each egg is thoroughly blended. Beat in 1 cup cheese. Place in pastry bag with ½-inch-diameter round tip and pipe 1-inch rounds on 2 greased baking sheets. Beat remaining egg. Brush tops of puffs with beaten egg and sprinkle with remaining cheese. Bake 20 to 25 minutes or until golden and crisp; turn off oven. Pierce each puff with a knife and return to cooling oven for 10 minutes to dry out. Remove and cool.

Drain approximately ¼ cup of liquid from salsa (reserve liquid for another use). Mix drained salsa with cream cheese and spoon filling into puffs.

Makes 36 appetizers

Italian-Topped Garlic Bread

Original Ranch® Spinach Dip

1 container (16 ounces) sour cream
   (2 cups)
1 box (10 ounces) frozen chopped
   spinach, thawed and squeezed dry
1 can (8 ounces) water chestnuts, rinsed,
   drained and chopped

1 packet (1 ounce) HIDDEN VALLEY®
   The Original Ranch® Salad Dressing
   & Seasoning Mix
1 loaf round French bread
   Fresh vegetables, for dipping

Stir together sour cream, spinach, water chestnuts and salad dressing & seasoning mix. Chill 30 minutes. Just before serving, cut top off bread and remove center, reserving firm bread pieces. Fill bread bowl with dip. Cut reserved bread into cubes. Serve dip with bread and vegetables.

Makes 2½ cups dip

Humpty Dumpty's Favorite Chicken Nachos

4 boneless, skinless chicken breast halves
   (about 1¼ pounds)
2 tablespoons CRISCO® Oil*
1 packet (1¼ ounces) taco seasoning mix
2 cloves garlic, crushed
1 bag (10½ ounces) tortilla chips

1 can (16 ounces) refried beans
1 jar (16 ounces) prepared mild or
   medium chunky salsa
3 cups (1½ (8-ounce) packages) shredded
   Mexican pasteurized process cheese

Use your favorite Crisco Oil product.

Rinse chicken; pat dry. Cut into ¾-inch cubes. Combine oil, taco seasoning mix and garlic in medium bowl. Add chicken. Stir to coat.

Heat large nonstick skillet on medium heat. Add chicken, half at a time. Stir-fry about 5 minutes or until browned and no longer pink in center, reducing heat if necessary. Remove from skillet with slotted spoon.

Heat oven to 425°F.

Spread chips evenly in two 15×10-inch jelly roll pans. Sprinkle chicken over chips. Combine beans and salsa. Spoon over chicken and chips. Sprinkle with cheese.

Bake for 6 to 7 minutes or until cheese melts. Serve warm.

Makes 6 servings

Original Ranch® Spinach Dip

The Ultimate Onion

3 cups cornstarch
3½ cups all-purpose flour, divided
6 teaspoons paprika, divided
2 teaspoons garlic salt
1 teaspoon salt
1½ teaspoons black pepper, divided
2 bottles (24 ounces) beer

4 to 6 Colossal onions (4 inches in diameter)
2 teaspoons garlic powder
¾ teaspoon cayenne pepper, divided
1 pint mayonnaise (2 cups)
1 pint sour cream (2 cups)
½ cup chili sauce

1. For batter, mix cornstarch, 1½ cups flour, 2 teaspoons paprika, garlic salt, salt and 1 teaspoon black pepper in large bowl. Add beer; mix well. Set aside.

2. Cut about ¾-inch off top of each onion; peel onions. Being careful not to cut through bottom, cut onions into 12 to 16 wedges.

3. Soak cut onions in ice water for 10 to 15 minutes. If onions do not "bloom," cut petals slightly deeper. Meanwhile, prepare seasoned flour mixture. Combine remaining 2 cups flour, remaining 4 teaspoons paprika, garlic powder, remaining ½ teaspoon black pepper and ¼ teaspoon cayenne pepper in large bowl; mix well.

4. Dip cut onions into seasoned flour; remove excess by carefully shaking. Dip in batter; remove excess by carefully shaking. Separate "petals" to coat thoroughly with batter. (If batter begins to separate, mix thoroughly before using.)

5. Gently place onions, one at a time, in fryer basket and deep-fry at 375°F 1½ minutes. Turn onion over and fry 1 to 1½ minutes or until golden brown. Drain on paper towels. Place onion upright in shallow bowl and remove about 1 inch of "petals" from center of onion.

6. To prepare Creamy Chili Sauce, combine mayonnaise, sour cream, chili sauce and remaining ½ teaspoon cayenne pepper in large bowl; mix well. Serve warm onions with Creamy Chili Sauce.

Makes about 24 servings

Favorite recipe from **National Onion Association**

The Ultimate Onion

7-Layer Ranch Dip

1 envelope LIPTON® RECIPE SECRETS®
    Ranch Soup Mix
1 container (16 ounces) sour cream
1 cup shredded lettuce
1 medium tomato, chopped (about 1 cup)
1 can (2.25 ounces) sliced pitted ripe
    olives, drained

¼ cup chopped red onion
1 can (4.5 ounces) chopped green chilies,
    drained
1 cup shredded Cheddar cheese (about
    4 ounces)

1. In 2-quart shallow dish, combine soup mix and sour cream.

2. Evenly layer remaining ingredients, ending with cheese. Chill, if desired. Serve with tortilla chips.

Makes 7 cups dip

Prep Time: 15 minutes

Maple Baked Ribs

¼ cup I CAN'T BELIEVE IT'S NOT
    BUTTER!® Spread
2 cloves garlic, finely chopped
½ cup ketchup
⅓ cup pure maple syrup or pancake syrup

2 tablespoons firmly packed brown sugar
2 tablespoons white vinegar
2 teaspoons hot pepper sauce
2½ to 3 pounds baby back ribs or spareribs

Preheat oven to 400°F.

In small saucepan, melt I Can't Believe It's Not Butter! Spread over medium heat and cook garlic, stirring occasionally, 1 minute. Stir in ketchup, syrup, brown sugar, vinegar and hot pepper sauce. Bring to a boil over high heat. Reduce heat to low and simmer 2 minutes.

In bottom of broiler, without rack, arrange ribs. Pour maple sauce over ribs. Cover with aluminum foil and bake 45 minutes. Remove foil and bake an additional 10 minutes, basting once with sauce. With knife, slice between ribs and toss with sauce in bottom of pan. *Makes 4 servings*

7-Layer Ranch Dip

Spicy Shrimp Cocktail

2 tablespoons olive or vegetable oil
¼ cup finely chopped onion
1 tablespoon chopped green bell pepper
1 clove garlic, minced
1 can (8 ounces) CONTADINA® Tomato
    Sauce

1 tablespoon chopped pitted green olives,
    drained
¼ teaspoon red pepper flakes
1 pound cooked shrimp, chilled

1. Heat oil in small skillet. Add onion, bell pepper and garlic; sauté until vegetables are tender. Stir in tomato sauce, olives and red pepper flakes.

2. Bring to a boil; simmer, uncovered, for 5 minutes. Cover.

3. Chill thoroughly. Combine sauce with shrimp in small bowl. *Makes 6 servings*

Molded Seafood Mousse

¾ cup boiling water
1 package (4-serving size) JELL-O® Brand
    Lemon Flavor Gelatin Dessert
¼ teaspoon salt
1 cup BREAKSTONE'S® Sour Cream
½ cup KRAFT® Mayo: Real Mayonnaise or
    MIRACLE WHIP® Salad Dressing

2 tablespoons horseradish
2 tablespoons lemon juice
2 tablespoons grated onion
2 cups seafood*
1½ teaspoons dill weed

Suggested Seafood:1 can (15 or 16 ounces) red salmon, drained and flaked, 2 cans (6 ounces each) crabmeat, drained and flaked, 2 cups chopped cooked shrimp, 2 cups chopped imitation crabmeat.

STIR boiling water into gelatin and salt in large bowl at least 2 minutes until completely dissolved. Stir in sour cream, mayonnaise, horseradish, lemon juice and onion. Refrigerate about 1½ hours or until thickened (spoon drawn through leaves definite impression). Stir in seafood and dill weed. Spoon into 4-cup mold.

REFRIGERATE 3 hours or until firm. Unmold. Serve as an appetizer with crackers and raw vegetables. *Makes 12 servings*

Spicy Shrimp Cocktail

Sweet Pepper Pizza Fingers

---

2 tablespoons margarine or butter
2 large red, green and/or yellow bell
    peppers, thinly sliced
1 clove garlic, finely chopped
1 envelope LIPTON® RECIPE SECRETS®
    Onion Soup Mix

1 cup water
1 package (10 ounces) refrigerated pizza
    crust
1½ cups shredded mozzarella cheese (about
    6 ounces)

Preheat oven to 425°F.

In 12-inch skillet, melt margarine over medium heat; cook peppers and garlic, stirring occasionally, 5 minutes or until peppers are tender. Stir in soup mix blended with water. Bring to a boil over high heat. Reduce heat to low and simmer uncovered 6 minutes or until liquid is absorbed. Remove from heat; set aside to cool 5 minutes.

Meanwhile, on large baking sheet sprayed with nonstick cooking spray, roll out pizza crust into 12×8-inch rectangle. Sprinkle 1 cup mozzarella cheese over crust; top with cooked pepper mixture, spreading to edges of dough. Top with remaining ½ cup mozzarella cheese. Bake 10 minutes or until crust is golden brown and topping is bubbly. Remove from oven and let stand 5 minutes. To serve, cut into 4×1-inch strips. *Makes about 24 appetizers*

Tip: Serve as a main dish by cutting pizza into Sicilian-style square pieces.

Pineapple-Almond Cheese Spread

---

2 cans (8 ounces each) DOLE® Crushed
    Pineapple
1 package (8 ounces) cream cheese,
    softened
4 cups (16 ounces) shredded sharp
    Cheddar cheese
½ cup mayonnaise

1 tablespoon soy sauce
1 cup chopped natural almonds, toasted
½ cup finely chopped DOLE® Green Bell
    Pepper
¼ cup minced green onions or chives
    DOLE® Celery stalks or assorted breads

• Drain pineapple. In large bowl, beat cream cheese until smooth; beat in Cheddar cheese, mayonnaise and soy sauce until smooth. Stir in pineapple, almonds, green pepper and onions. Refrigerate, covered. Use to stuff celery stalks or serve as spread with assorted breads. Serve at room temperature. *Makes 4 cups spread*

Sweet Pepper Pizza Fingers

Skewered Antipasto

1 jar (8 ounces) SONOMA® marinated
    dried tomatoes
1 pound (3 medium) new potatoes,
    cooked until tender
1 cup drained cooked egg tortellini and/or
    spinach tortellini
1 tablespoon chopped fresh chives *or*
    1 teaspoon dried chives

1 tablespoon chopped fresh rosemary *or*
    1 teaspoon dried rosemary
2 cups bite-sized vegetable pieces (such as
    celery, bell peppers, radishes, carrots,
    cucumber, green onions)

Drain oil from tomatoes into medium bowl. Place tomatoes in small bowl; set aside. Cut potatoes into 1-inch cubes. Add potatoes, tortellini, chives and rosemary to oil in medium bowl. Stir to coat with oil; cover and marinate 1 hour at room temperature. To assemble, alternately thread tomatoes, potatoes, tortellini and vegetables onto 6-inch skewers.   *Makes 12 to 14 skewers*

Cheesy Quiche Bites

36 RITZ® Crackers, finely crushed (about
    1½ cups crumbs)
3 tablespoons margarine or butter, melted
2 cups KRAFT® Shredded Cheddar Cheese
    (8 ounces)
½ cup chopped roasted red peppers

4 eggs, beaten
¾ cup milk
½ cup GREY POUPON® Dijon or
    COUNTRY DIJON® Mustard
¼ cup chopped fresh parsley
¼ cup KRAFT® Grated Parmesan Cheese

1. Mix cracker crumbs and margarine or butter; press onto bottom of greased 13×9×2-inch pan. Bake at 350°F for 8 to 10 minutes or until golden. Remove from oven; let stand for 5 minutes.

2. Sprinkle half the Cheddar cheese over crust; top with peppers and remaining Cheddar cheese.

3. Blend eggs, milk, mustard and parsley in small bowl; pour evenly over cheese in prepared pan. Sprinkle with Parmesan cheese. Bake at 350°F for 30 to 35 minutes or until set. Let stand 10 minutes; cut into 2×1½-inch bars. Serve warm.   *Makes 32 appetizers*

Prep Time: 30 minutes
Bake Time: 38 minutes
Total Time: 1 hour and 8 minutes

Skewered Antipasto

Savory Bruschetta

¼ cup olive oil
1 clove garlic, minced
1 loaf (1 pound) French bread, cut in half lengthwise
1 package (8 ounces) PHILADELPHIA® Cream Cheese, softened

3 tablespoons KRAFT® 100% Grated Parmesan Cheese
2 tablespoons chopped pitted Niçoise olives
1 cup chopped plum tomatoes
Fresh basil leaves

MIX oil and garlic; spread on cut surfaces of bread. Bake at 400°F for 8 to 10 minutes or until toasted. Cool.

MIX cream cheese and Parmesan cheese with electric mixer on medium speed until blended. Stir in olives. Spread on cooled bread halves.

TOP with tomatoes and basil leaves. Cut into slices.   *Makes 2 dozen appetizers*

Prep Time: 15 minutes
Bake Time: 10 minutes

Quick Sausage Appetizers

½ pound BOB EVANS® Italian Roll Sausage
⅓ cup mozzarella cheese
¼ cup sour cream

3 tablespoons mayonnaise
2 tablespoons chopped green onion
½ teaspoon Worcestershire sauce
10 slices white bread*

Party rye or thinly sliced French bread may be used instead of white bread. Double recipe to have enough sausage mixture.

Preheat broiler. Crumble and cook sausage in medium skillet until browned. Drain on paper towels. Transfer sausage to small bowl; stir in mozzarella cheese, sour cream, mayonnaise, green onion and Worcestershire sauce. Cut crusts from bread. Cut each bread slice into 4 squares; spread about 1 teaspoon sausage mixture onto each square. Arrange squares on ungreased baking sheet; place under hot broiler just until cheese melts and topping bubbles. (Be careful not to burn corners and edges.) Serve hot.   *Makes 40 appetizer squares*

Note: Quick Sausage Appetizers may be made ahead and refrigerated overnight or frozen up to 1 month before broiling.

Savory Bruschetta

Buffalo Hot Wings

24 TYSON® Individually Fresh Frozen®
    Chicken Wings
½ teaspoon salt
⅛ teaspoon black pepper

2 tablespoons butter
2 tablespoons hot sauce
½ teaspoon white vinegar

PREP: Preheat oven to 450°F. Line 15×11×1-inch baking pan with foil; spray with nonstick cooking spray. CLEAN: Wash hands. Arrange chicken in single layer on prepared pan. Sprinkle with salt and pepper. CLEAN: Wash hands.

COOK: Bake chicken 30 to 40 minutes or until internal juices of chicken run clear. (Or insert instant-read meat thermometer in thickest part of chicken. Temperature should read 170°F.) Meanwhile, in small saucepan, melt butter over medium heat. Add hot sauce and vinegar. Spread sauce over cooked chicken.

SERVE: Serve chicken with blue cheese dressing.

CHILL: Refrigerate leftovers immediately.

Makes 6 servings

Prep Time: 5 minutes
Cook Time: 40 minutes

Cheese Fondue

1½ cups dry white wine
8 ounces (2 cups) Gruyère *or* Swiss cheese,
    shredded
2 tablespoons flour

1 teaspoon TABASCO® brand Pepper
    Sauce
⅛ teaspoon salt
French bread cubes

Heat wine in 2-quart saucepan over low heat until boiling. Meanwhile, toss cheese with flour in medium bowl until blended.

Gradually add the cheese mixture to saucepan, stirring constantly until cheese melts. Stir in TABASCO® Sauce and salt. Serve immediately with French bread cubes for dipping.

Makes 2 servings

Hearty Fondue: Substitute 4 teaspoons TABASCO® New Orleans Style Steak Sauce for TABASCO® brand Pepper Sauce.

Ham-Chive Fondue: Stir ⅓ cup diced cooked ham and 1 tablespoon snipped chives into melted cheese mixture.

Spinach-Artichoke Cheese Squares

1 box (11 ounces) pie crust mix
1 container (15 ounces) part-skim ricotta
  cheese
½ cup grated Parmesan cheese
4 eggs
¼ cup plain dry bread crumbs
¼ cup *French's®* Napa Valley Style Dijon
  Mustard

1 teaspoon dried Italian seasoning
2 packages (10 ounces each) frozen
  chopped spinach, thawed and
  squeezed dry
1 jar (12 ounces) marinated artichoke
  hearts, drained and chopped
4 green onions, thinly sliced
½ cup chopped pimiento, well drained

1. Preheat oven to 400°F. Coat 15×10×1-inch baking pan with nonstick cooking spray. Toss pie crust mix with ⅓ cup cold water in large bowl until moistened and crumbly. Press mixture firmly onto bottom of prepared pan using floured bottom of measuring cup. Prick with fork. Bake 20 minutes or until golden.

2. Combine cheeses, eggs, bread crumbs, mustard and Italian seasoning in large bowl until well blended. Stir in vegetables; mix well. Spoon over baked crust, spreading evenly.

3. Bake 20 minutes or until toothpick inserted into center comes out clean. Cool on wire rack 15 minutes. Cut into squares. Serve warm or at room temperature. *Makes 24 servings*

Prep Time: 25 minutes
Bake Time: 40 minutes

Guacamole

2 avocados, mashed
¼ cup red salsa (mild or hot, according to
  taste)
3 tablespoons NEWMAN'S OWN® Salad
  Dressing

2 tablespoons lime or lemon juice
1 clove garlic, finely minced
Salt
Black pepper

Combine all ingredients and mix well. Chill for 1 to 2 hours tightly covered. Serve with tortilla chips. *Makes about 2 cups guacamole*

Snappy Shrimp Zingers

2 cups finely chopped cooked, shelled shrimp
½ cup all-purpose flour
3 tablespoons finely chopped green onions
3 tablespoons finely chopped red bell pepper
1 tablespoon minced fresh parsley
1 tablespoon fresh lemon juice

2¼ teaspoons GEBHARDT® Hot Pepper Sauce
2 teaspoons Cajun seasoning
½ teaspoon salt
1 egg, slightly beaten
1 cup fine dry bread crumbs
2 cups WESSON® Canola Oil

In medium bowl, combine *first 9* ingredients, ending with salt; blend well. Add egg and blend until thoroughly combined. (Mixture will be sticky.) Shape mixture into 12 (3×¾-inch) stick-shaped pieces. Gently roll *each* piece in bread crumbs. In a large skillet, heat oil to 325°F. Gently place shrimp sticks into oil and fry until crisp and golden brown. Drain on paper towels. Serve with your favorite dipping sauce or a squeeze of lemon. *Makes about 12 zingers*

Ritz® Stuffed Mushrooms

20 medium mushrooms
2 tablespoons finely chopped onion
2 tablespoons finely chopped red bell pepper

3 tablespoons margarine or butter
14 RITZ® Crackers, finely crushed (about ½ cup crumbs)
½ teaspoon dried basil leaves

1. Remove stems from mushrooms; finely chop ¼ cup stems.

2. Cook and stir chopped stems, onion and bell pepper in margarine or butter in skillet over medium heat until tender. Stir in crumbs and basil.

3. Spoon crumb mixture into mushroom caps; place on baking sheet. Bake at 400°F for 15 minutes or until hot. *Makes 20 appetizers*

Prep Time: 20 minutes
Cook Time: 15 minutes
Total Time: 35 minutes

Snappy Shrimp Zingers

Party Chicken Sandwiches

1½ cups finely chopped cooked chicken
1 cup MIRACLE WHIP® or MIRACLE WHIP LIGHT Dressing
1 can (4 ounces) chopped green chilies, drained

¾ cup KRAFT® Shredded Sharp Cheddar Cheese
¼ cup finely chopped onion
36 party rye or pumpernickel bread slices

HEAT broiler.

MIX chicken, dressing, chilies, cheese and onion. Spread evenly onto bread slices.

BROIL 5 minutes or until lightly browned. Serve hot.   *Makes 3 dozen sandwiches*

Prep Time: 10 minutes
Broil Time: 5 minutes

Make-ahead: Prepare chicken mixture as directed; cover. Refrigerate. When ready to serve, spread bread with chicken mixture. Broil as directed.

Savory Cheese Ball

1 package (8 ounces) PHILADELPHIA® Cream Cheese, softened
1 package (8 ounces) KRAFT® Shredded Sharp Cheddar Cheese
¾ cup crumbled KRAFT® Natural Blue Cheese Crumbles

¼ cup chopped green onions
2 tablespoons milk
1 teaspoon Worcestershire sauce
PLANTERS® Finely Chopped Walnuts, Pecans, Cashews or Almonds

MIX cheeses, green onions, milk and Worcestershire sauce until well blended; cover. Refrigerate 1 to 2 hours.

SHAPE into ball; roll in nuts. Serve with TRISCUIT® Crackers and apple or pear slices.

Makes 2⅔ cups spread

Prep Time: 5 minutes plus refrigerating

Great Substitutes: Substitute 1 package (4 ounces) ATHENOS® Traditional Crumbled Feta Cheese for blue cheese.

Party Chicken Sandwiches

Chili Chip Party Platter

1 pound ground beef	1 bag (8 to 9 ounces) tortilla chips or corn
1 medium onion, chopped	chips
1 package (1.48 ounces) LAWRY'S® Spices	1½ cups (6 ounces) shredded cheddar cheese
& Seasonings for Chili	1 can (2¼ ounces) sliced pitted black
1 can (6 ounces) tomato paste	olives, drained
1 cup water	½ cup sliced green onions

In medium skillet, cook ground beef until browned and crumbly; drain fat. Add onion, Spices & Seasonings for Chili, tomato paste and water; mix well. Bring to a boil over medium-high heat; reduce heat to low and simmer, uncovered, 15 minutes, stirring occasionally. Serve over tortilla chips. Top with cheddar cheese, olives and green onions. *Makes 4 servings*

Serving Suggestion: Serve with a cool beverage and sliced melon.

Smoked Turkey Roll-Ups

2 packages (4 ounces each) herb-flavored	2 green onions, minced
soft spreadable cheese	¼ cup roasted red peppers, drained and
4 flour (8-inch diameter) tortillas*	finely chopped
2 packages (6 ounces each) smoked turkey	
breast slices	

*To keep flour tortillas soft while preparing turkey roll-ups, cover with a slightly damp cloth.

1. Spread one package of cheese evenly over tortillas. Layer turkey slices evenly over cheese, overlapping turkey slices slightly to cover each tortilla. Spread remaining package of cheese evenly over turkey slices. Sprinkle with green onions and red peppers.

2. Roll up each tortilla jelly-roll style. Place roll-ups, seam side down, in resealable plastic bag; refrigerate several hours or overnight.

3. To serve, cut each roll-up crosswise into ½-inch slices to form pinwheels. If desired, arrange pinwheels on serving plate and garnish with red pepper slices in center.

Makes 56 appetizer servings

Favorite recipe from **National Turkey Federation**

Chili Chip Party Platter

Shrimp Toast

¾ pound medium-size raw shrimp, peeled,
    deveined and minced
3 green onions, minced
1 tablespoon chopped fresh cilantro
1 teaspoon minced fresh ginger root
1 teaspoon KIKKOMAN® Soy Sauce
1 teaspoon dry sherry

1 teaspoon Oriental sesame oil
½ teaspoon salt
1 tablespoon cornstarch
1 egg, slightly beaten
8 slices day-old white bread, edges
    trimmed
2 cups vegetable oil

Combine shrimp, green onions, cilantro, ginger, soy sauce, sherry, sesame oil and salt in medium bowl. Blend in cornstarch. Stir in egg; blend thoroughly. Cut each bread slice diagonally in half to form triangles. Spread shrimp mixture evenly over bread, spreading out to edges. Heat vegetable oil in wok or large skillet over medium-high heat to 360°F. (Oil is ready when bread cube dropped into oil rises to surface.) Add 2 or 3 triangles to hot oil, shrimp side down. Deep-fry about 30 seconds until edges begin to brown; turn over and deep-fry about 30 seconds longer, or until golden brown and crispy. Drain on paper towels, shrimp side down; keep warm. Repeat procedure with remaining triangles. To serve, cut each shrimp triangle diagonally in half. *Makes about 8 appetizer servings*

Sweet and Sour Meatballs

Meatballs
    ½ cup instant rice
    2 pounds lean ground beef
    1 egg
    1 cup soft butter-flavored cracker crumbs*
    2 tablespoons oil

Sauce
    1½ cups barbecue sauce
    1 cup (12-ounce jar) SMUCKER'S®
        Pineapple Topping
    ¼ cup firmly packed brown sugar

You may substitute croutons or stuffing mix for the crackers.

Prepare rice according to package directions.

Meanwhile, combine ground beef, egg and cracker crumbs; mix well. Add cooked rice; mix thoroughly. Shape into 1½- or 2-inch meatballs. Cook in oil over medium heat until browned, turning occasionally. If necessary, drain grease from skillet.

Combine all sauce ingredients; mix until brown sugar is dissolved. Pour over meatballs. Cover and simmer over low heat for 30 to 45 minutes or until meatballs are no longer pink in center. Serve with toothpicks. *Makes 4 to 6 servings*

Shrimp Toast

Deviled Eggs

12 large eggs, room temperature
1 tablespoon vinegar
Lettuce leaves

Filling
3 tablespoons *Frank's® RedHot®* Cayenne
Pepper Sauce

2 tablespoons mayonnaise
2 tablespoons sour cream
½ cup minced celery
¼ cup minced red onion
¼ teaspoon garlic powder

1. Place eggs in a single layer in bottom of large saucepan; cover with water. Add vinegar to water. Bring to a full boil. Immediately remove from heat. Cover; let stand 15 minutes. Drain eggs and rinse with cold water. Set eggs in bowl of ice water; cool.

2. To peel eggs, tap against side of counter. Gently remove shells, holding eggs under running water. Slice eggs in half lengthwise; remove yolks to medium bowl. Arrange whites on lettuce-lined platter.

3. To make Filling, add *Frank's RedHot* Sauce, mayonnaise and sour cream to egg yolks in bowl. Mix until well blended and creamy. Stir in celery, onion and garlic powder; mix well. Spoon about 1 tablespoon filling into each egg white. Garnish with parsley, capers or caviar, if desired. Cover with plastic wrap; refrigerate 30 minutes before serving. *Makes 12 servings (about 1½ cups filling)*

Tip: Filling may be piped into whites through large star-shaped pastry tip inserted into corner of plastic bag.

Piggy Wraps

1 package HILLSHIRE FARM® Lit'l
Smokies

2 (8-ounce) cans refrigerated crescent roll
dough, cut into small triangles

Preheat oven to 400°F.

Wrap individual Lit'l Smokies in dough triangles. Bake 5 minutes or until golden brown.

Makes about 50 hors d'oeuvres

Note: Piggy Wraps may be frozen. To reheat in microwave, microwave at HIGH 1½ minutes or at MEDIUM-HIGH (70% power) 2 minutes. When reheated in microwave, dough will not be crisp.

Hot Artichoke Dip

1 envelope LIPTON® RECIPE SECRETS®
  Onion Soup Mix*
1 can (14 ounces) artichoke hearts,
  drained and chopped

1 cup HELLMANN'S® or BEST FOODS®
  Mayonnaise
1 container (8 ounces) sour cream
1 cup shredded Swiss or mozzarella cheese

Also terrific with LIPTON® RECIPE SECRETS® Savory Herb with Garlic, Golden Onion, or Onion Mushroom Soup Mix.

1. Preheat oven to 350°F. In 1-quart casserole, combine all ingredients.

2. Bake uncovered 30 minutes or until heated through.

3. Serve with your favorite dippers. *Makes 3 cups dip*

Prep Time: 5 minutes
Bake Time: 30 minutes

Cold Artichoke Dip: Omit Swiss cheese. Stir in, if desired, ¼ cup grated Parmesan cheese. Do not bake.

Recipe Tip: When serving hot dip for a party, try baking it in 2 smaller casseroles. When the first casserole is empty, replace it with the second one, fresh from the oven.

Chicken Wings Teriyaki

½ cup teriyaki sauce
¼ cup HOLLAND HOUSE® Sherry
  Cooking Wine
2 tablespoons oil
2 tablespoons honey
1 teaspoon finely chopped peeled ginger

½ teaspoon five spice powder
¼ teaspoon sesame oil
2 cloves garlic, finely chopped
2 pounds chicken wings
¼ cup sliced scallions
1 tablespoon toasted sesame seeds

Heat oven to 375°F. In small bowl, combine teriyaki sauce, cooking wine, oil, honey, ginger, five spice powder, sesame oil and garlic. Pour into 13×9-inch pan. Add chicken wings, turning to coat all sides. Bake for 35 to 45 minutes or until chicken is tender and cooked through, turning once and basting occasionally with sauce.* Sprinkle with scallions and sesame seeds. *Makes 24 appetizers*

Do not baste during last 5 minutes of cooking.

❧ *Traditional Breads* ❧

Apple Cinnamon Rolls

5 to 5½ cups all-purpose flour
½ cup sugar
2 envelopes FLEISCHMANN'S®
   RapidRise™ Yeast
1 teaspoon salt
½ cup water

½ cup milk
¼ cup butter or margarine
3 large eggs
   Apple Filling (recipe follows)
   Cinnamon-Sugar Topping (recipe
   follows)

In large bowl, combine 1 cup flour, sugar, undissolved yeast, and salt. Heat water, milk, and butter until very warm (120° to 130°F). Gradually add to dry ingredients. Beat 2 minutes at medium speed of electric mixer, scraping bowl occasionally. Add eggs and 1 cup flour; beat 2 minutes at high speed, scraping bowl occasionally. Stir in enough remaining flour to make soft dough. Knead on lightly floured surface until smooth and elastic, about 8 to 10 minutes. Cover; let rest 10 minutes.

Divide dough into 2 equal portions. Roll each portion into 12×8-inch rectangle. Spread Apple Filling evenly over dough. Beginning at long end of each, roll up tightly jelly-roll style. Pinch seams to seal. Cut each roll into 12 equal pieces. Place, cut sides up, in greased 9-inch round pans. Cover; let rise in warm, draft-free place until doubled in size, about 45 minutes. Sprinkle with Cinnamon-Sugar Topping.

Bake at 375°F for 25 to 30 minutes or until done. Remove from pans; serve warm.

Makes 24 rolls

Apple Filling: Combine 2 large cooking apples, chopped, 2 tablespoons all-purpose flour, ¾ cup sugar, and ¼ cup butter or margarine in medium saucepan; bring to a boil over medium high heat. Cook 3 minutes. Reduce heat to medium-low; cook 10 minutes, stirring constantly until thick. Stir in 1 teaspoon ground cinnamon and ½ teaspoon nutmeg. Cool completely.

Cinnamon-Sugar Topping: Combine ¾ cup sugar, 1 teaspoon ground cinnamon, and ½ teaspoon nutmeg. Stir until well-blended.

Apple Cinnamon Rolls

Onion Buckwheat Bread

1 pound diced white onions
3 tablespoons olive oil
4½ teaspoons yeast
1½ cups water, at 90°F
½ cup milk
6½ cups unbleached bread flour
½ cup buckwheat flour
5 teaspoons sea salt

1 tablespoon finely chopped fresh
   rosemary
3 ounces shredded Gouda or Cheddar
   cheese
Unbleached bread flour as needed for
   kneading
4 tablespoons poppy seeds or nigella seeds
   (onion seeds)

1. Sauté onions in olive oil over medium high heat until just browned, about 5 minutes. Set aside to cool.

2. Combine yeast with water; let sit 10 minutes until creamy.

3. Add milk to yeast mixture and stir to combine. Gradually add bread flour, buckwheat flour, salt, rosemary and onions. When mixture is well combined, add cheese and blend. The dough will be slightly sticky.

4. Knead dough about 10 minutes, until smooth and elastic. Add additional bread flour as needed if dough is too soft.

5. Lightly oil clean bowl. Place dough in bowl; cover and let rise until doubled in bulk, about 1½ to 2 hours.

6. Gently punch down dough and place on lightly floured surface. Cut dough in half and shape into round ball. Spritz top of each loaf with water, and press into poppy seeds or nigella seeds. Place on lightly floured sheet pan; cover and let rise until almost doubled in bulk, 45 minutes to 1 hour.

7. Preheat oven to 450°F. Slash top of loaves with razor and place in oven. Add steam for first 10 minutes. *Reduce heat to 400°F* and bake an additional 35 to 40 minutes. Cool loaves completely on rack.
Makes 2 (10-inch) round loaves

Favorite recipe from **National Onion Association**

Onion Buckwheat Bread

Focaccia

1 cup water
1 tablespoon olive oil, plus additional for
   brushing
1 teaspoon salt
1 tablespoon sugar
3 cups bread flour

2¼ teaspoons RED STAR® Active Dry Yeast
Suggested toppings: sun-dried tomatoes,
   grilled bell pepper slices, sautéed
   onion rings, fresh and dried herbs of
   any combination, grated hard cheese

Bread Machine Method
Place room temperature ingredients, except toppings, in pan in order listed. Select dough cycle. Check dough consistency after 5 minutes of kneading, making adjustments if necessary.

Hand-Held Mixer Method
Combine yeast, 1 cup flour, sugar and salt. Combine water and 1 tablespoon oil; heat mixture to 120° to 130°F. Combine dry mixture and liquid mixture in mixing bowl on low speed. Beat 2 to 3 minutes on medium speed. By hand, stir in enough remaining flour to make firm dough. Knead on floured surface 5 to 7 minutes or until smooth and elastic. Add additional flour, if necessary.

Stand Mixer Method
Combine yeast, 1 cup flour, sugar and salt. Combine water and 1 tablespoon oil; heat mixture to 120° to 130°F. Combine dry mixture and liquid mixture in mixing bowl with paddle or beaters 4 minutes on medium speed. Gradually add remaining flour and knead with dough hook 5 to 7 minutes or until smooth and elastic. Add additional flour, if necessary.

Food Processor Method
Combine yeast, 1 cup flour, sugar and salt. Combine water and 1 tablespoon oil. Put dry mixture in processing bowl with steel blade. While motor is running, add liquid mixture. Process until mixed. Continue processing, adding remaining flour until dough forms a ball. Add additional flour, if necessary.

Rising, Shaping, and Baking
Place dough in lightly oiled bowl and turn to grease top. Cover; let rise until dough tests ripe.* Turn dough onto lightly floured surface; punch down to remove air bubbles. On lightly floured surface, shape dough into a ball. Place on greased cookie sheet. Flatten to 14-inch circle. With knife, cut circle in dough about 1 inch from edge, cutting almost through to cookie sheet. Pierce center with fork. Cover; let rise about 15 minutes. Brush with oil and sprinkle with desired toppings. Bake in preheated 375°F oven 25 to 30 minutes or until golden brown. Remove from cookie sheet to cool. Serve warm or cold.

Makes 1 (14-inch) loaf

Place two fingers into the dough and them remove them. If the holes remain the dough is ripe and ready to punch down.

Focaccia

Tropical Carrot Bread

Bread
  ⅓ CRISCO® Stick or ⅓ cup CRISCO®
    all-vegetable shortening plus
    additional for greasing
  ¾ cup firmly packed brown sugar
  4 egg whites, slightly beaten
  2¼ cups all-purpose flour
  1 tablespoon plus 2 teaspoons baking
    powder
  ¾ teaspoon ground cinnamon
  ¼ teaspoon ground ginger

  ¼ teaspoon salt (optional)
  1¼ cups uncooked old-fashioned or quick
    oats
  1 cup shredded carrots
  1 can (8 ounces) crushed pineapple in
    unsweetened juice
  ½ cup raisins

Topping
  2 tablespoons uncooked old-fashioned or
    quick oats

1. Heat oven to 350°F. Grease 9×5×3-inch loaf pan.

2. For bread, combine shortening and brown sugar in large bowl. Beat at medium speed of electric mixer or stir with fork until well blended. Stir in egg whites. Beat until fairly smooth.

3. Combine flour, baking powder, cinnamon, ginger and salt in medium bowl. Stir into egg mixture. Stir in oats. Add carrots and pineapple with juice. Stir until just blended. Stir in raisins. Spoon into loaf pan.

4. For topping, sprinkle oats over top.

5. Bake at 350°F for 70 to 80 minutes or until toothpick inserted in center comes out clean. Cool 10 minutes in pan on rack. Loosen from sides. Remove from pan. Cool completely on rack.

Makes 1 loaf (12 servings)

Kitchen Hint: A loaf of homemade bread makes a great gift—especially when it's given in a new loaf pan. Just add a wooden spoon and the recipe, wrap it all up in a festive towel and tie it with ribbon.

Tropical Carrot Bread

Top Choice White Bread

5½ to 6 cups all-purpose flour
3 tablespoons sugar
2 envelopes FLEISCHMANN'S®
    RapidRise™ Yeast

2 teaspoons salt
1½ cups water
½ cup milk
2 tablespoons butter or margarine

In large bowl, combine 2 cups flour, sugar, undissolved yeast, and salt. Heat water, milk, and butter until very warm (120° to 130°F); stir into dry ingredients. Beat 2 minutes at medium speed of electric mixer, scraping bowl occasionally. Stir in 1 cup flour; beat at high speed for 2 minutes, scraping bowl occasionally. Stir in enough remaining flour to make soft dough. Knead on lightly floured surface until smooth and elastic, about 8 to 10 minutes. Cover; let rest 10 minutes.

Divide dough in half. Roll each half into 12×7-inch rectangle. Beginning at short end of each rectangle, roll up tightly as for jelly roll. Pinch seams and ends to seal. Place seam sides down, in 2 greased 8½×4½-inch loaf pans. Cover; let rise in warm, draft-free place until doubled in size, about 45 minutes.

Bake at 400°F for 25 to 30 minutes or until done. Remove from pans; cool on wire rack.

Makes 2 loaves

Mallomar® Sticky Buns

1 (8-ounce) package refrigerated crescent
    roll dough
8 MALLOMARS® Chocolate Cakes

Powdered sugar glaze and melted
    semisweet chocolate, optional

1. Separate crescent roll dough into 8 triangles.

2. Wrap each dough triangle around one cake, pinching seams to seal. Place in 8-inch round cake pan.

3. Bake at 375°F for 15 to 17 minutes or until golden brown. Cool in pan on wire rack for 15 minutes. Remove from pan to serving plate; drizzle with powdered sugar glaze and melted chocolate if desired. Serve warm.

Makes 8 buns

Prep Time: 25 minutes
Cook Time: 15 minutes

Top Choice White Bread

Chocolate Chunk Cinnamon Coffee Cake

1 package (12 ounces) BAKER'S®
   Semi-Sweet Chocolate Chunks
¾ cup chopped nuts
2 cups sugar, divided
1½ teaspoons cinnamon
2⅔ cups flour
1½ teaspoons baking soda
¾ teaspoon CALUMET® Baking Powder
½ teaspoon salt
¾ cup (1½ sticks) butter, softened
1 teaspoon vanilla
3 eggs
1½ cups BREAKSTONE'S® or KNUDSEN®
   Sour Cream

HEAT oven to 350°F. Grease 13×9-inch baking pan.

MIX chocolate, nuts, ⅔ cup sugar and cinnamon; set aside. Mix flour, baking soda, baking powder and salt; set aside.

BEAT butter, remaining 1⅓ cups sugar and vanilla in large bowl with electric mixer on medium speed until light and fluffy. Add eggs, 1 at a time, beating well after each addition. Add flour mixture alternately with sour cream, beating after each addition until smooth. Spoon ½ of the batter into prepared pan. Top with ½ of the chocolate-nut mixture. Repeat layers.

BAKE 40 to 45 minutes or until toothpick inserted in center comes out clean. Cool in pan on wire rack.
Makes 16 servings

Potato Dill Biscuits

1 medium COLORADO potato, peeled
   and chopped
½ cup water
2 cups all-purpose flour
1 tablespoon baking powder
2 teaspoons sugar
1 teaspoon dried dill weed
½ teaspoon cream of tartar
½ teaspoon salt
¼ cup shortening
¼ cup butter

In small saucepan combine chopped potato and ½ cup water. Cover and cook over medium heat about 10 minutes or until potato is tender. *Do not drain.* Mash until smooth. Add additional water to measure 1 cup. In mixing bowl combine flour, baking powder, sugar, dill, cream of tartar and salt. Cut in shortening and butter until mixture resembles coarse crumbs. Add potato mixture. Stir just until mixture clings together. On lightly floured surface, knead dough 10 or 12 times. Pat into 8-inch square. Cut into 16 squares. Place biscuits on baking sheet. Bake in 450°F oven 10 to 12 minutes or until lightly browned. Serve warm.
Makes 16 biscuits

Favorite recipe from **Colorado Potato Administrative Committee**

Chocolate Chunk Cinnamon Coffee Cake

Hot Cross Buns

1 package (¼ ounce) active dry yeast
¼ cup warm water (105° to 115°F)
¾ cup warm milk
¼ cup GRANDMA'S® Molasses
4 tablespoons (½ stick) butter, softened
2 eggs
1½ teaspoons salt

3½ cups all-purpose flour, divided
1 teaspoon cinnamon
½ teaspoon nutmeg
¼ teaspoon allspice
½ cup currants or raisins
2 tablespoons chopped candied citron

1. In large bowl, stir yeast into water and let stand several minutes to dissolve. Combine milk, molasses, butter, eggs and salt in large bowl; beat well. Add yeast mixture; mix well. Beat in 1½ cups flour, cinnamon, nutmeg and allspice. Cover bowl and let rise about 1 hour or until bubbly or double in bulk.

2. Add remaining 2 cups flour and blend well, adding additional flour if necessary to make dough firm enough to handle. Turn onto floured surface; knead dough until firm and elastic. Add currants and citron during last 5 minutes of kneading. Place dough in greased bowl; cover and let rise until double in bulk.

3. Heat oven to 375°F. Punch dough down; turn onto lightly floured surface. Roll into 14×10-inch rectangle, about ½ inch thick. Cut dough with 2½- to 3-inch round cutter; place buns about 1 inch apart on greased baking sheets. Gather up scraps, reroll and continue cutting until all dough has been used. Let rise, uncovered, until double in bulk.

4. Just before baking, use floured scissors to snip cross in tip of each bun, cutting about ½ inch deep. Bake about 15 minutes or until tops of buns are golden brown. Remove from oven and transfer to rack to cool.

Makes 12 buns

Fred's Raspberry Cream Cheese Coffee Cake

2¼ cups all-purpose flour
1 cup sugar, divided
¾ cup butter or margarine, cut into 12 pieces
½ teaspoon baking powder
½ teaspoon baking soda
¼ teaspoon salt
¾ cup sour cream
2 eggs, divided

1 teaspoon almond extract
1 (8-ounce) package cream cheese, softened
½ teaspoon grated lemon peel
½ teaspoon vanilla
½ cup SMUCKER'S® Seedless Red Raspberry Jam
½ cup slivered almonds

Grease and flour bottom and side of 10-inch springform pan. In large bowl, combine flour and ¾ cup of the sugar. Using pastry blender, cut in butter until mixture resembles coarse crumbs. Reserve 1 cup crumb mixture.

To remaining crumb mixture, add baking powder, baking soda, salt, sour cream, 1 of the eggs and almond extract; blend well. Spread batter over bottom and 2 inches up side of prepared pan. Batter should be about ¼ inch thick on side.

Combine cream cheese, remaining ¼ cup sugar, remaining egg, lemon peel and vanilla; blend well. Spread over batter in pan. Spoon jam evenly over cream cheese filling.

Combine reserved crumb mixture and almonds. Sprinkle over top.

Bake at 350°F for 45 to 55 minutes or until cream cheese filling is set and crust is deep golden brown. Cool 15 minutes. Remove side of pan. Serve warm or cool. Refrigerate leftovers.

Makes 12 servings

Monkey Bread

½ pound butter, melted
2 teaspoons LAWRY'S® Garlic Powder with Parsley

4 packages (9.5 ounces each) refrigerated buttermilk biscuits

In medium bowl, combine butter and Garlic Powder with Parsley; mix well. Separate biscuits and dip each into butter to coat. In tube pan, place one layer of dipped biscuits in bottom, slightly overlapping each biscuit. Arrange remaining biscuits in zig-zag fashion, some towards center and some towards outside edge of pan. Use all biscuits in as many layers as needed. Pour half of remaining butter over biscuits. Bake, uncovered, in 375°F oven 15 to 20 minutes. Invert onto serving platter and pour remaining butter over bread. Serve warm. *Makes 10 to 12 servings*

Old-Fashioned Cake Doughnuts

3¾ cups all-purpose flour
1 tablespoon baking powder
1 teaspoon ground cinnamon
¾ teaspoon salt
½ teaspoon ground nutmeg
3 eggs
¾ cup granulated sugar

1 cup applesauce
2 tablespoons butter, melted
1 quart vegetable oil
2 cups sifted powdered sugar
3 tablespoons milk
½ teaspoon vanilla
Colored sprinkles (optional)

Combine flour, baking powder, cinnamon, salt and nutmeg in medium bowl. Beat eggs in large bowl with electric mixer at high speed until frothy. Gradually beat in granulated sugar. Continue beating at high speed 4 minutes until thick and lemon colored, scraping down side of bowl once. Reduce speed to low; beat in applesauce and butter.

Beat in flour mixture until well blended. Divide dough into halves. Place each half on large piece of plastic wrap. Pat each half into 5-inch square; wrap in plastic wrap. Refrigerate 3 hours or until well chilled.

Pour oil into large Dutch oven. Place deep-fry thermometer in oil. Heat oil over medium heat until thermometer registers 375°F. Adjust heat as necessary to maintain temperature at 375°F. To prepare glaze, stir together powdered sugar, milk and vanilla in small bowl until smooth. Cover; set aside. Roll out 1 dough half to ⅜-inch thickness. Cut dough with floured 3-inch doughnut cutter; repeat with remaining dough. Reserve doughnut holes. Reroll scraps; cut dough again.

Place 4 doughnuts and holes in hot oil. Cook 2 minutes or until golden brown, turning often. Remove with slotted spoon; drain on paper towels. Repeat with remaining doughnuts and holes. Spread glaze over warm doughnuts; decorate with sprinkles, if desired.

Makes 12 doughnuts and holes

Old-Fashioned Cake Doughnuts

Braided Sandwich Ring

Dough
3/4 cup buttermilk, at 80°F
2 large eggs, at room temperature
2 tablespoons vegetable oil
3 tablespoons sugar
1 1/2 teaspoons salt
4 cups bread flour
2 1/4 teaspoons RED STAR® Active Dry Yeast

Glaze
1 egg
1 tablespoon milk
1 tablespoon sesame or poppy seeds

Filling
Mayonnaise, lettuce, sliced tomatoes, onion rings, sliced olives, sliced deli meats, sliced cheeses, Dijon mustard

Bread Machine Method
Place dough ingredients in pan in order listed. Select dough cycle. Check dough consistency after 5 minutes of kneading making adjustments if necessary.

Hand-Held Mixer Method
Combine 1 cup flour, sugar, yeast and salt. Heat buttermilk to 120° to 130°F. Combine flour mixture, buttermilk, 2 eggs and oil in mixing bowl on low speed. Beat 2 to 3 minutes on medium speed. By hand, stir in enough remaining flour to make firm dough. Knead on floured surface 5 to 7 minutes or until smooth and elastic. Use additional flour, if necessary. Place dough in lightly oiled bowl and turn to grease top. Cover; let rise until dough tests ripe.*

Stand Mixer Method
Combine 1 cup flour, sugar, yeast and salt. Heat buttermilk to 120° to 130°F. Combine flour mixture, buttermilk, 2 eggs and oil in mixing bowl with paddle or beaters 4 minutes on medium speed. Gradually add remaining flour and knead with dough hook 5 to 7 minutes or until smooth and elastic. Use additional flour, if necessary. Place dough in lightly oiled bowl and turn to grease top. Cover; let rise until dough tests ripe.*

Shaping and Baking
Punch down dough. Divide into three parts. On lightly floured surface, roll each third into 24-inch rope. On greased cookie sheet lightly sprinkled with cornmeal, loosely braid ropes from center to ends. Shape into circle; fasten ends by pinching dough together. Cover; let rise until indentation remains after touching.

For glaze, combine remaining 1 egg and milk; gently brush risen dough. Sprinkle with sesame seeds. Bake in preheated 375°F oven 25 to 35 minutes or until golden brown; cool.

Using serrated knife, slice ring crosswise to create large sandwich. Spread bottom half with mayonnaise; arrange filling ingredients on top of mayonnaise. Spread top section with mustard; place on top of filling. Slice into serving portions.   *Makes 1 sandwich ring*

Place two fingers into the dough and then remove them. If the holes remain the dough is ripe and ready to punch down.

Braided Sandwich Ring

English-Style Scones

3 eggs, divided
½ cup heavy cream
1½ teaspoons vanilla
2 cups all-purpose flour
2 teaspoons baking powder
¼ teaspoon salt
¼ cup cold butter

¼ cup finely chopped pitted dates
¼ cup golden raisins or currants
1 teaspoon water
6 tablespoons no-sugar-added orange
    marmalade fruit spread
6 tablespoons softly whipped cream or
    crème fraîche

Preheat oven to 375°F. Beat two eggs with cream and vanilla; set aside. Combine flour, baking powder and salt in medium bowl. Cut in butter with pastry blender or two knives until mixture resembles coarse crumbs. Stir in dates and raisins. Add egg mixture; mix just until dry ingredients are moistened. With floured hands, knead dough four times on lightly floured surface. Place dough on greased cookie sheet; pat into 8-inch circle. With sharp wet knife, gently score dough into six wedges, cutting ¾ of the way into dough. Beat remaining egg with water; brush lightly over dough. Bake 18 to 20 minutes or until golden brown. Cool 5 minutes on wire rack. Cut into wedges. Serve warm with marmalade and whipped cream.

Makes 6 scones

Harvest Mini Chip Muffins

¼ cup (½ stick) butter or margarine
1 cup sugar
1 cup canned pumpkin
2 eggs
2¼ cups all-purpose flour
2 teaspoons baking powder
½ teaspoon baking soda

¾ teaspoon pumpkin pie spice
½ teaspoon salt
½ cup milk
1 cup HERSHEY'S MINI CHIPS™
    Semi-Sweet Chocolate Chips
½ cup chopped pecans

1. Heat oven to 350°F. Grease or line muffin cups (2½ inches in diameter) with paper bake cups.

2. Beat butter and sugar in large bowl until creamy. Add pumpkin and eggs; blend well. Stir together flour, baking powder, baking soda, pumpkin pie spice and salt; add alternately with milk to pumpkin mixture, beating after each addition just until blended. Stir in small chocolate chips and pecans. Fill muffin cups ⅔ full with batter.

3. Bake 20 to 25 minutes or until wooden pick inserted in center comes out clean. Serve warm.

Makes about 2 dozen muffins

English-Style Scone

Banana Pecan Braid

Dough
- 3 cups bread flour
- ½ cup chopped dates or pitted dates, snipped
- ½ cup chopped pecans, toasted
- ¼ cup sugar
- 2 teaspoons FLEISCHMANN'S® Bread Machine Yeast
- ½ teaspoon salt
- 3 tablespoons butter or margarine, cut up
- 3 tablespoons milk
- 3 tablespoons water (70° to 80°F)
- ½ cup mashed ripe banana
- 1 large egg

Topping
- 1 tablespoon sugar
- ½ teaspoon ground cardamom *or*
- ¼ teaspoon ground allspice

Add dough ingredients to bread machine pan in the order suggested by manufacturer. Select dough/manual cycle. When cycle is complete, remove dough to floured surface. If necessary, knead in additional flour to make dough easy to handle.

Divide dough into 3 equal pieces; roll each to 15-inch rope. Braid 3 ropes together, pinching ends to seal. Place on greased baking sheet. Cover and let rise in warm, draft-free place until doubled in size, about 1 hour. In small bowl, combine topping ingredients; sprinkle over loaf. Bake at 375°F for 25 to 30 minutes or until done. Remove from baking sheet; cool on wire rack.   *Makes 1 loaf*

Note: Dough can be prepared in all size bread machines.

Cranberry Brunch Muffins

- 1 cup chopped fresh cranberries
- ⅓ cup plus ¼ cup sugar, divided
- 2 cups all-purpose flour
- 2 teaspoons baking powder
- ¾ teaspoon salt
- ½ cup butter
- ¾ cup orange juice
- 1 egg, lightly beaten
- 1 teaspoon vanilla
- 2 tablespoons butter, melted

Preheat oven to 400°F. Grease 12-cup muffin pan. Combine cranberries and 1 tablespoon sugar in small bowl. Blend flour, ⅓ cup sugar, baking powder and salt in large bowl. Cut in ½ cup butter until mixture is crumbly. Stir in orange juice, egg and vanilla just until ingredients are moistened. Fold in cranberry mixture; spoon batter into prepared pan.

Bake 20 to 25 minutes or until golden. Cool 5 minutes before removing from pan. Dip tops of muffins in melted butter; sprinkle with remaining 3 tablespoons sugar. Serve warm.

Makes 12 muffins

Banana Pecan Braid

Lots o' Chocolate Bread

⅔ cup packed light brown sugar
½ cup butter, softened
1½ cups miniature semi-sweet chocolate
    chips, divided
2 eggs
2½ cups all-purpose flour
1½ cups applesauce

1 teaspoon baking soda
1 teaspoon baking powder
½ teaspoon salt
1½ teaspoons vanilla
½ cup chocolate chips
1 tablespoon shortening (do not use
    butter, margarine, spread or oil)

Preheat oven to 350°F. Grease 5 (5½×3-inch) mini loaf pans. Beat brown sugar and butter in large bowl with electric mixer until creamy. Melt 1 cup miniature chocolate chips; cool slightly and add to sugar mixture with eggs. Add flour, applesauce, baking soda, baking powder, salt and vanilla; beat until well mixed. Stir in remaining ½ cup miniature chocolate chips. Spoon batter into prepared pans; bake 35 to 40 minutes or until center crack is dry to the touch. Cool 10 minutes before removing from pans.

Place ½ cup chocolate chips and shortening in small microwavable bowl. Microwave at HIGH 1 minute; stir. If necessary, microwave at HIGH an additional 15 seconds at a time, stirring after each heating. Drizzle warm loaves with glaze. Cool completely. *Makes 5 mini loaves*

Super Brown Bread

2 cups warm water (105° to 115°F)
2 packages active dry yeast
1½ cups whole wheat flour
2½ to 3 cups bread flour, divided
½ cup rolled oats

½ cup packed brown sugar
¼ cup wheat germ
¼ cup vegetable oil
¼ cup molasses
2 teaspoons salt

In large bowl, combine water and yeast. Let stand until dissolved, about 5 minutes. Add whole wheat flour, 1 cup bread flour, oats, brown sugar, wheat germ, oil, molasses and salt. Beat until smooth. Add additional bread flour to make soft dough.

Knead 10 minutes or until smooth. Place in greased bowl, turning to grease top; cover and let rise until doubled.

Form into two loaves; place in two 8×4-inch greased loaf pans and let rise until doubled. Bake at 450°F for 10 minutes. *Reduce oven temperature to 325°F; bake 35 minutes.*

Makes 2 loaves (16 slices each)

Favorite recipe from **North Dakota Wheat Commission**

Lots o' Chocolate Bread

Soda Bread

1½ cups whole wheat flour
1 cup all-purpose flour
½ cup rolled oats
¼ cup sugar
1½ teaspoons baking powder
½ teaspoon baking soda

¼ teaspoon ground cinnamon
⅓ cup raisins (optional)
¼ cup walnuts (optional)
1¼ cups low-fat buttermilk
1 tablespoon vegetable oil

Preheat oven to 375°F. Combine whole wheat flour, all-purpose flour, oats, sugar, baking powder, baking soda and cinnamon in large bowl. Stir in raisins and walnuts, if desired. Gradually stir in buttermilk and oil until dough forms. Knead in bowl for 30 seconds. Spray loaf pan with nonstick cooking spray; place dough in pan. Bake 40 to 50 minutes or until wooden toothpick inserted in center comes out clean.

Makes 16 slices

Favorite recipe from **The Sugar Association, Inc.**

Peach Streusel Coffee Cake

Streusel
½ cup QUAKER® Oats (quick or old fashioned, uncooked)
⅓ cup sugar
3 tablespoons margarine, melted
½ teaspoon ground cinnamon
⅛ teaspoon ground nutmeg (optional)

Coffee Cake
1 cup sugar
½ cup (1 stick) margarine, softened

1½ teaspoons vanilla
4 egg whites
1½ cups all-purpose flour
¾ cup QUAKER® Oats (quick or old fashioned, uncooked)
1 tablespoon baking powder
½ teaspoon baking soda
¾ cup light sour cream
1 (16-ounce) can sliced peaches, drained
or 1 cup sliced fresh peaches

Heat oven to 350°F. Spray 9-inch square baking pan with no-stick cooking spray or grease lightly. For streusel, combine all ingredients; mix well. Set aside. For coffee cake, beat sugar, margarine and vanilla until fluffy. Add egg whites; mix until smooth. Combine flour, oats, baking powder and baking soda; mix well. Add to sugar mixture alternately with sour cream, beginning and ending with dry ingredients; mix well after each addition. Spread into prepared pan. Pat canned peach slices dry with paper towels; arrange over batter. Sprinkle with streusel. Bake 50 to 55 minutes or until wooden pick inserted in center comes out clean. Serve warm.

Makes 16 servings

Soda Bread

Corn Bread

1 cup all-purpose flour	**½ teaspoon salt**
1 cup yellow cornmeal	**1 cup milk**
⅓ cup sugar	**⅓ cup vegetable oil**
2 teaspoons baking powder	**1 egg**

1. Preheat oven to 400°F. Grease 8-inch square baking pan.

2. Combine flour, cornmeal, sugar, baking powder and salt in large bowl; set aside. Combine milk, oil and egg in small bowl until blended. Stir milk mixture into flour mixture just until moistened. Spread batter evenly into prepared pan.

3. Bake 20 to 25 minutes or until golden brown and toothpick inserted in center comes out clean. Cut into squares. Serve warm. *Makes 9 servings*

Corn Muffins: Preheat oven to 400°F. Prepare batter as directed in steps 1 and 2, except spoon batter into 12 (2½-inch) greased or paper-lined muffin cups. Bake 20 minutes or until golden brown and toothpick inserted in center comes out clean. Immediately remove from pan; cool on wire rack 10 minutes. Serve warm. Makes 12 muffins.

Double Apple Bran Cereal Muffins

1¼ cups flour	**1 egg**
1 tablespoon CALUMET® Baking Powder	**½ cup applesauce**
¼ teaspoon ground cinnamon	**1 small apple, peeled, cored and finely**
¼ teaspoon salt	**chopped (1 cup)**
2 cups POST® Bran Flakes Cereal	**⅓ cup firmly packed brown sugar**
1 cup fat free milk	**2 tablespoons margarine, melted**

HEAT oven to 400°F. Spray 12-cup muffin pan with no stick cooking spray.

MIX flour, baking powder, cinnamon and salt in large bowl. Mix cereal and milk in another bowl; let stand 3 minutes.

BEAT egg in small bowl; stir in applesauce, chopped apple, sugar and margarine. Stir into cereal mixture. Add to flour mixture; stir just until moistened. (Batter will be lumpy.) Spoon batter into prepared muffin pan, filling each cup ⅔ full.

BAKE 20 minutes or until golden brown. Serve warm. *Makes 12 muffins*

Challah

1-Pound Loaf
½ cup water
1 large egg
2 tablespoons margarine, cut up
1 teaspoon salt
2 cups bread flour
4 teaspoons sugar
1½ teaspoons FLEISCHMANN'S® Bread
    Machine Yeast
1 yolk of large egg
1 tablespoon water

1½-Pound Loaf
¾ cup water
1 large egg
3 tablespoons margarine, cut up
1¼ teaspoons salt
3 cups bread flour
2 tablespoons sugar
2 teaspoons FLEISCHMANN'S® Bread
    Machine Yeast
1 yolk of large egg
1 tablespoon water

Add water, egg, margarine, salt, bread flour, sugar and yeast to bread machine pan in the order suggested by manufacturer. Select dough/manual cycle. When cycle is complete, remove dough from machine to lightly floured surface. If necessary, knead in enough additional flour to make dough easy to handle. (For 1½-pound recipe, divide dough in half to make 2 loaves.)

For each loaf, divide dough into 2 pieces, one about ⅔ of the dough and the other about ⅓ of the dough. Divide larger piece into 3 equal pieces; roll into 12-inch ropes. Place ropes on greased baking sheet. Braid by bringing left rope under center rope; lay it down. Bring right rope under new center rope; lay it down. Repeat to end. Pinch ends to seal. Divide remaining piece into 3 equal pieces. Roll into 10-inch ropes; braid. Place small braid on top of large braid. Pinch ends firmly to seal and to secure to large braid. Cover and let rise in warm, draft-free place until almost doubled in size, 15 to 20 minutes. Lightly beat egg yolk and 1 tablespoon water; brush over braids.

Bake at 375°F for 25 to 30 minutes or until done, covering with foil after 15 minutes to prevent excess browning. (For even browning when baking two loaves, switch positions of baking sheets halfway through baking.) Remove from baking sheets; cool on wire racks.   *Makes 1 or 2 loaves*

❈ Hearty Soups ❈

Chicken Tortilla Soup

1 clove garlic, minced
1 can (14½ ounces) chicken broth
1 jar (16 ounces) mild chunky-style salsa
2 tablespoons *Frank's® RedHot®* Cayenne Pepper Sauce
1 package (10 ounces) fully cooked carved chicken breasts

1 can (8¾ ounces) whole kernel corn, undrained
1 tablespoon chopped fresh cilantro (optional)
1 cup crushed tortilla chips
½ cup (2 ounces) shredded Monterey Jack cheese

1. Heat *1 teaspoon oil* in large saucepan over medium-high heat. Cook garlic 1 minute or until tender. Add broth, *¾ cup water,* salsa and *Frank's RedHot* Sauce. Stir in chicken, corn and cilantro. Heat to boiling. Reduce heat to medium-low. Cook, covered, 5 minutes.

2. Stir in tortillas and cheese. Serve hot.   *Makes 4 servings*

Prep Time: 5 minutes
Cook Time: 6 minutes

Chicken Tortilla Soup

Veg•All® Italian Soup

2 tablespoons butter
1 cup diced onion
1 cup shredded cabbage
2 cups water
2 cans (14½ ounces each) stewed tomatoes
1 can (15 ounces) VEG•ALL® Original
    Mixed Vegetables, drained

1 tablespoon chopped fresh parsley
½ teaspoon dried basil
½ teaspoon dried oregano
½ teaspoon black pepper

In large saucepan, melt butter. Stir in onion and cabbage. Heat for 2 minutes. Add water; cover and simmer for 10 minutes. Stir in tomatoes, Veg•All, and seasonings. Simmer for 10 minutes.

Makes 6 servings

Mama Mia Minestrone Magnifico

2 tablespoons extra-virgin olive oil
8 ounces crimini mushrooms, cut into
    ½-inch pieces (3 cups)
1 yellow summer squash (6 ounces), cut
    into ½-inch cubes (1¼ cups)
½ small eggplant, cut into ½-inch cubes
    (1 cup)
4 ounces green beans, cut diagonally into
    ½-inch pieces (1 cup)
6 cups water
1 (26-ounce) jar NEWMAN'S OWN®
    Roasted Garlic and Peppers Sauce

1 cup Burgundy wine
1 cup uncooked orzo pasta
1 (15½- to 19-ounce) can white kidney
    beans (cannellini), drained
4 medium tomatoes (1 pound), chopped
    (2 cups)
4 fresh basil leaves, chopped
1 tablespoon chopped fresh Italian parsley
¾ cup freshly grated Parmesan cheese
½ cup pine nuts, toasted

In 12-inch nonstick skillet, heat oil; sauté mushrooms, squash, eggplant and green beans over medium-high heat 10 minutes, stirring constantly, until golden and tender.

Combine water, pasta sauce and wine in 6-quart saucepot and bring to a boil. Add orzo and simmer 10 minutes, stirring occasionally.

Add sautéed vegetables, white beans, chopped tomatoes, basil and parsley; simmer 5 minutes, stirring occasionally.

Serve with Parmesan cheese and pine nuts to sprinkle on top.

Makes 8 servings

Veg•All® Italian Soup

Ranch Clam Chowder

¼ cup chopped onion
3 tablespoons butter or margarine
½ pound fresh mushrooms, sliced
2 tablespoons Worcestershire sauce
1½ cups half-and-half
1 can (10¾ ounces) cream of potato soup
¼ cup dry white wine

1 package (1 ounce) HIDDEN VALLEY®
   The Original Ranch® Salad Dressing
   & Seasoning Mix
1 can (10 ounces) whole baby clams,
   undrained
Chopped parsley

In 3-quart saucepan, cook onion in butter over medium heat until onion is soft but not browned. Add mushrooms and Worcestershire sauce. Cook until mushrooms are soft and pan juices have almost evaporated. In medium bowl, whisk together half-and-half, potato soup, wine and salad dressing mix until smooth. Drain clam liquid into dressing mixture; stir into mushrooms in pan. Cook, uncovered, until soup is heated through but not boiling. Add clams to soup; cook until heated through. Garnish each serving with parsley. *Makes 6 servings*

Butternut Squash Soup

2 tablespoons butter or margarine
1 medium onion, chopped
2 cloves garlic, minced
3 medium carrots, diced
2 stalks celery, diced
1 butternut squash, peeled, seeded and
   diced

1 medium potato, peeled and diced
3 cans (14½ ounces each) ready-to-serve
   chicken broth
½ cup honey
½ teaspoon dried thyme leaves, crushed
   Salt and pepper, to taste

In large pot, melt butter over medium heat. Stir in onion and garlic. Cook and stir until lightly browned, about 5 minutes. Stir in carrots and celery. Cook and stir until tender, about 5 minutes. Stir in squash, potato, chicken broth, honey and thyme. Bring mixture to a boil; reduce heat and simmer 30 to 45 minutes, or until vegetables are tender. Remove from heat and cool slightly. Working in small batches, transfer mixture to blender or food processor; process until smooth. Return puréed soup to pot. Season to taste with salt and pepper. Heat until hot and serve.

Makes 6 servings

Favorite recipe from **National Honey Board**

Ranch Clam Chowder

Chicken Vegetable Soup

1 bag SUCCESS® Rice
5 cups chicken broth
1½ cups chopped uncooked chicken
1 cup sliced celery
1 cup sliced carrots
½ cup chopped onion

¼ cup chopped fresh parsley
½ teaspoon black pepper
½ teaspoon dried thyme leaves, crushed
1 bay leaf
1 tablespoon lime juice

Prepare rice according to package directions.

Combine broth, chicken, celery, carrots, onion, parsley, pepper, thyme and bay leaf in large saucepan or Dutch oven. Bring to a boil over medium-high heat, stirring once or twice. Reduce heat to low; simmer 10 to 15 minutes or until chicken is no longer pink in center. Remove bay leaf; discard. Stir in rice and lime juice. Garnish, if desired.

Makes 4 servings

Corn and Potato Soup

2 tablespoons CRISCO® Oil*
1 medium onion, peeled and diced
1 tablespoon jarred minced garlic *or*
　2 large cloves garlic, peeled and
　minced
3 ears fresh corn, husked, kernels cut from
　cobs

1 large Idaho or russet potato (about
　½ pound), peeled and thinly sliced
1 can (14½ ounces) chicken broth
¼ teaspoon dried thyme leaves
¾ cup half-and-half
½ teaspoon salt
¼ teaspoon freshly ground black pepper

*Use your favorite Crisco Oil product.

1. Heat oil in 2-quart saucepan on medium-high heat. Add onion and garlic. Sauté 3 minutes, or until onion is translucent.

2. Add corn, potato, broth and thyme to pan. Bring to a boil. Cover pan. Reduce heat to low. Simmer 15 minutes, or until potato slices are breaking apart. Remove pan from heat. Mash soup with potato masher or fork; do not purée.

3. Add half-and-half, salt and pepper to pan. Bring to a boil on medium heat. Simmer 3 minutes. Stir occasionally.

Makes 4 servings

Prep Time: 10 minutes
Total Time: 35 minutes

Chicken Vegetable Soup

Quick Beef Soup

1½ pounds lean ground beef
1 cup chopped onion
2 cloves garlic, finely chopped
1 can (28 ounces) tomatoes, undrained
6 cups water
6 beef bouillon cubes

¼ teaspoon black pepper
1½ cups frozen peas, carrots and corn
    vegetable blend
½ cup uncooked orzo
French bread (optional)

Cook beef, onion and garlic in large saucepan over medium-high heat until beef is brown, stirring to separate meat; drain fat.

Purée tomatoes with juice in covered blender or food processor. Add tomatoes with juices, water, bouillon cubes and pepper to meat mixture. Bring to a boil; reduce heat to low. Simmer, uncovered, 20 minutes. Add vegetables and orzo. Simmer 15 minutes more. Serve with French bread.

Makes 6 servings

Favorite recipe from **North Dakota Beef Commission**

Potato Basil Soup

½ cup WESSON® Vegetable Oil
3 cups chopped celery
1½ cups chopped onions
1 teaspoon fresh minced garlic
1 quart chicken broth
3 to 4 cups peeled and diced russet
    potatoes (about 3 large potatoes)

¼ cup chopped fresh parsley
¼ cup chopped fresh basil
¼ teaspoon pepper
Grated Fontina cheese

In large saucepan, heat Wesson Oil until hot; sauté celery, onions and garlic until tender. Stir in chicken broth, potatoes, parsley, basil and pepper; bring to a boil and reduce heat. Simmer, covered, for 20 minutes or until potatoes are tender. Pour *half* of mixture into blender; purée until smooth. Set aside. Pour *remaining* soup into blender; blend until coarsely chopped. Combine both mixtures. Ladle soup into bowls; garnish with Fontina cheese and additional parsley if desired.

Makes 8 cups soup

Prep Time: 10 minutes
Cook Time: 20 minutes

Quick Beef Soup

Black Bean Soup

2 tablespoons vegetable oil
1 large onion, chopped
3 large cloves garlic, minced
4 cans (15 to 19 ounces each) black beans, undrained
2 cans (14½ ounces each) reduced-sodium chicken broth

⅓ cup *Frank's® RedHot®* Cayenne Pepper Sauce
¼ cup minced fresh cilantro
2 teaspoons ground cumin

1. Heat oil in 4- to 5-quart saucepan. Add onion and garlic; cook until tender. Stir in beans with liquid, broth, *Frank's RedHot* Sauce, cilantro and cumin.

2. Bring to a boil. Reduce heat; simmer, partially covered, 30 minutes, stirring often.

3. Remove 1 cup soup. Place in blender; cover securely and process until smooth. Return to saucepan; stir. Serve soup in individual soup bowls. Top with dollop of sour cream, if desired.

Makes 10 servings

Prep Time: 10 minutes
Cook Time: 35 minutes

Note: This soup freezes well. Freeze leftovers in individual portions. Thaw and reheat in microwave.

Cabbage Soup

1 pound BOB EVANS® Italian or Original Recipe Roll Sausage
3 cups water
1 (14-ounce) can beef broth
1 (10¾-ounce) can condensed tomato soup
1 small head cabbage, coarsely chopped
1 medium onion, chopped

¾ teaspoon salt
½ teaspoon black pepper
¼ teaspoon paprika
1 bay leaf
1 (16-ounce) can dark red kidney beans, rinsed and drained
Parmesan cheese for garnish (optional)

Crumble and cook sausage in medium skillet until browned. Drain off any drippings. Combine sausage and all remaining ingredients except beans and cheese in large saucepan; bring to a boil over high heat. Reduce heat to low; cover and simmer 35 minutes or until cabbage is tender. Remove bay leaf. Add beans; cook until heated through. Serve in individual soup bowls and garnish with Parmesan cheese, if desired. Refrigerate leftovers.

Makes 8 servings

Tomato-Lentil Soup

2 tablespoons olive oil
2 cups chopped onion
1 cup sliced celery
1 carrot, peeled, sliced
6 cups water
1 cup dry lentils
1 can (6 ounces) CONTADINA® Tomato
    Paste
½ cup dry red wine or chicken broth

¼ cup chopped fresh parsley *or*
    1 tablespoon dried parsley flakes
3 small chicken bouillon cubes
1 teaspoon salt
½ teaspoon Worcestershire sauce
¼ teaspoon black pepper
    Shredded or grated Parmesan cheese
    (optional)

1. Heat oil over medium-high heat in large saucepan. Add onion, celery and carrot; sauté until vegetables are tender.

2. Stir in water, lentils, tomato paste, wine, parsley, bouillon cubes, salt, Worcestershire sauce and pepper. Bring to a boil.

3. Reduce heat to low; simmer, uncovered, 45 to 50 minutes or until lentils are tender. Sprinkle with Parmesan cheese, if desired.

Makes 9 cups soup

Prep Time: 8 minutes
Cook Time: 55 minutes

Hot & Sour Soup

1 can (10½ ounces) condensed chicken
    broth
2 soup cans water
2 tablespoons cornstarch
2 tablespoons KIKKOMAN® Soy Sauce
2 tablespoons distilled white vinegar

⅛ teaspoon ground red pepper (cayenne)
1 egg, beaten
½ block firm tofu, drained and cut into
    ½-inch cubes
⅓ cup thinly sliced green onions and tops

Blend chicken broth, water, cornstarch, soy sauce, vinegar and red pepper in medium saucepan. Bring to a boil over high heat, stirring constantly until slightly thickened. Gradually pour egg into boiling soup, stirring constantly in 1 direction. Add tofu and green onions; cook only until tofu is heated through. Serve immediately.

Makes 5 (1-cup) servings

Vegetable and Shrimp Chowder

1½ cups diced Spanish onions
½ cup sliced carrots
½ cup diced celery
2 tablespoons margarine or butter
2 cups peeled and diced baking potatoes
1 (10-ounce) package frozen corn

5 cups chicken broth
½ pound small shrimp, peeled and deveined
⅓ cup GREY POUPON® Dijon Mustard
¼ cup chopped fresh parsley

1. Cook and stir onions, carrots and celery in margarine or butter in large saucepan over medium heat for 3 to 4 minutes or until tender. Add potatoes, corn and chicken broth; heat to a boil.

2. Reduce heat; simmer for 20 to 25 minutes or until potatoes are tender. Add shrimp, mustard and parsley; cook for 5 minutes more or until shrimp are cooked. Garnish as desired. Serve warm.

Makes 8 servings

Hearty Beef and Mushroom Soup

¾ pound sirloin beef sandwich steak
3 tablespoons butter or margarine, divided
1 small onion, chopped
1 package (6 ounces) sliced portobello mushrooms, cut into 1-inch chunks

1 large carrot, sliced
1 box UNCLE BEN'S® Brown & Wild Rice Mushroom Recipe
3 cans (14½ ounces each) beef broth
1 tablespoon chopped fresh parsley

1. Slice beef into 1-inch-wide strips; cut strips into 1-inch pieces.

2. Melt 2 tablespoons butter in large saucepan or Dutch oven over medium-high heat. Add onion and mushrooms; cook 2 minutes. Add remaining 1 tablespoon butter, beef and carrot; cook 2 minutes or until beef is no longer pink.

3. Add rice, contents of seasoning packet and broth. Bring to a boil. Cover; reduce heat and simmer 25 minutes or until rice is tender. Stir in parsley just before serving.   *Makes 4 (1½-cup) servings*

Cook's Tip: If sliced portobello mushrooms are not available, substitute 2 medium portobello mushrooms cut into chunks. Or, substitute 6 ounces button mushrooms, cut into quarters.

Vegetable and Shrimp Chowder

Creamy Gazpacho

1 cup undiluted evaporated skimmed milk
1 can (14.5 ounces) CONTADINA®
    Recipe Ready Diced Tomatoes
2 cups tomato juice
3 tablespoons lemon juice
2 tablespoons olive oil
1 clove garlic, minced
½ teaspoon salt
¼ teaspoon ground black pepper

¼ teaspoon red pepper sauce
2 cups (2 medium) peeled, seeded and
    diced cucumbers
½ cup diced green bell pepper
½ cup diced onion
    Garnishes: Plain low-fat or nonfat
    yogurt, diced cucumber, bell pepper
    and onion (optional)

1. Place evaporated skimmed milk, tomatoes, tomato juice, lemon juice, olive oil, garlic, salt, pepper and red pepper sauce in blender; cover and blend thoroughly. (Blender container will be very full.)

2. Pour into serving bowl or tureen and add cucumber, bell pepper and onion; stir thoroughly.

3. Chill. Serve cold; garnish as desired.

Makes about 7 (1-cup) servings

Prep Time: 10 minutes
Chill Time: 2 hours or overnight

Italian Vegetable Soup

1 package KNORR® Recipe Classics™
    Tomato Basil Soup, Dip and Recipe
    Mix
4 cups water

2 cups sliced fennel or broccoli florets
1 large zucchini, diced (about 2 cups)
1 teaspoon dried oregano
    Grated Parmesan cheese (optional)

• In 4-quart dutch oven, combine recipe mix, water, fennel, zucchini and oregano. Stirring occasionally, bring to a boil over medium-high heat.

• Reduce heat, cover and simmer, stirring occasionally, 15 minutes or until vegetables are tender.

• If desired, sprinkle lightly with Parmesan cheese

Makes 6 (1-cup) servings

Prep Time: 20 minutes
Cook Time: 25 minutes

Creamy Gazpacho

Hearty Tortellini Soup

1 small red onion, chopped
2 medium carrots, chopped
2 ribs celery, thinly sliced
1 small zucchini, chopped
2 plum tomatoes, chopped
2 cloves garlic, minced
2 cans (14½ ounces *each*) chicken broth

1 can (15 to 19 ounces) red kidney beans, rinsed and drained
2 tablespoons *French's*® Worcestershire Sauce
1 package (9 ounces) refrigerated tortellini pasta

1. Heat *2 tablespoons oil* in 6-quart saucepot or Dutch oven over medium-high heat. Add vegetables, tomatoes and garlic. Cook and stir 5 minutes or until vegetables are crisp-tender.

2. Add broth, *½ cup water,* beans and Worcestershire. Heat to boiling. Stir in pasta. Return to boiling. Cook 5 minutes or until pasta is tender, stirring occasionally. Serve with crusty bread and grated Parmesan cheese, if desired.

Makes 4 servings

Prep Time: 15 minutes
Cook Time: 10 minutes

Onion Soup with Pasta

3 cups sliced onions
3 cloves garlic, minced
½ teaspoon sugar
2 cans (14½ ounces each) reduced-sodium beef broth

½ cup uncooked small pasta stars
2 tablespoons dry sherry
¼ teaspoon salt
⅛ teaspoon black pepper
Grated Parmesan cheese

1. Spray large saucepan with nonstick cooking spray; heat over medium heat until hot. Add onions and garlic. Cook, covered, 5 to 8 minutes or until onions are wilted. Stir in sugar; cook about 15 minutes or until onion mixture is very soft and browned.

2. Add broth to saucepan; bring to a boil. Add pasta and simmer, uncovered, 6 to 8 minutes or until tender. Stir in sherry, salt and pepper. Ladle soup into bowls; sprinkle lightly with Parmesan cheese.

Makes 4 first-course servings

Hearty Tortellini Soup

Beef Barley Soup

¾ pound boneless beef top round, excess
    fat trimmed, cut into ½-inch pieces
3 cans (about 14 ounces each) defatted
    low sodium beef broth*
1 can (14½ ounces) no-salt-added
    tomatoes
2 cups ½-inch unpeeled potato cubes
1½ cups ½-inch green bean slices
1 cup chopped onion

1 cup sliced carrots
½ cup pearled barley
1 tablespoon cider vinegar
2 teaspoons caraway seeds, lightly crushed
2 teaspoons dried marjoram leaves,
    crushed
2 teaspoons dried thyme leaves, crushed
½ teaspoon salt
½ teaspoon black pepper

To defat beef broth, skim fat from surface of broth with spoon. Or, place can of broth in refrigerator at least 2 hours ahead of time. Before using, remove fat that has hardened on surface of broth.

Coat large saucepan with nonstick cooking spray; heat over medium heat. Add beef; cook and stir until browned on all sides. Add beef broth, tomatoes, potatoes, green beans, onion, carrots, barley, vinegar, caraway seeds, marjoram, thyme, salt and pepper; bring to a boil over high heat. Reduce heat to low. Simmer, covered, about 2 hours or until beef is fork-tender, uncovering saucepan during last 30 minutes of cooking.

Makes 4 servings

Pea Soup

2 tablespoons butter or margarine
1 medium onion, chopped
1 bag (16 ounces) BIRDS EYE® frozen
    Green Peas

1 can (13¾ ounces) chicken broth
½ teaspoon dried tarragon

• Melt butter in medium saucepan over medium-high heat. Add onion; cook until tender, about 3 minutes.

• Add peas, chicken broth and tarragon. Bring to boil; reduce heat to medium. Cover and cook 4 minutes.

• Transfer mixture to blender; blend until smooth. Strain, if desired. Serve hot or cold.

Makes about 3 servings

Prep Time: 5 minutes
Cook Time: 15 minutes

Meatball & Pasta Soup

2 cans (14½ ounces each) chicken broth
4 cups water
1 can (15 ounces) crushed tomatoes
1 package (15 ounces) frozen precooked
    Italian style meatballs, not in sauce
1 envelope LIPTON® RECIPE SECRETS®
    Onion Soup Mix

½ teaspoon garlic powder
1 cup uncooked mini pasta (such as
    conchigliette or ditalini)
4 cups fresh baby spinach leaves

1. In 6-quart saucepot, bring broth, water, crushed tomatoes, meatballs, soup mix and garlic powder to a boil over medium-high heat.

2. Add pasta and cook 5 minutes or until pasta is almost tender. Stir in spinach. Reduce heat to medium and simmer uncovered 2 minutes or until spinach is wilted and pasta is tender. Serve, if desired, with Parmesan cheese.
Makes 8 servings

Prep Time: 10 minutes
Cook Time: 15 minutes

Velvety Leek & Wild Rice Soup

½ pound zucchini, peeled and coarsely
    chopped
½ pound fennel, coarsely chopped
2 large leeks, chopped (white part only)
2 tablespoons butter

4 tablespoons chopped fresh dill, divided
4 cups chicken broth
    Salt and white pepper to taste
1 cup heavy cream
3 cups cooked wild rice

In large saucepan, cook zucchini, fennel and leeks in butter over medium heat 10 to 15 minutes. Add 3 tablespoons dill, broth, salt and pepper. Simmer, uncovered, 20 minutes. Remove from heat; purée in food processor or blender (in batches if necessary). When ready to serve, return to saucepan over low heat. Add cream, adjust seasonings and heat through. *Do not boil.* In bottom of each shallow soup bowl, mound ½ cup wild rice in center. Ladle soup around rice and garnish with remaining 1 tablespoon dill.
Makes 6 servings

Favorite recipe from **Minnesota Cultivated Wild Rice Council**

SPAM™ Vegetable Soup with Cheese-Topped Croutons

1½ cups chopped carrots
1 cup chopped onion
1 tablespoon vegetable oil
5 cups chicken broth
3 cups chopped cabbage
1 cup diced, unpeeled potatoes
½ teaspoon dried thyme leaves
1 (12-ounce) can SPAM® Luncheon Meat, cubed

Cheese-Topped Croutons

1¼ cups (5 ounces) shredded Swiss cheese
⅓ cup mayonnaise or salad dressing
2 tablespoons grated Parmesan cheese
2 tablespoons sliced green onion
6 slices sourdough bread, toasted

In 3- or 4-quart saucepan over medium heat, sauté carrots and chopped onion in oil 5 to 10 minutes or until onion is golden. Stir in broth, cabbage, potatoes and thyme. Bring to a boil. Cover. Reduce heat and simmer 30 minutes or until vegetables are tender. Stir in SPAM®. Simmer 2 minutes.

Meanwhile, heat broiler. In small bowl, combine Swiss cheese, mayonnaise, Parmesan cheese and green onion. Spread over each bread slice. Ladle soup into oven-proof bowls.* Top each with a bread slice. Place bowls on baking sheet. Broil 3 minutes or until cheese mixture just begins to brown.

Makes 6 servings

*If bowls are not oven-proof, place bread slices on baking sheet and broil, then place on top of soup.

SPAM™ *Vegetable Soup with Cheese-Topped Crouton*

Mushroom and Rice Soup

1 bag SUCCESS® Rice
2 tablespoons olive oil
2 cups sliced fresh mushrooms
1 cup chopped onion
1 cup diagonally sliced green onions

5 cups chicken broth
1 teaspoon pepper
1 teaspoon dried thyme leaves, crushed
1 tablespoon dry sherry

Prepare rice according to package directions.

Heat oil in large saucepan or Dutch oven over medium heat. Add mushrooms and onions; cook and stir until tender. Add broth, pepper and thyme. Reduce heat to low; simmer until thoroughly heated, 5 to 7 minutes. Stir in rice and sherry; heat thoroughly, stirring occasionally. Garnish, if desired.

Makes 4 servings

Quick and Zesty Vegetable Soup

1 pound lean ground beef
½ cup chopped onion
   Salt and pepper
2 cans (14½ ounces each) DEL MONTE®
   Italian Recipe Stewed Tomatoes

2 cans (14 ounces each) beef broth
1 can (14½ ounces) DEL MONTE® Mixed
   Vegetables
½ cup uncooked medium egg noodles
½ teaspoon dried oregano

1. Brown meat with onion in large pot. Cook until onion is tender; drain. Season to taste with salt and pepper.

2. Stir in remaining ingredients. Bring to boil; reduce heat.

3. Cover and simmer 15 minutes or until noodles are tender.

Makes 8 servings

Prep Time: 5 minutes
Cook Time: 15 minutes

Mushroom and Rice Soup

Aztec Corn Soup

2 packages (10 ounces each) frozen whole
   kernel corn
3½ cups chicken broth
¼ teaspoon salt
1 large tomato, peeled and seeded

¼ cup coarsely chopped onion
½ teaspoon dried oregano leaves
2 tablespoons butter or margarine
½ cup heavy cream
   Green bell pepper strips (optional)

Combine corn, broth and salt in 3-quart saucepan. Bring to a boil over high heat. Reduce heat to low. Cover and simmer 4 to 5 minutes until corn is tender. Remove ½ cup corn from saucepan with slotted spoon; set aside. Process remaining soup until smooth, half at a time, in blender. Return soup to saucepan.

Process tomato, onion and oregano in blender until smooth. Heat butter over medium heat until hot; add tomato mixture. Cook and stir 4 to 5 minutes or until thickened.

Add tomato mixture to corn mixture in saucepan; bring to a boil over high heat. Reduce heat to low; simmer uncovered, 5 minutes.

Remove soup from heat; gradually stir in cream. Heat over very low heat 30 seconds or just until hot. Do not boil. Ladle into bowls. Garnish with reserved corn and green bell pepper.

Makes 4 to 6 servings

Country Vegetable Soup

3 cans (13¾ ounces each) chicken broth
1 cup water
1 package (4½ ounces) creamy chicken,
   rice and sauce mix

½ teaspoon dried basil
1 bag (16 ounces) BIRDS EYE® frozen
   Farm Fresh Mixtures Broccoli, Green
   Beans, Pearl Onions and Red Peppers

• Bring broth, water, rice and sauce mix, and basil to boil in large saucepan over high heat.

• Reduce heat to medium. Cook, uncovered, 7 minutes.

• Add vegetables; cook 6 to 7 minutes or until rice and vegetables are tender.   *Makes 4 servings*

Prep Time: 5 minutes
Cook Time: 15 minutes

Aztec Corn Soup

Chicken Wild Rice Soup

⅓ cup instant nonfat dry milk
2 tablespoons cornstarch
2 teaspoons low sodium instant chicken
    bouillon
¼ teaspoon dried onion flakes
¼ teaspoon dried basil leaves, crushed
¼ teaspoon dried thyme leaves, crushed

⅛ teaspoon ground pepper
4 cups low sodium chicken broth, divided
½ cup sliced celery
½ cup sliced carrots
½ cup chopped onion
2 cups cooked wild rice
1 cup cooked cubed chicken breasts

In small bowl, combine dry milk, cornstarch, bouillon, onion flakes, basil, thyme and pepper. Stir in small amount of chicken broth; set aside. In large saucepan, combine remaining broth, celery, carrots and onion. Cook until vegetables are crisp-tender. Gradually add dry milk mixture. Stir in wild rice and chicken. Simmer 5 to 10 minutes.   *Makes 8 servings*

Favorite recipe from **Minnesota Cultivated Wild Rice Council**

Vegetable Medley Soup

1 package KNORR® Recipe Classics™
    Vegetable Soup, Dip and Recipe Mix
5 cups water
1 medium onion, sliced into thin wedges
1 cup sliced mushrooms
1 tablespoon barbecue sauce *or* 1 teaspoon
    Worcestershire sauce

⅛ to ¼ teaspoon ground black pepper
2 cups diagonally sliced fresh asparagus *or*
    1 package (10 ounces) frozen cut
asparagus

• In 4-quart Dutch oven or saucepot, combine recipe mix, water, onion, mushrooms, barbecue sauce and pepper.

• Bring to a boil over medium-high heat, stirring occasionally. Reduce heat to low and simmer covered 10 minutes, stirring occasionally.

• Add asparagus and simmer 5 minutes or until vegetables are tender.   *Makes 6 (1-cup) servings*

Prep Time: 5 minutes
Cook Time: 20 minutes

Calico Minestrone Soup

2 cans (14 ounces each) chicken broth
¼ cup uncooked small shell pasta
1 can (14½ ounces) DEL MONTE®
    Italian Recipe Stewed Tomatoes
1 can (8¾ ounces) *or* 1 cup kidney beans,
    drained

½ cup chopped cooked chicken or beef
1 carrot, cubed
1 stalk celery, sliced
½ teaspoon dried basil, crushed

1. Bring broth to boil in large saucepan; stir in pasta and boil 5 minutes.

2. Add remaining ingredients.

3. Reduce heat; cover and simmer 20 minutes. Garnish with grated Parmesan cheese, if desired.

Makes approximately 6 servings (1 cup each)

Prep Time: 5 minutes
Cook Time: 25 minutes

Matzo Ball Soup

4 eggs
1 cup matzo meal
¼ cup margarine, melted and cooled
2 tablespoons water
1 tablespoon grated raw onion

½ teaspoon salt
⅛ teaspoon white pepper *or* ¼ teaspoon
    black pepper
2 quarts chicken broth
Chopped fresh parsley (optional)

In large bowl, beat eggs on medium speed of electric mixer. Add matzo meal, margarine, water, onion, salt and pepper. Mix at low speed until well blended. Let stand 15 to 30 minutes. With wet hands, form mixture into 12 (2-inch) balls. Bring 8 cups water to a boil in Dutch oven. Drop matzo balls, one at a time, into boiling water. Reduce heat. Cover; simmer 35 to 40 minutes or until matzo balls are cooked through. Remove from Dutch oven with slotted spoon; drain well. Discard water.

In same Dutch oven, bring broth to a boil over high heat. Add matzo balls; reduce heat. Simmer, covered, 5 minutes or until matzo balls are heated through. Garnish with parsley.

Makes 6 servings

❈ *Delightful Salads* ❈

Waldorf Salad with Turkey and Apricot

Dressing
⅓ cup SMUCKER'S® Apricot Preserves
½ cup nonfat plain yogurt
2 tablespoons lemon juice
1 tablespoon chopped dried tarragon, chives, parsley or curry powder
1 teaspoon Dijon mustard
½ teaspoon grated lemon peel
½ teaspoon salt
⅛ teaspoon freshly ground pepper

Salad
1 pound boneless skinless turkey or chicken, cooked and cubed*
1 cup diced unpeeled red apple
1 cup diced unpeeled green apple
1 cup diced celery
¼ cup raisins
6 lettuce leaves
1 tablespoon chopped fresh parsley or chives

Deli turkey breast may be used in this recipe. Ask the deli to slice the turkey into ¾- or 1-inch slices, then cube the meat at home before adding it to the salad.

Combine all dressing ingredients; stir until well blended. Add turkey or chicken, apples, celery and raisins. Toss to coat the salad ingredients. Season with additional salt and/or pepper, if desired.

Place lettuce leaf on each of 6 serving plates. Top each with mound of salad. Garnish each salad with chopped fresh parsley or chives.   *Makes 6 servings*

Note: This also makes an excellent sandwich filling for pita (pocket) breads.

Waldorf Salad with Turkey and Apricot

Black Bean and Mango Chicken Salad

1 can (16 ounces) black beans, drained, rinsed
1 package (10 ounces) frozen corn, thawed
1 cup chopped ripe mango
½ pound boneless skinless chicken breasts, grilled, cut up

½ cup chopped red pepper
⅓ cup chopped fresh cilantro
⅓ cup chopped red onion
¼ cup lime juice
1 envelope GOOD SEASONS® Italian Salad Dressing Mix

TOSS all ingredients in large bowl. Refrigerate.

SERVE with baked tortilla chips, if desired.

Makes 4 servings

Prep Time: 10 minutes plus refrigerating

Ginger Fruit Salad

⅓ cup HELLMANN'S® or BEST FOODS® Real or Light Mayonnaise or Low Fat Mayonnaise Dressing
2 tablespoons orange juice
⅛ teaspoon ground ginger

2 medium oranges, sectioned
1 kiwifruit, peeled and sliced
1 cup fresh raspberries
Sliced star fruit for garnish (optional)
Pomegranate seeds for garnish (optional)

1. In medium bowl combine mayonnaise, orange juice and ginger.

2. Arrange orange sections, kiwi slices and raspberries on 4 serving plates. Spoon dressing over fruit. Garnish with sliced star fruit and pomegranate seeds, if desired.

Makes 4 servings

Black Bean and Mango Chicken Salad

Pasta Salad with Pesto

1 package BOB EVANS® Italian Grillin'
    Sausage (approximately 5 links)
1 pound uncooked penne pasta
1 tablespoon butter or margarine
2 cloves garlic, peeled
2 cups fresh basil leaves
½ cup fresh parsley leaves
2 tablespoons pine nuts

½ cup olive oil
¼ cup freshly grated Parmesan cheese
¼ teaspoon black pepper
2 cups seeded and diced Roma tomatoes
1 small green bell pepper, chopped
1 cup whole ripe olives
1 cup (4 ounces) cubed mozzarella cheese
Red leaf lettuce for garnish (optional)

Cook sausage in large skillet or on grill until browned; let cool. Cut in half lengthwise; cut each half into ¼-inch slices and set aside. Cook penne according to package directions; drain. Toss in large bowl with butter to prevent sticking.

To prepare pesto sauce, place garlic cloves in food processor with metal blade or in blender; process until smooth. Add basil and parsley; process until finely chopped. Add pine nuts; process until finely chopped. With motor running, slowly add olive oil in fine, steady stream. Add Parmesan cheese and black pepper; process until well blended, scraping down side as needed.

To assemble salad, toss sausage, tomatoes, bell pepper, olives and mozzarella cheese with penne. Gradually stir in pesto until salad is moist but not saturated. Serve salad on lettuce-lined platter, if desired. Refrigerate leftovers.

Makes 8 servings

Healthy Carrot Salad

4 cups shredded carrots
¼ cup raisins
¼ cup chopped walnuts
½ cup orange juice

¼ cup plain yogurt
1 tablespoon vegetable oil
¾ teaspoon LAWRY'S® Seasoned Salt
½ teaspoon LAWRY'S® Lemon Pepper

In medium bowl, combine carrots, raisins and walnuts. In small bowl, combine remaining ingredients; mix well. Add to carrot mixture; mix lightly to coat.

Makes 6 servings

Serving Suggestion: A cool side-dish salad for sandwiches or a terrific salad to serve on a picnic.

Pasta Salad with Pesto

Grilled Chicken Spinach Salad

2 boneless skinless chicken breasts, grilled, cut into strips
5 cups torn spinach
1 cup sliced mushrooms
½ cup thinly sliced red onion wedges

4 slices OSCAR MAYER® Bacon, crisply cooked, crumbled
1 cup KRAFT FREE CATALINA® Fat Free Dressing

TOSS all ingredients except dressing in large bowl. Serve with dressing.

Makes 6 servings

Prep Time: 15 minutes

Tip: Substitute grilled shrimp for grilled chicken.

Tangy Cherry Coleslaw

Dressing
¼ cup granulated sugar
½ teaspoon dry mustard
½ teaspoon celery seed
  Dash salt
⅓ cup vegetable oil
¼ cup lime juice
3 tablespoons honey

Salad
1 (16-ounce) bag coleslaw mixture
1 cup shredded carrots
1 cup dried tart cherries
½ cup chopped green onions

For dressing, combine sugar, dry mustard, celery seed and salt in small mixing bowl; mix well. Whisk in oil, lime juice and honey until well blended and sugar is dissolved.

For salad, combine coleslaw mixture, carrots, dried cherries and green onions in large mixing bowl. Pour dressing over coleslaw mixture; mix until well combined. Refrigerate 30 minutes before serving.

Makes 6 to 8 servings

Favorite recipe from **Cherry Marketing Institute**

Grilled Chicken Spinach Salad

Bow Tie Pasta Salad

1 package (16 ounces) uncooked bow ties, rotini, ziti or other shaped pasta
1 bag (16 ounces) BIRDS EYE® frozen Farm Fresh Mixtures Broccoli, Cauliflower and Carrots*
1 cup Italian, creamy Italian or favorite salad dressing
1 bunch green onions, thinly sliced
1 cup pitted ripe olives, halved (optional)

Or, substitute any other Birds Eye® frozen Farm Fresh Mixtures variety.

• Cook pasta according to package directions; drain.

• Cook vegetables according to package directions; drain.

• Combine pasta and vegetables with remaining ingredients in large bowl. Cover and chill until ready to serve.
Makes about 8 side-dish servings

Prep Time: 5 minutes
Cook Time: 20 minutes

Serving Suggestion: Use this recipe as the base for a variety of main-dish salads, adding sliced salami and small cubes of cheese or cooked chicken, turkey or seafood to the pasta and vegetables.

Insalata Rustica

Mustard Dressing (recipe follows)
4 cups torn iceberg lettuce
4 cups torn romaine lettuce
1 bunch watercress, stems removed and leaves torn
2 tomatoes, sliced
6 radishes, sliced
2 large fresh California peaches, halved, pitted and cut into wedges

Prepare Mustard Dressing; set aside. Combine iceberg lettuce, romaine lettuce and watercress in large salad bowl. Arrange tomatoes, radishes and peaches in attractive pattern on top. Drizzle with Mustard Dressing.
Makes 6 servings

Mustard Dressing: Combine ¾ cup chicken broth, 3 tablespoons white wine vinegar, 4 teaspoons Dijon-style mustard, 1 teaspoon olive oil, 2 teaspoons minced garlic and ½ teaspoon sugar in jar with tight-fitting lid. Cover; shake well.

*Favorite recipe from **California Tree Fruit Agreement***

Bow Tie Pasta Salad

Vegetable Potato Salad

1 envelope LIPTON® RECIPE SECRETS®
   Vegetable Soup Mix
1 cup HELLMANN'S® or BEST FOODS®
   Mayonnaise

2 teaspoons white vinegar
2 pounds red or all-purpose potatoes,
   cooked and cut into chunks
¼ cup red onion, finely chopped (optional)

1. In large bowl, combine soup mix, mayonnaise and vinegar.

2. Add potatoes and onion; toss well. Chill 2 hours.

Makes 6 servings

Prep Time: 20 minutes
Chill Time: 2 hours

Tasty Taco Salad

1 pound lean ground pork
1 can (8 ounces) whole tomatoes,
   undrained, cut up
¼ cup chopped onion
2 to 3 teaspoons chili powder, or to taste
¼ teaspoon garlic powder

Salt and pepper
1 head iceberg lettuce
2 fresh tomatoes, cut into wedges
¼ cup (1 ounce) shredded Cheddar cheese
   Corn chips, crushed (optional)

In heavy 10-inch skillet, brown ground pork over medium heat; drain. Stir in undrained canned tomatoes, onion, chili powder and garlic powder. Bring to a boil; reduce heat and simmer, uncovered, until most liquid evaporates, about 15 minutes, stirring occasionally. Season to taste with salt and pepper. Meanwhile, line four individual salad bowls with large lettuce leaves; tear remaining lettuce into bite-size pieces. Divide among bowls. Spoon about ½ cup pork mixture over lettuce in each bowl. Arrange fresh tomato wedges on salad; sprinkle with cheese and crushed corn chips, if desired.

Makes 4 servings

Prep Time: 25 minutes
Cook Time: 20 minutes

Favorite recipe from **National Pork Board**

Vegetable Potato Salad

Neon Turkey Pasta Salad

2 cups cubed cooked BUTTERBALL®
  Breast of Young Turkey
2 cups tri-colored rotini pasta, cooked and
  drained
1 small zucchini, sliced
2 small tomatoes, cut into wedges
½ cup chunked yellow bell pepper

½ cup chunked red bell pepper
½ cup chunked green bell pepper
½ cup crumbled feta cheese
1 can (2¼ ounces) sliced ripe olives,
  drained
⅓ cup fresh basil leaves, cut into strips
1 cup prepared Italian salad dressing

Combine turkey, pasta, vegetables, cheese, olives and basil in large bowl. Toss with salad dressing. Chill at least 2 hours before serving.

Makes 6 servings

Prep Time: 20 minutes plus chilling time

Watergate Salad

1 package (4-serving size) JELL-O®
  Pistachio Flavor Instant Pudding
  & Pie Filling
1 can (20 ounces) crushed pineapple in
  juice, undrained

1 cup miniature marshmallows
½ cup chopped nuts
2 cups thawed COOL WHIP® Whipped
  Topping

STIR pudding mix, pineapple with juice, marshmallows and nuts in large bowl until well blended. Gently stir in whipped topping.

REFRIGERATE 1 hour or until ready to serve. Garnish as desired.

Makes 8 servings

Prep Time: 10 minutes
Refrigerate Time: 1 hour

Neon Turkey Pasta Salad

Hot German Potato Salad

1½ pounds new or boiling-type potatoes, cut into ¾-inch cubes
1⅓ cups water, divided
½ teaspoon salt
½ pound bacon, cut crosswise into strips
2 tablespoons cider vinegar
4 teaspoons sugar
1 tablespoon *French's*® Worcestershire Sauce

2 teaspoons cornstarch
¼ teaspoon ground black pepper
1⅓ cups *French's*® French Fried Onions, divided
1 cup chopped green bell pepper
1 cup chopped celery
¼ cup chopped pimiento

Place potatoes, 1 cup water and salt in 3-quart microwave-safe dish. Cover and microwave on HIGH 15 minutes or until potatoes are tender, stirring once. Drain in colander; set aside.

Place bacon in same dish. Microwave, uncovered, on HIGH 5 minutes or until bacon is crisp, stirring once. Remove bacon with slotted spoon; set aside. Pour off all but ¼ cup bacon drippings. Stir in remaining ⅓ cup water, vinegar, sugar, Worcestershire, cornstarch and black pepper. Microwave, uncovered, on HIGH 1 to 2 minutes or until dressing has thickened, stirring once.

Return potatoes to dish. Add ⅔ cup French Fried Onions, bell pepper, celery, pimiento and reserved bacon; toss well to coat evenly. Microwave, uncovered, on HIGH 2 minutes. Stir. Sprinkle with remaining ⅔ *cup* onions. Microwave on HIGH 1 minute or until onions are golden. Serve warm.

Makes 6 side-dish servings

Prep Time: 20 minutes
Cook Time: 25 minutes

Sunshine Fruit and Avocado Salad

5 small oranges, peeled
2 ripe small avocados, halved, pitted and peeled
1 tablespoon lemon juice
4 shallots, chopped
¼ cup golden raisins
1 tablespoon chopped fresh cilantro *or*
  ½ teaspoon ground coriander

1 teaspoon chopped fresh thyme *or*
  ½ teaspoon dried thyme leaves
3 tablespoons FILIPPO BERIO® Olive Oil
  Juice of 1 small orange
2 tablespoons dry sherry
1 tablespoon honey
  Salt and freshly ground black pepper

Cut oranges into ½-inch-thick round slices. Cut avocados into ¼-inch-thick slices; brush with lemon juice. Arrange orange and avocado slices in layers in serving bowl, sprinkling each layer with shallots, raisins, cilantro and thyme.

In small bowl, whisk together olive oil, orange juice, sherry and honey. Pour dressing over salad. Cover; refrigerate at least 1 hour before serving. Season to taste with salt and pepper.

Makes 6 servings

Cobb Salad

  Red leaf lettuce
8 cups mixed torn salad greens
1 cup prepared HIDDEN VALLEY® The Original Ranch® with Bacon Salad Dressing
1 can (16 ounces) thin asparagus spears
¼ pound cooked turkey, cut into strips

¼ pound cooked ham, cut into strips
¼ pound (about 4 slices) American cheese, cut into strips
4 hard-cooked eggs, sliced
4 radishes, thinly sliced
  Freshly ground black pepper

Line 4 salad plates with lettuce leaves; divide salad greens among plates. Pour ¼ cup of the salad dressing into individual containers. Place in center of each plate. Arrange asparagus, turkey, ham, cheese, eggs and radishes in spoke fashion around dressing. Sprinkle with pepper.

Makes 4 servings

Mexican Taco Salad

1 pound ground beef or turkey
1 cup (1 small) chopped onion
1 cup ORTEGA® Salsa Prima-Thick
   & Chunky Mild
¾ cup water
1 package (1¼ ounces) ORTEGA® Taco
   Seasoning Mix
1¾ cups (15-ounce can) kidney or pinto
   beans, rinsed and drained
½ cup (4-ounce can) ORTEGA® Diced
   Green Chiles

6 tortilla shells *or* 3 cups (3 ounces)
   tortilla chips
6 cups shredded lettuce, *divided*
   Chopped tomatoes (optional)
¾ cup (3 ounces) shredded nacho & taco
   blend cheese, *divided*
   Sour cream (optional)
   Guacamole (optional)
   ORTEGA® Thick & Smooth Taco Sauce

COOK beef and onion until beef is brown; drain. Stir in salsa, water and seasoning mix. Bring to a boil. Reduce heat to low; cook for 2 to 3 minutes. Stir in beans and chiles.

LAYER ingredients as follows in *each* shell: *1 cup* lettuce, *¾ cup* meat mixture, tomatoes, *2 tablespoons* cheese and sour cream. Serve with guacamole and taco sauce. *Makes 6 servings*

Easy Cole Slaw

2 tablespoons CRISCO® Oil*
¼ cup granulated sugar
¼ cup cider vinegar
1 tablespoon prepared mustard

½ teaspoon salt
¼ teaspoon freshly ground black pepper
1 bag (1 pound) cole slaw mix (or
   shredded cabbage)

Use your favorite Crisco Oil product.

1. Combine oil, sugar, vinegar, mustard, salt and pepper in small saucepan. Place pan on medium heat. Simmer for 3 minutes.

2. Place cole slaw mix in mixing bowl. Toss with hot dressing. Let stand for 20 minutes. Serve with slotted spoon. *Makes 4 servings*

Prep Time: 10 minutes
Total Time: 30 minutes

Note: This cole slaw can also be made up to 2 days in advance and refrigerated, tightly covered. Drain before serving.

Mexican Taco Salad

Cool-as-a-Cucumber Salad

4 cups cooked UNCLE BEN'S®
    ORIGINAL CONVERTED® Brand
    Rice
1 cup finely chopped seeded cucumber
¾ cup plain yogurt or sour cream

2 tablespoons finely chopped onion
1 tablespoon balsamic vinegar
2 teaspoons dried dill weed
1 teaspoon salt
¼ teaspoon black pepper

1. Rinse hot cooked rice under cold running water to cool; drain.

2. In large bowl, combine rice with remaining ingredients; mix well. Cover and refrigerate until well chilled to allow flavors to blend, about 4 hours.
Makes 6 servings

Tomato and Goat Cheese Salad

Salad
1 package (16 ounces) uncooked
    BARILLA® medium shells
2 cups cherry tomato halves (red and
    yellow, if desired)
½ cup crumbled goat cheese
    Baby Boston lettuce or mesclun mix

Dressing
½ cup balsamic vinegar
½ cup chopped red onion
¼ cup olive oil
1 tablespoon chopped fresh parsley
1 teaspoon Dijon mustard
    Salt and black pepper to taste

Prepare shells according to package directions; drain.

Combine cooked shells with tomatoes and goat cheese in large bowl; mix gently but thoroughly.

For dressing, combine vinegar, onion, oil, parsley, mustard, salt and pepper in small bowl; mix well. Add dressing to shell mixture and toss well.

Serve immediately over beds of lettuce.
Makes 4 to 6 servings

Variation: To make this salad a main dish, top with sliced, grilled chicken.

Tip: The flavor of goat cheese, or chèvre, can range from mild to strong. Choose a brand that suits your taste.

Cool-as-a-Cucumber Salad

Grilled Steak Salad

¾ cup Italian salad dressing
¼ cup LA CHOY® Soy Sauce
4 (4-ounce) boneless beef tenderloin
 steaks

8 large mushrooms, stems removed
6 cups salad greens

In small bowl, combine salad dressing and soy sauce; mix well. In resealable plastic bag, combine steaks, mushroom caps and ¼ cup soy sauce mixture; marinate 15 minutes. Grill steak over medium-hot heat, basting often with marinade, 5 minutes on each side or to desired doneness. Grill mushrooms last 5 minutes of cooking time. Discard remaining marinade. Serve sliced steak and mushrooms over salad greens and dress with remaining soy sauce mixture.   *Makes 4 servings*

Open Range Black Eyed Peas and Pasta Salad

Dressing
 ¼ cup red wine vinegar
 1½ tablespoons WESSON® Vegetable Oil
 1½ tablespoons country-style Dijon
  mustard
 1 tablespoon sugar
 2 teaspoons grated fresh orange peel
 1 teaspoon minced fresh garlic
 ¾ teaspoon ground cumin
 ½ teaspoon salt
 ¼ teaspoon cayenne pepper

Salad
 ½ pound multi-colored wagon wheel pasta,
  cooked according to package directions
 1 can (15 ounces) black eyed peas, rinsed
  and drained
 1 can (14.5 ounces) HUNT'S® Choice-Cut
  Diced Tomatoes, undrained
 ⅔ cup sliced black olives
 ⅔ cup chopped red or green bell pepper
 ½ cup sliced green onions
 ¼ cup chopped fresh cilantro

1. Place *all* dressing ingredients in food processor or blender. Process until smooth and well blended.

2. In large bowl, combine *all* salad ingredients. Add dressing and toss gently to mix and coat.

3. Cover and refrigerate at least 1 hour or overnight to allow flavors to blend. Gently toss salad before serving.   *Makes 10 (6-ounce) servings*

Tip: Add a little kick to this salad by adding red pepper flakes and hot pepper sauce. For another variation, try chopped parsley and fresh oregano instead of cilantro.

Grilled Steak Salad

Salmon Broccoli Waldorf Salad

1 bag (16 ounces) BIRDS EYE® frozen
    Broccoli Cuts
1 large Red Delicious apple, chopped
¼ cup thinly sliced green onions

½ cup bottled creamy roasted garlic, ranch
    or blue cheese dressing
1 can (14¾ ounces) salmon, drained and
    flaked

• In large saucepan, cook broccoli according to package directions; drain and rinse under cold water in colander.

• In large bowl, toss together broccoli, apple, onions and dressing. Gently stir in salmon; add pepper to taste.

Makes 4 servings

Prep Time: 5 minutes
Cook Time: 7 minutes

Pasta Waldorf Salad: Increase salad dressing to 1 cup. Add 6 cups cooked pasta with the salmon.

Serving Suggestion: Serve over lettuce leaves and sprinkle with toasted nuts.

BIRDS EYE IDEA: To prevent cut fruits and vegetables, such as apples and artichokes, from discoloring, try rubbing them with a lemon wedge.

Fruit & Feta Salad with Raspberry Vinaigrette

1 package (10 ounces) mixed salad greens
1 can (11 ounces) mandarin orange
    segments, drained
½ cup thinly sliced red onion
1 cup coarsely chopped walnuts, toasted

1 package (4 ounces) ATHENOS®
    Crumbled Feta Cheese
¾ cup KRAFT LIGHT DONE RIGHT!®
    Raspberry Vinaigrette Dressing

TOSS greens, oranges, onion, nuts and cheese in large bowl. Add dressing; toss to coat.

Makes 6 servings

Prep Time: 20 minutes

How to Toast Nuts: Spread nuts in single layer on cookie sheet. Bake at 350°F for 7 minutes or until lightly toasted, stirring occasionally.

Salmon Broccoli Waldorf Salad

Tuna Salad Elegante

1 round bread loaf (about 1½ pounds)
1 can (12 ounces) STARKIST® Tuna, drained and flaked
6 spears cooked asparagus, trimmed and cut into 2-inch pieces
2 hard-cooked eggs, chopped
½ cup sliced pitted ripe and stuffed green olives

⅓ cup chopped green onions
⅓ cup reduced-calorie mayonnaise or salad dressing
¼ cup plain low-fat yogurt
2 tablespoons red wine vinegar
1 teaspoon dried tarragon, crushed
1 teaspoon dried basil, crushed
Lettuce leaves

With a sharp knife, cut a 1-inch-thick slice from top of bread loaf. Reserve to use later for the lid. Then, hollow out loaf, making a 1-inch shell. If preparing ahead, wrap shell and bread top in plastic wrap. Save bread for another use.

To make salad, in a large bowl toss together tuna, asparagus, eggs, olives and onions. In a small bowl stir together mayonnaise, yogurt, vinegar, tarragon and basil. Spoon over salad; toss well to coat. If preparing ahead, cover and chill.

To serve salad, line bread shell with lettuce leaves. Spoon tuna mixture into shell. Add bread top, if desired. Serve with flat crackers or party bread.

Makes 5 to 6 main-dish or about 30 appetizer servings

Prep Time: 30 minutes

Three-Bean Salad

1 (15½-ounce) can red kidney beans
1 (14½-ounce) can cut green beans
1 (14½-ounce) can yellow wax beans
1 green bell pepper, seeded and chopped
1 medium onion, chopped

2 ribs celery, sliced
¾ cup cider vinegar
⅓ cup FILIPPO BERIO® Olive Oil
2 tablespoons sugar
Salt and freshly ground black pepper

Rinse and drain kidney beans; drain green and wax beans. In large bowl, combine beans, bell pepper, onion and celery. In small bowl, whisk together vinegar, olive oil and sugar. Pour over bean mixture; toss until lightly coated. Cover; refrigerate several hours or overnight before serving. Season to taste with salt and black pepper. Store salad, covered, in refrigerator up to 1 week.

Makes 10 to 12 servings

Tuna Salad Elegante

Parsley Ham and Pasta Salad

2 cups uncooked elbow macaroni
2 cups (12 ounces) CURE 81® ham, cut into strips
1 cup sliced celery
½ cup sliced green onions

1 cup mayonnaise or salad dressing
1 cup packed parsley, finely chopped
¼ cup grated Parmesan cheese
¼ cup white wine vinegar
1 clove garlic, minced

Cook macaroni according to package directions. In large bowl, combine ham, macaroni, celery and green onions. In small bowl, combine mayonnaise, parsley, cheese, vinegar and garlic; toss with pasta. Cover and refrigerate 1 to 2 hours to blend flavors. *Makes 6 to 8 servings*

Tossed Salad with Honey Mustard Vinaigrette

⅓ cup red wine, balsamic or champagne vinegar
3 tablespoons *French's®* Sweet & Tangy Honey Mustard or Napa Valley Style Dijon Mustard
1 tablespoon packed brown sugar
2 teaspoons *French's®* Worcestershire Sauce
⅔ cup olive oil

2 tablespoons minced herbs (parsley, basil, tarragon or chives)
12 cups mesclun salad greens, thoroughly washed
3 cups cut-up vegetables (broccoli, bell pepper and carrots)
1⅓ cups *French's®* French Fried Onions

1. Combine vinegar, mustard, sugar and Worcestershire in blender. Cover; process until well mixed. Gradually add oil, processing until smooth. Stir in herbs. Season to taste with salt and pepper.

2. Toss salad greens and vegetables with dressing just before serving. Sprinkle salad with French Fried Onions. *Makes 6 servings (1 cup dressing)*

Prep Time: 10 minutes

Tip: Toast French Fried Onions in microwave 1 minute for extra crispness.

Parsley Ham and Pasta Salad

Sweet Potato Salad

2 pounds sweet potatoes, peeled and
    cubed
2 tablespoons lemon juice
1 cup HELLMANN'S® or BEST FOODS®
    Real or Light Mayonnaise or Low Fat
    Mayonnaise Dressing
2 tablespoons orange juice
1 tablespoon honey
1 teaspoon grated orange peel

1 teaspoon chopped fresh ginger
¼ teaspoon salt
⅛ teaspoon nutmeg
1 cup coarsely chopped pecans
1 cup sliced celery
⅓ cup chopped pitted dates
    Lettuce leaves
1 can (11 ounces) mandarin orange
    sections, drained

1. In medium saucepan cook potatoes 8 to 10 minutes in boiling, salted water just until tender. (Do not overcook.) Drain. Toss with lemon juice.

2. In large bowl combine mayonnaise, orange juice, honey, orange peel, ginger, salt and nutmeg. Stir in warm potatoes, pecans, celery and dates. Cover; chill.

3. To serve, spoon salad onto lettuce-lined platter. Arrange orange sections around salad. Garnish as desired.

Makes 6 servings

Chinese Chicken Salad

3 cups cooked rice, cooled
1½ cups cooked chicken breast cubes (about
    1 whole breast)
1 cup sliced celery
1 can (8 ounces) sliced water chestnuts,
    drained
½ cup sliced fresh mushrooms
¼ cup sliced green onions

¼ cup chopped red bell pepper
¼ cup sliced black olives
2 tablespoons vegetable oil
2 tablespoons lemon juice
1 tablespoon soy sauce
½ teaspoon ground ginger
¼ to ½ teaspoon ground white pepper
    Lettuce leaves

Combine rice, chicken, celery, water chestnuts, mushrooms, onions, bell pepper and olives in large bowl. Place oil, lemon juice, soy sauce, ginger and white pepper in small jar with lid; shake well. Pour over rice mixture. Toss lightly. Serve on lettuce leaves.

Makes 4 servings

Favorite recipe from **USA Rice Federation**

Sweet Potato Salad

❈ *Unbeatable Sides* ❈

Potatoes au Gratin

**4 to 6 medium unpeeled baking potatoes
 (about 2 pounds)**
**2 cups (8 ounces) shredded Cheddar
 cheese**
1 cup (4 ounces) shredded Swiss cheese
2 tablespoons butter or margarine

3 tablespoons all-purpose flour
2½ cups milk
2 tablespoons Dijon mustard
¼ teaspoon salt
¼ teaspoon black pepper

1. Preheat oven to 400°F. Grease 13×9-inch baking dish.

2. Cut potatoes into thin slices. Layer potatoes in prepared dish. Top with cheeses.

3. Melt butter in medium saucepan over medium heat. Stir in flour; cook 1 minute. Stir in milk, mustard, salt and pepper; bring to a boil. Reduce heat and cook, stirring constantly, until mixture thickens. Pour milk mixture over cheese. Cover pan with foil.

4. Bake 30 minutes. Remove foil and bake 15 to 20 minutes more until potatoes are tender and top is brown. Remove from oven and let stand 10 minutes before serving. *Makes 6 to 8 servings*

Potatoes au Gratin

Stir-Fry Vegetables

¼ cup GRANDMA'S® Molasses
¼ cup chicken broth
2 tablespoons soy sauce
4 teaspoons cornstarch
1 tablespoon minced ginger
1 teaspoon minced garlic

⅛ teaspoon ground red pepper
1 tablespoon canola oil
2 pounds fresh vegetables, cut into bite-sized pieces (celery, zucchini, onion, peppers, Chinese cabbage and snow peas)

In large bowl, combine molasses, broth, soy sauce, cornstarch, ginger, garlic and red pepper. Set aside. Heat oil in wok or large heavy skillet. Add vegetables and stir-fry 2 minutes until crisp and tender. Mix in molasses mixture. Cook just until sauce thickens and vegetables are well coated.

Makes 4 to 6 servings

Campbell's® Parmesan Potatoes

1 can (10¾ ounces) CAMPBELL'S®
    Condensed Cheddar Cheese Soup
½ cup milk
½ cup grated Parmesan cheese
¼ teaspoon pepper

4 medium white potatoes, cut in 1-inch pieces (about 4 cups)
1 can (2.8 ounces) *French's® Taste Toppers™* French Fried Onions (1⅓ cups)

1. In greased shallow 2-quart baking dish mix soup, milk, cheese and pepper. Stir in potatoes and *½ can Taste Toppers.*

2. Bake at 400°F. for 40 minutes or until potatoes are tender. Sprinkle remaining *Taste Toppers* over potatoes. Bake 5 minutes more or until *Taste Toppers* are golden.

Makes 4 servings

Prep Time: 5 minutes
Cook Time: 45 minutes

BBQ Corn Wheels

4 ears corn on the cob, husked and
    cleaned
3 red, green or yellow bell peppers, cut
    into large chunks

¾ cup barbecue sauce
½ cup honey
¼ cup _French's_® Worcestershire Sauce
    Vegetable cooking spray

1. Cut corn into ½-inch slices. Alternately thread corn and pepper chunks onto four metal skewers. (Pierce tip of skewer through center of corn wheel to thread.) Combine barbecue sauce, honey and Worcestershire.

2. Coat kabobs with vegetable cooking spray. Grill kabobs on greased rack over medium heat for 5 minutes. Cook 5 minutes more until corn is tender, turning and basting with barbecue sauce mixture. Serve any extra sauce on the side with grilled hamburgers, steaks or chicken.

Makes 4 servings

Prep Time: 10 minutes
Cook Time: 10 minutes

Campbell's® Creamy Vegetable Medley

1 can (10¾ ounces) CAMPBELL'S®
    Condensed Cream of Celery Soup _or_
    98% Fat Free Cream of Celery Soup
½ cup milk

2 cups broccoli flowerets
2 medium carrots, sliced (about 1 cup)
1 cup cauliflower flowerets

1. In medium saucepan mix soup, milk, broccoli, carrots and cauliflower. Over medium heat, heat to a boil.

2. Reduce heat to low. Cover and cook 15 minutes or until vegetables are tender, stirring occasionally.

Makes 6 servings

Prep Time: 15 minutes
Cook Time: 20 minutes

BBQ Corn Wheels

Orzotto with Herbs and Mushrooms

1 medium onion, chopped
2 tablespoons minced garlic
4 tablespoons olive oil
1 package (16 ounces) BARILLA® Orzo
3 cups chicken broth
1¾ cups (4 ounces) assorted mushrooms, sliced
½ cup *each* red, green and yellow bell peppers, finely chopped
1 tablespoon dried Italian seasoning
½ cup white wine
⅓ cup heavy whipping cream
4 ounces herbed cheese spread, at room temperature
1 (4-ounce) piece prosciutto ham, diced
Salt and pepper
Grated Parmesan cheese

1. Cook onion and garlic in olive oil in Dutch oven or large pot over medium heat until onion is transparent.

2. Add orzo to Dutch oven; cook and stir 1 minute. Add chicken broth; heat to boiling. Reduce heat to low; cook about 7 to 8 minutes, stirring frequently, until orzo is tender but still firm. Add mushrooms, peppers and Italian seasoning; cook over medium heat, stirring frequently, until pasta and vegetables are just tender.

3. Stir in wine, cream and herbed cheese. Cook over low heat until smooth, stirring constantly. Stir in prosciutto; add salt and pepper to taste.

4. Remove from heat; cover and let stand 5 minutes. Serve with cheese. *Makes 8 to 10 servings*

Oven-Roasted Vegetables

1½ pounds assorted cut-up fresh vegetables*
3 tablespoons I CAN'T BELIEVE IT'S NOT BUTTER!® Spread, melted
2 cloves garlic, finely chopped
1 tablespoon chopped fresh oregano leaves *or* 1 teaspoon dried oregano leaves, crushed
Salt and ground black pepper to taste

*Use any combination of the following: zucchini, red, green or yellow bell peppers, Spanish or red onions, white or portobello mushrooms and carrots.

Preheat oven to 450°F.

In bottom of broiler pan, without rack, combine all ingredients. Roast 20 minutes or until vegetables are tender, stirring once. *Makes 4 servings*

Orzotto with Herbs and Mushrooms

Broccoli-Walnut Noodles

12 ounces extra-wide curly "no yolk" noodles
2 pounds broccoli (florets and peeled stems, cut into ½-inch slices)
2 tablespoons olive oil

½ cup chopped California walnuts
Juice of 1 lemon
Juice of ½ orange
Grated zest of 1 lemon
½ teaspoon ground pepper

1. Cook noodles until al dente (about 5 minutes).

2. Steam broccoli until tender (3 to 5 minutes).

3. Heat olive oil in large skillet over medium-high heat; add walnuts. Sauté about 1 minute.

4. Combine noodles and broccoli. Add walnut-oil mixture; toss well. Add citrus juices, zest and pepper; toss well.

Makes 4 servings

Serving Suggestion: Serve with tomato salad and crusty bread.

Variation: Add ½ cup diced smoked turkey, low-fat chicken sausage or seasoned tofu.

Favorite recipe from **Walnut Marketing Board**

Pineapple Wild Rice

1 cup uncooked brown rice
½ cup uncooked wild rice
¼ cup margarine
2 cups sliced fresh mushrooms
1 cup chopped onion
1 cup finely chopped DOLE® Fresh Pineapple

1 cup finely chopped dried apricots
½ cup toasted pine nuts
1 teaspoon chopped fresh thyme *or*
¼ teaspoon dried thyme leaves

• Cook brown rice and wild rice according to package directions, omitting oils.

• Melt margarine in large skillet. Stir in mushrooms and onion, cooking 10 minutes or until onion is tender.

• Stir pineapple, apricots, pine nuts and thyme into skillet. Stir in rices. Heat through. Serve hot or at room temperature. Garnish with fresh thyme sprig, if desired. Serve with lamb and green beans.

Makes 10 servings

Broccoli-Walnut Noodles

Citrus Asparagus

Orange Sauce
- 2 teaspoons reduced-fat margarine
- 1 clove garlic, minced
- Juice of 1 large orange (about ⅓ cup)
- 1¼ teaspoons balsamic vinegar
- ¼ teaspoon Dijon mustard
- ½ teaspoon grated orange peel
- Salt (optional)

Asparagus
- Nonstick olive oil cooking spray
- 1 small onion, diced
- 1 pound fresh asparagus, lower half of stalks peeled*
- ⅔ cup diced red bell pepper
- ½ cup water

*If using pencil-thin asparagus, do not peel. Reduce cooking time to 4 to 5 minutes.

1. For Orange Sauce, heat margarine in small saucepan over medium heat. Add garlic; cook and stir 2 minutes or until soft. Stir in orange juice; bring to a boil. Add vinegar and mustard; reduce heat and simmer 2 minutes. Remove from heat and add orange peel. Season to taste with salt, if desired. Reserve and keep warm.

2. For asparagus, spray medium saucepan with cooking spray; heat over medium-high heat. Add onion; cook and stir 2 minutes. Add asparagus, bell pepper and water. Reduce heat to medium-low. Cover and simmer 7 minutes or until asparagus is crisp-tender. Remove vegetables with slotted spoon to serving dish; serve with reserved Orange Sauce. *Makes 4 servings*

Pesto Double-Stuffed Potatoes

- 4 large Idaho Potatoes, baked
- ½ cup part-skim ricotta cheese
- ⅓ cup prepared pesto
- ¼ teaspoon salt
- ¼ teaspoon pepper
- Nonstick cooking spray

1. Preheat oven to 450°F.

2. Cut ½ inch from long side of each potato into bowl; scoop out inside of potato, leaving ¼-inch-thick shell. With fork or potato masher, mash cooked potato in bowl. Stir in ricotta, pesto, salt and pepper until well-blended. Spoon potato mixture into potato shells, dividing evenly, heaping on top if necessary.

3. Lightly spray cookie sheet with nonstick cooking spray; place stuffed potatoes on cookie sheet. Bake until golden brown and heated through, about 10 to 15 minutes. *Makes 4 servings*

Prep & Cook Time: 45 minutes

Favorite recipe from **Idaho Potato Commission**

Citrus Asparagus

Almond Fried Rice

2 tablespoons vegetable oil
¾ cup thinly sliced green onions and tops
½ cup diced red bell pepper
1 egg, beaten

3 cups cold cooked rice
2 ounces diced cooked ham (about ½ cup)
2 tablespoons KIKKOMAN® Soy Sauce
½ cup slivered blanched almonds, toasted

Heat oil in hot wok or large skillet over medium-high heat. Add green onions and bell pepper; stir-fry 1 minute. Add egg and scramble. Stir in rice and cook until heated through, gently separating grains. Add ham and soy sauce; cook and stir until mixture is well blended. Just before serving, stir in almonds. Garnish as desired.

Makes 4 servings

Baked Eggplant with Cheese

6 or 7 small eggplants, sliced into
  ½-inch-thick slices
1 egg, beaten
1 cup bread crumbs
2 tablespoons olive oil
  Salt to taste
  Ground black pepper to taste
1 tablespoon dried parsley

1 can (5 ounces) sliced mushrooms,
  drained
1 can (15 ounces) chunky tomato sauce
6 thin slices tomato
8 ounces shredded Wisconsin Scamorze
  or Mozzarella cheese
1 teaspoon grated onion
  Fresh basil leaves for garnish

Preheat oven to 375°F. Dip eggplant slices in egg, then into bread crumbs. Heat olive oil in skillet; brown eggplant lightly on both sides. Arrange in buttered baking dish. Season to taste with salt and pepper; sprinkle with parsley and sliced mushrooms. Pour tomato sauce over eggplant. Top with tomato slices and cheese. Sprinkle grated onion over cheese. Bake 30 minutes or until cheese is melted.

Makes 8 servings

Favorite recipe from **Wisconsin Milk Marketing Board**

Almond Fried Rice

Roasted Fall Vegetables

2 cups small broccoli florets
1 large red bell pepper, cut into squares
1 cup cubed turnip (1-inch cubes)
½ cup diced onion
1 tablespoon balsamic vinegar or red wine vinegar
2 teaspoons olive oil

½ cup fat-free reduced-sodium chicken broth or water
4 sprigs fresh thyme *or* ¼ teaspoon dried thyme leaves
¼ teaspoon salt
Black pepper

1. Preheat oven to 425°F. Combine broccoli, bell pepper, turnip and onion in shallow heavy roasting pan.

2. Whisk together vinegar and oil; pour over vegetables, tossing to coat. Pour chicken broth around vegetables. Add thyme sprigs.

3. Roast vegetables about 30 minutes or until tender, stirring occasionally. Remove from oven. Season with salt and pepper.   *Makes 6 (⅓-cup) servings*

Macho Macaroni and Cheese

1 pound elbow macaroni
1 pound processed American cheese, grated
3 cups milk

2 teaspoons dry mustard
1 teaspoon TABASCO® brand Pepper Sauce

Preheat oven to 350°F. Cook macaroni according to package directions. Drain macaroni and combine with cheese; mix lightly. Place in buttered 2-quart casserole.

Blend milk, mustard and TABASCO® Sauce; pour over macaroni. Cover and bake 35 minutes. Uncover and bake 10 to 15 minutes or until top is lightly browned.   *Makes 8 to 10 servings*

Roasted Fall Vegetables

Hot and Spicy Spinach

1 red bell pepper, cut into 1-inch pieces
1 clove garlic, minced
1 pound prewashed fresh spinach, rinsed
    and chopped

1 tablespoon prepared mustard
1 teaspoon lemon juice
¼ teaspoon red pepper flakes

1. Spray large skillet with nonstick cooking spray; heat over medium heat. Add red bell pepper and garlic; cook and stir 3 minutes.

2. Add spinach; cook and stir 3 minutes or just until spinach begins to wilt.

3. Stir in mustard, lemon juice and red pepper flakes. Serve immediately.   *Makes 4 servings*

Cook's Tip: To obtain the maximum nutritional value from spinach, cook it for the shortest possible time. The vitamins in spinach and other greens are soluble in water and fats and are therefore lost during long cooking.

Mediterranean Red Potatoes

2 medium red potatoes, cut in half
    lengthwise, then crosswise into pieces
⅔ cup fresh or frozen pearl onions
    Nonstick garlic-flavored cooking spray
¾ teaspoon dried Italian seasoning

¼ teaspoon black pepper
1 small tomato, seeded and chopped
½ cup (2 ounces) crumbled feta cheese
2 tablespoons chopped black olives

Slow Cooker Directions

1. Place potatoes and onions in 1½-quart soufflé dish. Spray potatoes and onions with cooking spray; toss to coat. Add Italian seasoning and pepper; mix well. Cover dish tightly with foil.

2. Tear off 3 (18×3-inch) strips of heavy-duty aluminum foil. Cross strips so they resemble wheel spokes. Place soufflé dish in center of strips. Pull foil strips up and over dish and place dish into slow cooker.

3. Pour hot water to about 1½ inches from top of soufflé dish. Cover and cook on LOW 7 to 8 hours.

4. Use foil handles to lift dish out of slow cooker. Stir tomato, feta cheese and olives into potato mixture.   *Makes 4 servings*

Hot and Spicy Spinach

Broccoli & Rice au Gratin with Stilton Cheese

1 box UNCLE BEN'S CHEF'S RECIPE™
 Broccoli Rice Au Gratin Supreme
1 package (10 ounces) frozen broccoli
 florets
1 medium carrot, sliced
1 medium tomato, chopped

½ cup crumbled Stilton cheese
½ cup pecans, toasted and crumbled
¼ cup olive oil
2 tablespoons white wine vinegar
 Salt and coarsely ground black pepper
 to taste

CLEAN: Wash hands. Prepare rice according to package directions; transfer to serving dish. Meanwhile, cook broccoli and carrot in large saucepan of rapidly boiling water until crisp-tender. Drain and rinse under cold water. Arrange broccoli and carrot over rice. Sprinkle with tomato, cheese and pecans. Combine olive oil and vinegar in small bowl; whisk to blend. Drizzle over vegetables and rice. Season with salt and pepper.

Serve warm.

Refrigerate leftovers immediately.

Makes 6 servings

Captain's Choice Baked Beans

1 pound ground beef
1 can (16 ounces) baked beans
1 can (15½ ounces) dark red kidney
 beans, drained
1 can (15½ ounces) butter beans, drained
1 onion, chopped

½ cup packed brown sugar
½ cup MISSISSIPPI® Barbecue Sauce
1 tablespoon Worcestershire sauce
2 tablespoons prepared mustard
3 to 4 strips bacon (optional)

1. Preheat oven to 350°F. Brown ground beef; drain fat.

2. In 2-quart casserole, combine ground beef and remaining ingredients except bacon. Place bacon strips on top.

3. Bake at 350°F for 1¼ hours.

Makes 6 servings

Prep Time: 20 minutes
Bake Time: 1¼ hours

Broccoli & Rice au Gratin with Stilton Cheese

Roasted Idaho & Sweet Potatoes

1 envelope LIPTON® RECIPE SECRETS®
    Onion Soup Mix
2 medium all-purpose potatoes, peeled, if
    desired, and cut into large chunks
    (about 1 pound)

2 medium sweet potatoes or yams, peeled,
    if desired, and cut into large chunks
    (about 1 pound)
¼ cup olive or vegetable oil

1. Preheat oven to 425°F. In large plastic bag or bowl, combine all ingredients. Close bag and shake, or toss in bowl, until potatoes are evenly coated.

2. In 13×9-inch baking or roasting pan, arrange potatoes; discard bag.

3. Bake uncovered, stirring occasionally, 40 minutes or until potatoes are tender and golden.

Makes 4 servings

Vegetables Italiano

2 tablespoons olive oil
1 cup sliced peeled carrots
¾ cup halved onion slices
2 cloves garlic, minced
1 can (14.5 ounces) CONTADINA®
    Stewed Tomatoes, undrained

3 cups sliced zucchini
1 cup fresh mushrooms, halved
¼ teaspoon salt, or to taste
⅛ teaspoon ground black pepper

1. Heat oil in large skillet. Add carrots, onion and garlic; sauté for 3 minutes.

2. Stir in tomatoes and juice, zucchini, mushrooms, salt and pepper.

3. Bring to a boil. Reduce heat to low; simmer, uncovered, for 5 to 6 minutes or until vegetables are crisp-tender. Serve over pasta, if desired.

Makes 4 side-dish servings

Prep Time: 8 minutes
Cook Time: 10 minutes

Roasted Idaho & Sweet Potatoes

Zesty Mixed Vegetables

8 ounces green beans
½ small head cauliflower
2 green onions with tops
1 or 2 jalapeño or Thai chili peppers*
2 tablespoons vegetable oil
2 cloves garlic, chopped
8 ounces peeled fresh baby carrots

1 cup ⅓-less-salt chicken broth, divided
1 tablespoon cornstarch
1 teaspoon sugar
¼ teaspoon salt
2 tablespoons oyster sauce
Red and yellow bell pepper strips for garnish

Jalapeño and other chili peppers can sting and irritate the skin; wear rubber gloves when handling peppers and do not touch eyes. Wash hands after handling.

• Trim ends from beans; discard. Cut beans diagonally into thirds or quarters. Cut cauliflower into florets. Cut onions into ½-inch pieces, keeping white part and green tops of onions separate. Cut jalapeño in half lengthwise. Remove stem and seeds. Cut jalapeño crosswise into thin slices.

• Heat wok over high heat about 1 minute or until hot. Drizzle oil into wok and heat 30 seconds. Add white part of onions, beans, cauliflower, jalapeño and garlic; stir-fry until tender. Add carrots and ¾ cup broth. Cover; bring to a boil. Reduce heat to low; cook until carrots and beans are crisp-tender.

• Combine cornstarch, sugar and salt in cup; stir in remaining ¼ cup broth and oyster sauce until smooth. Stir into wok. Cook until sauce boils and thickens. Stir in green onion tops. Transfer to serving dish. Garnish, if desired.   *Makes 4 servings*

Note: Jalapeños are small, dark green chilies, normally 2 to 3 inches long and ¾ inch wide with a slightly tapered end. Jalapeño flavor varies from hot to very hot. Use 1 or 2 in this dish depending on your preference.

Zesty Mixed Vegetables

Vegetable Couscous

3 cups water
1 package KNORR® Recipe Classics™
    Vegetable Soup, Dip and Recipe Mix
2 tablespoons BERTOLLI® Olive Oil or
    I CAN'T BELIEVE IT'S NOT
    BUTTER!® Spread

1 package (10 ounces) plain couscous
    (about 1½ cups)
¼ cup chopped fresh parsley (optional)
    Pine nuts, slivered almonds or raisins
    (optional)

• In 2-quart saucepan, bring water, recipe mix and olive oil to a boil, stirring frequently. Reduce heat; cover and simmer 2 minutes.

• Stir couscous into saucepan until evenly moistened. Remove from heat; cover and let stand 5 minutes.

• Fluff couscous with fork. Spoon into serving dish. Garnish, if desired, with chopped parsley and nuts or raisins.

Makes 5 cups couscous

Prep Time: 5 minutes
Cook Time: 10 minutes

Chili Bean Del Monte®

¾ cup sliced green onions, divided
1 can (15 ounces) pinto beans, drained
1 can (14½ ounces) DEL MONTE® Zesty
    Chili Style Chunky Tomatoes
1 can (8¾ ounces) *or* 1 cup kidney beans,
    drained

½ to 1 teaspoon minced jalapeño pepper
½ teaspoon ground cumin
¼ teaspoon garlic powder
¼ cup shredded sharp Cheddar cheese

1. Set aside ¼ cup green onions for garnish. In large skillet, combine remaining ½ cup green onions with remaining ingredients except cheese.

2. Bring to a boil; reduce heat to medium. Cook 5 minutes. Serve with cheese and reserved onions.

Makes 3 servings (approximately ¾ cup each)

Prep and Cook Time: 15 minutes

Vegetable Couscous

Pepper and Squash Gratin

2 medium russet potatoes, unpeeled
2 small yellow squash, thinly sliced
2 small zucchini, thinly sliced
2 cups frozen pepper stir-fry blend, thawed
1 teaspoon dried oregano leaves

½ teaspoon salt
  Black pepper to taste
½ cup grated Parmesan cheese or shredded reduced-fat sharp Cheddar cheese
1 tablespoon butter or margarine, cut into 8 pieces

Preheat oven to 375°F. Coat 12×8-inch glass baking dish with nonstick cooking spray. Pierce potatoes several times with fork. Microwave at HIGH (100% power) 3 minutes; cut into thin slices.

Layer half of potatoes, yellow squash, zucchini, pepper stir-fry blend, oregano, salt, black pepper and cheese in prepared baking dish. Repeat layers and top with butter. Cover tightly with foil; bake 25 minutes or until vegetables are just tender. Remove foil and bake 10 minutes or until lightly browned.

Makes 8 servings

Cheesy Corn Bake

3 eggs, well beaten
1 can (16 ounces) creamed corn
¾ cup unseasoned dry bread crumbs
¾ cup (3 ounces) shredded Cheddar cheese
½ medium green bell pepper, chopped
½ cup hot milk

1 tablespoon chopped onion
1 teaspoon LAWRY'S® Seasoned Salt
¾ teaspoon LAWRY'S® Seasoned Pepper
¼ teaspoon LAWRY'S® Garlic Powder with Parsley

In large bowl, combine all ingredients. Pour into ungreased 2-quart casserole. Bake in 350°F oven 1 hour. Let stand 10 minutes before serving.

Makes 6 servings

Serving Suggestion: Serve with meat loaf, baked chicken or fried fish.

Hint: Serve topped with prepared LAWRY'S® Original Style Spaghetti Sauce for extra flavor.

Pepper and Squash Gratin

Southwestern Rice

1 cup uncooked converted rice
1 can (15 ounces) black beans, rinsed and
    drained
1 can (8 ounces) corn, drained
1 packet (1 ounce) HIDDEN VALLEY®
    The Original Ranch® Salad Dressing
    & Seasoning Mix

¾ cup (3 ounces) diced Monterey Jack
    cheese
½ cup seeded, diced tomato
¼ cup sliced green onions

Cook rice according to package directions, omitting salt. During last five minutes of cooking time, quickly uncover and add beans and corn; cover immediately. When rice is done, remove saucepan from heat; add salad dressing & seasoning mix and stir. Let stand 5 minutes. Stir in cheese, tomato and onions. Serve immediately. *Makes 6 servings*

Herbed Cheese Mashed Potatoes

¼ cup chopped green onions
2 cloves garlic, minced
2 tablespoons FLEISCHMANN'S®
    Original Margarine
2 pounds potatoes, peeled, cubed and
    cooked

½ cup plain nonfat yogurt
½ cup skim milk
½ cup shredded Swiss cheese (2 ounces)

1. Cook and stir green onions and garlic in margarine in large saucepan over medium-high heat until green onions are tender.

2. Add hot cooked potatoes, yogurt, milk and cheese. Mash until smooth and well blended. Serve immediately. *Makes 6 servings*

Prep Time: 20 minutes
Cook Time: 20 minutes
Total Time: 40 minutes

Southwestern Rice

Golden Apple Sweet Potato Bake

2 pounds (about 3 large) sweet potatoes or yams	¼ cup butter or margarine
Water	1 tablespoon lemon juice
⅓ cup apple juice or orange juice	¼ teaspoon grated lemon peel
¼ cup packed brown sugar	2 Washington Golden Delicious apples

In saucepan, cover potatoes with boiling water; cook, covered, about 35 minutes or until barely tender. Combine remaining ingredients except apples in small saucepan. Bring to a boil; simmer 10 minutes. Peel and cut potatoes into ¼-inch slices. Arrange in buttered 2-quart baking dish. Core and slice apples into ¼-inch wedges; arrange over potatoes. Pour apple juice mixture over apples. Bake at 325°F about 30 minutes, basting occasionally. *Makes about 6 servings*

Microwave Directions: Place potatoes in microwave-proof dish; cover with plastic wrap. Microwave at HIGH 10 minutes or until tender; turn dish once. Combine apple juice, brown sugar, butter, lemon juice and peel in 1-quart microwave-proof container; cover with plastic wrap. Microwave at HIGH 3 minutes. Slice apples and potatoes and arrange in buttered 2-quart microwave-proof dish as above. Pour apple juice mixture over apples; cover with plastic wrap. Microwave at HIGH 5 minutes or until thoroughly heated, basting and turning dish once.

Favorite recipe from **Washington Apple Commission**

Manwich Baked Noodles

4 cups cooked pasta	1½ cups shredded Cheddar cheese, divided
3 cups HUNT'S® Original Manwich	PAM® Cooking Spray

In large bowl, combine pasta, prepared Manwich and 1 cup cheese. Pour into baking dish sprayed with cooking spray; sprinkle remaining ½ cup cheese over top. Bake, covered, at 350°F 30 minutes. Remove cover; bake, uncovered, 10 minutes or until hot and bubbling. *Makes 4 to 6 servings*

Ritz® Cracker Stuffing

1 cup coarsely chopped mushrooms or broccoli
½ cup chopped onion
½ cup chopped celery
¼ cup margarine or butter
4 Stay Fresh Packs RITZ® Crackers, coarsely crushed (about 7 cups crumbs)

2 cups PLANTERS® Walnuts, Pecans or Almonds, coarsely chopped
¼ cup chopped fresh parsley
1 tablespoon poultry seasoning
½ teaspoon ground black pepper
1 (14½-ounce) can chicken broth
2 eggs, beaten

1. Cook mushrooms or broccoli, onion and celery in margarine or butter in large skillet over medium heat until tender.

2. Mix cracker crumbs, nuts, parsley, poultry seasoning, pepper and vegetable mixture in large bowl. Add broth and eggs, tossing until well combined. Spoon into 2-quart baking dish or pan; cover.

3. Bake at 325°F for 30 to 40 minutes or until heated through. Or use as a stuffing for turkey, chicken or pork. *Makes about 6 cups*

Microwave Directions: In 2½-quart microwave-proof bowl, combine mushrooms or broccoli, onion, celery and margarine or butter; cover. Microwave at HIGH (100%) power for 3 to 4 minutes or until tender. Stir in remaining ingredients as above; cover. Microwave at HIGH for 10 to 12 minutes or until hot, stirring after 6 minutes.

Mint-Glazed Carrots & Snow Peas

1 tablespoon margarine
3 medium carrots, sliced thin diagonally
½ pound fresh snow peas, trimmed
2 tablespoons sugar

1 tablespoon fresh lemon juice
1 tablespoon chopped fresh mint leaves *or* 1 teaspoon dried mint, crushed

In large nonstick skillet, melt margarine over medium heat. Add carrots; cook and stir 3 to 4 minutes. Add peas, sugar, lemon juice and mint. Cook and stir 1 to 2 minutes or until vegetables are glazed and crisp-tender. *Makes 4 servings*

Favorite recipe from **The Sugar Association, Inc.**

❧ *Meaty Main Dishes* ❧

Beef Kabobs over Lemon Rice

½ **pound boneless beef sirloin steak, cut**
    into 1-inch cubes
1 **small zucchini, sliced**
1 **small yellow squash, sliced**
1 **small red bell pepper, cut into squares**
1 **small onion, cut into chunks**

¼ **cup Italian dressing**
1 **cup hot cooked rice**
2 **teaspoons fresh lemon juice**
1 **tablespoon snipped fresh parsley**
¼ **teaspoon seasoned salt**

Combine beef and vegetables in large resealable plastic food storage bag; add dressing. Seal bag and marinate 4 to 6 hours in refrigerator, turning bag occasionally. Thread beef and vegetables alternately onto 4 metal skewers. Grill over medium coals, or broil, 5 to 7 minutes or to desired doneness, turning occasionally. Combine rice and remaining ingredients. Serve kabobs over rice mixture.

Makes 2 servings

Favorite recipe from **USA Rice Federation**

Beef Kabobs over Lemon Rice

Grilled Sherry Pork Chops

¼ cup HOLLAND HOUSE® Sherry
  Cooking Wine
¼ cup GRANDMA'S® Molasses

2 tablespoons soy sauce
4 pork chops, 1 inch thick

In plastic bowl, combine sherry, molasses and soy sauce; pour over pork chops. Cover; refrigerate 30 minutes. Prepare grill. Drain pork chops; save marinade. Grill pork chops over medium-high heat 20 to 30 minutes or until pork is no longer pink in center, turning once and brushing frequently with marinade. Discard any remaining marinade.*   *Makes 4 servings*

Do not baste during last 5 minutes of grilling.

Spaghetti Pie

6 ounces spaghetti, cooked and well
  drained
2 eggs, lightly beaten
8 ounces ground beef
½ cup chopped onion

¾ cup spaghetti sauce
⅓ cup A.1.® Steak Sauce
8 ounces POLL-Y® Ricotta Cheese
2 tablespoons KRAFT® Grated Parmesan
  Cheese

1. Mix spaghetti with eggs until well blended; press on bottom and side of lightly greased 9-inch pie plate with spoon to form crust. Set aside.

2. Cook ground beef and onion in skillet over medium-high heat until meat is no longer pink, stirring to break up meat; pour off fat. Stir in spaghetti sauce and steak sauce. Heat to a boil; reduce heat to low. Cook, uncovered, for 1 to 2 minutes or until slightly thickened. Remove from heat.

3. Spread ricotta cheese into prepared crust; top with meat mixture.

4. Bake at 350°F for 25 to 30 minutes or until hot. Sprinkle with Parmesan cheese; bake for 5 minutes more. Let stand for 5 minutes before serving.   *Makes 6 servings*

Grilled Sherry Pork Chop

Campbell's® Country Skillet Supper

1 pound ground beef
1 medium onion, chopped (about ½ cup)
⅛ teaspoon garlic powder *or* 1 clove garlic, minced
1 can (10¾ ounces) CAMPBELL'S® Condensed Golden Mushroom Soup
1 can (10½ ounces) CAMPBELL'S® Condensed Beef Broth
1 can (14½ ounces) diced tomatoes
1 small zucchini, sliced (about 1 cup)
½ teaspoon dried thyme leaves, crushed
1½ cups *uncooked* corkscrew pasta

1. In medium skillet over medium-high heat, cook beef, onion and garlic powder until beef is browned, stirring to separate meat. Pour off fat.

2. Add soup, broth, tomatoes, zucchini and thyme. Heat to a boil. Stir in pasta. Reduce heat to low. Cook 15 minutes or until pasta is done, stirring often. *Makes 4 servings*

Prep Time: 5 minutes
Cook Time: 25 minutes

Mediterranean Burgers

1½ pounds ground beef
¼ cup (1 ounce) shredded mozzarella cheese
2 tablespoons grated Parmesan cheese
2 tablespoons chopped kalamata olives
1 tablespoon chopped fresh parsley
1 tablespoon diced tomato
2 teaspoons dried oregano leaves
1 teaspoon black pepper
4 hamburger buns, split

Prepare grill for direct cooking.

Shape beef into eight ¼-inch-thick burger patties.

Combine cheeses, olives, parsley, tomato, oregano and pepper in small bowl. Place ¼ of cheese mixture on top of 1 burger patty; spread to within ½ inch of edge. Top cheese mixture with another burger patty; seal edges to enclose filling. Repeat with remaining cheese mixture and burger patties.

Place burgers on grid. Grill, covered, over medium heat 8 to 10 minutes for medium or until desired doneness, turning halfway through grilling time.

Remove burgers from grill. Place burgers between buns. *Makes 4 servings*

Campbell's® Country Skillet Supper

Harvest Pork Roast

¼ cup WESSON® Best Blend Oil	3½ to 4 pounds boned pork shoulder roast, trimmed
2½ cups cubed onions (½-inch dice)	
1½ teaspoons fresh minced garlic	4 large Red Delicious apples, quartered and cored
¾ cup honey	
¼ cup Dijon mustard	3 acorn squash, sliced horizontally 1½ inches thick
1½ teaspoons coarsely ground pepper	
WESSON® No-Stick Cooking Spray	1 cup fresh cranberries

Preheat oven to 350°F. In large skillet, heat Wesson® Oil. Add onions and garlic; sauté until onions are crisp-tender. Remove from heat. Add honey, mustard and pepper to onions and garlic in skillet; mix well. Spray large roasting pan with Wesson® Cooking Spray. Place pork roast in center of roasting pan. Pour onion mixture evenly over roast. Bake, covered, for 1½ hours, basting often with pan juices. Arrange apples and squash around roast. Baste roast, apples and squash several times with pan juices; cover. Bake an additional hour, basting occasionally, or until apples and squash are tender. Sprinkle cranberries evenly over dish. Bake, uncovered, for 10 minutes.

Makes 4 to 6 servings

Tip: If fresh cranberries are not available, use ⅔ cup dried cranberries.

Sloppy Joes

1 pound BOB EVANS® Italian Roll Sausage	2 tablespoons Dijon mustard
	2 tablespoons cider vinegar
1 medium onion, chopped	1 tablespoon sugar
½ green bell pepper, chopped	1 teaspoon minced garlic
½ cup ketchup	8 sandwich buns, split and toasted

Crumble sausage into medium skillet. Add onion and pepper. Cook over medium heat until sausage is browned, stirring occasionally. Drain off any drippings. Stir in all remaining ingredients except buns. Bring to a boil. Reduce heat to low; simmer 30 minutes. Serve hot on buns. Refrigerate leftovers.

Makes 8 servings

Harvest Pork Roast

Beef Bourguignon

1 boneless beef sirloin steak, ½ inch thick,
 trimmed and cut into ½-inch pieces
 (about 3 pounds)
½ cup all-purpose flour
4 slices bacon, diced
3 cups Burgundy wine or beef broth
2 medium carrots, diced
1 teaspoon dried marjoram leaves
½ teaspoon dried thyme leaves

½ teaspoon salt
 Black pepper to taste
1 bay leaf
2 tablespoons vegetable oil
20 to 24 fresh pearl onions
8 small new red potatoes, cut into quarters
8 to 10 mushrooms, sliced
3 cloves garlic, minced

Coat beef with flour, shaking off excess. Set aside.

Cook and stir bacon in 5-quart Dutch oven over medium-high heat until partially cooked. Brown half of beef with bacon in Dutch oven over medium-high heat. Remove with slotted spoon; set aside. Brown remaining beef. Pour off drippings. Return beef and bacon to Dutch oven.

Stir in wine, carrots, marjoram, thyme, salt, pepper and bay leaf. Bring to a boil over high heat. Reduce heat to low. Cover and simmer 10 minutes.

Meanwhile, heat oil in large saucepan over medium-high heat. Add onions, potatoes, mushrooms and garlic; cook and stir about 10 minutes. Add to Dutch oven. Cover and simmer 50 minutes or until meat is fork-tender. Discard bay leaf before serving. *Makes 10 to 12 servings*

Grilled Teriyaki Lamb Chops

2 pounds lamb chops (rib, shoulder or
 loin), ½ to ¾ inch thick
½ cup KIKKOMAN® Teriyaki Marinade
 & Sauce

3 tablespoons minced fresh parsley
2 tablespoons dry white wine
2 cloves garlic, pressed
½ teaspoon pepper

Place lamb chops in single layer in large shallow pan. Combine teriyaki sauce, parsley, wine, garlic and pepper; pour over chops. Turn chops over to coat both sides well. Marinate 45 minutes, turning chops over occasionally. Reserving marinade, remove chops; place on grill 4 to 5 inches from hot coals. Cook 4 minutes on each side for medium-rare, or to desired doneness, turning over and brushing occasionally with reserved marinade. (Or, place lamb chops on rack of broiler pan. Broil 4 to 5 inches from heat 5 minutes; turn over. Brush with reserved marinade. Broil 5 minutes longer for medium-rare, or to desired doneness.) *Makes 4 servings*

Beef Bourguignon

Campbell's® Simply Delicious Meat Loaf

1½ pounds ground beef
½ cup Italian-seasoned dry bread crumbs
1 egg, beaten

1 can (10¾ ounces) CAMPBELL'S®
Condensed Golden Mushroom Soup
¼ cup water

1. Mix beef, bread crumbs and egg *thoroughly.* In medium baking pan shape firmly into 8- by 4-inch loaf.

2. Bake at 350°F. for 30 minutes. Spread *½ can* soup over top of meat loaf. Bake 30 minutes more or until meat loaf is no longer pink (160°F.).

3. In small saucepan mix *2 tablespoons* drippings, remaining soup and water. Heat through. Serve with meat loaf.

Makes 6 servings

Prep Time: 5 minutes
Cook Time: 1 hour 5 minutes

California Stew

2 pounds cubed beef or lamb stew meat,
cut into 1-inch pieces
2 tablespoons salad oil
1 package (1⅝ ounces) LAWRY'S® Beef
Stew Seasoning Mix
Water

1 cup dry red wine
12 small boiling onions, peeled
1 bunch carrots, peeled and cut into
1-inch pieces
3 medium zucchini, cut into 1-inch pieces
2 large tomatoes, peeled and quartered

In large Dutch oven, brown meat in oil; drain fat. Add Beef Stew Seasoning Mix, 1 cup water and wine. Bring to a boil over medium-high heat; reduce heat to low, cover and simmer 1½ hours. Pierce each end of onions with fork to retain shape while cooking. Add onions and carrots to beef; cover and continue simmering 10 minutes. Add remaining ingredients, cover and continue simmering 20 minutes or until vegetables are tender.

Makes 6 servings

Microwave Oven Method

In 3-quart glass casserole dish, combine meat, Beef Stew Seasoning Mix, ½ cup water and wine. Cover with plastic wrap, venting one corner. Microwave on HIGH 10 minutes. Pierce each end of onions with fork to retain shape while cooking. Add all vegetables except tomatoes. Cover again and microwave on HIGH 10 minutes; stir and re-cover. Microwave at 50% power 45 minutes or until carrots are just tender. Stir in tomatoes during last 4 minutes.

Left to right: Campbell's® Parmesan Potatoes (page 124) and Campbell's® Simply Delicious Meat Loaf

Italian Stir-Fried Lamb

12 ounces boneless American lamb, leg or sirloin, thinly bias-sliced into strips about 3 inches long
¾ cup chicken broth
¼ cup dry white wine or water
2 tablespoons pesto
4 teaspoons cornstarch
½ teaspoon dried oregano leaves
1 tablespoon vegetable oil
1 (9-ounce) package frozen Italian-style green beans, thawed
½ cup thinly sliced carrots
1 cup sliced fresh mushrooms
1 cup cherry tomato halves
4 ounces linguine or fettuccine, cooked
2 tablespoons grated Parmesan cheese

In small bowl, stir together chicken broth, wine, pesto, cornstarch and oregano; set aside. Preheat wok or large skillet over high heat; add oil. Stir-fry green beans and carrots 4 minutes. Add mushrooms; stir-fry 1 to 2 minutes or until vegetables are crisp-tender. Remove vegetables from wok; set aside.

Add lamb strips to wok. Stir-fry about 3 minutes or until slightly pink. Remove lamb from wok; add to reserved vegetable mixture. Return vegetable mixture and meat to wok. Stir cornstarch mixture; add to wok. Cook and stir until thickened and bubbly. Stir in tomatoes. Cook 1 minute. Serve over hot cooked pasta; sprinkle with cheese. *Makes 4 servings*

Prep Time: 15 minutes
Cook Time: 20 minutes

Favorite recipe from **American Lamb Council**

Pork, Beans and Sausage Skillet Dinner

7 ounces low-fat Polska kielbasa sausage, cut into 1-inch pieces
2 cups frozen mixed vegetables
1 can (15 ounces) VAN CAMP'S® Pork and Beans
1 can (10¾ ounces) reduced-fat, reduced-sodium condensed tomato soup
2 cups cooked rice

1. In large skillet, brown sausage; drain.

2. Add vegetables, Van Camp's Beans and soup. Bring to a soft boil, reduce heat, cover, and simmer 10 minutes, stirring occasionally.

3. Stir in rice and heat through. *Makes 6 (10-ounce) servings*

Italian Stir-Fried Lamb

Marinated Steak with Parslied Rice

½ cup CRISCO® Oil*
⅓ cup soy sauce
¾ teaspoon ginger
1 clove garlic, minced *or* ⅛ teaspoon garlic powder

1 beef top round steak, ¾ to 1 inch thick (about 2 pounds)
5⅓ cups hot cooked rice (cooked without salt or fat)
⅓ cup chopped fresh parsley

*Use your favorite Crisco Oil product.

1. Combine oil, soy sauce, ginger and garlic in shallow baking dish. Add meat, turning to coat all surfaces. Refrigerate at least 30 minutes, turning meat after 15 minutes and spooning marinade over meat.

2. Heat broiler or prepare grill.

3. Remove meat from marinade; discard marinade. Broil or grill meat to desired doneness. Cut diagonally into very thin slices.

4. Toss hot rice with parsley. Serve with meat. Garnish, if desired.   *Makes 8 servings*

Layered Noodle Bake

1 can (26½ ounces) DEL MONTE® Spaghetti Sauce with Green Peppers and Mushrooms
1 package (12 ounces) extra-wide noodles, cooked
1 pound ground beef or turkey, browned and drained

1 pint (16 ounces) ricotta or cottage cheese
1 package (8 ounces) shredded mozzarella cheese

1. Preheat oven to 350°F.

2. Spread thin layer of sauce onto bottom of shallow 3-quart baking pan. Arrange half of noodles over sauce; cover with half of remaining sauce. Cover with meat, ricotta cheese and half of mozzarella cheese; top with layers of remaining noodles, sauce and mozzarella cheese.

3. Bake, uncovered, about 25 minutes or until heated through. Garnish, if desired.

Makes 4 to 6 servings

Marinated Steak with Parslied Rice

Beef & Mushroom Stroganoff

1 pound boneless sirloin or top round
   steak, thinly sliced
½ teaspoon ground black pepper
2 tablespoons margarine or butter, divided
3 cups (8 ounces) sliced mushrooms
½ cup chopped onion

1 (14½-ounce) can beef broth
½ cup milk
1 (4.8-ounce) package PASTA RONI®
   Parmesano
¾ cup frozen peas
⅓ cup sour cream

1. Sprinkle steak with pepper. In large skillet over medium-high heat, melt 1 tablespoon margarine. Add steak; sauté 2 minutes or until no longer pink. Remove from skillet; set aside.

2. In same skillet over medium heat, melt remaining 1 tablespoon margarine. Add mushrooms and onion; sauté 6 minutes.

3. Add beef broth and milk; bring to a boil. Stir in pasta, steak, peas and Special Seasonings. Reduce heat to medium-low. Gently boil, uncovered, 4 to 6 minutes or until pasta is tender, stirring frequently. Stir in sour cream; let stand 5 minutes before serving. *Makes 4 servings*

Prep Time: 10 minutes
Cook Time: 20 minutes

Reuben Casserole

1 can (10¾ ounces) condensed cream of
   mushroom soup, undiluted
¾ cup milk
¼ cup chopped onion
1½ teaspoons prepared mustard
1 can (16 ounces) sauerkraut, rinsed and
   drained

1 package (8 ounces) uncooked noodles
1 pound HILLSHIRE FARM® Polska
   Kielbasa, cut into ½-inch pieces
1 cup (4 ounces) shredded Swiss cheese
½ cup bread crumbs
2 tablespoons butter, melted

Preheat oven to 350°F.

Grease 13×9-inch baking pan. Combine soup, milk, onion and mustard in medium bowl. Spread sauerkraut onto bottom of prepared pan, pressing firmly. Add noodles. Spoon soup mixture evenly over noodles; cover with Polska Kielbasa. Top with cheese. Combine bread crumbs and butter in small bowl; sprinkle over cheese. Cover tightly. Bake 1 hour or until noodles are tender.

Makes 6 servings

Heartland Crown Roast of Pork

1 (8- to 9-pound) crown roast of pork
1 pound ground pork, cooked, drained
5 cups dry bread cubes
1 can (14½ ounces) chicken broth
1 cup walnut halves, toasted
½ cup chopped onion
½ cup chopped celery

1 teaspoon salt
¼ teaspoon *each* ground cinnamon and
   allspice
⅛ teaspoon pepper
2 cups sliced fresh or thawed frozen
   rhubarb
½ cup sugar

Place roast in shallow pan. Roast at 350°F until temperature on meat thermometer reaches 155°F, about 1½ hours. Remove roast from oven. Let stand 10 minutes before slicing to serve.

Meanwhile, combine ground pork, bread cubes, broth, walnuts, onion, celery and seasonings; mix well. Combine rhubarb and sugar in medium saucepan; bring to a boil. Pour over bread mixture; mix lightly. Spoon into buttered 2-quart casserole. Cover; bake at 350°F for 1½ hours. Serve with pork roast.   *Makes 16 servings*

Favorite recipe from **National Pork Board**

Lawry's® Home-Baked Ribs

2 tablespoons LAWRY'S® Seasoned Salt
6 pounds lean baby back ribs
1½ cups lemon juice
½ bottle (3.5 ounces) liquid smoke

1 bottle (16 ounces) barbecue sauce
Syrup from 1 can (16 ounces) peaches*
   (about ½ cup)

*Peaches can be refrigerated for later use.

Sprinkle Seasoned Salt onto both sides of ribs. In large resealable plastic food storage bag, place ribs. In medium bowl, combine lemon juice and liquid smoke. Pour over ribs; seal bag. Marinate in refrigerator at least 2 hours or overnight, turning occasionally. Remove ribs from marinade; discard used marinade. Place ribs in shallow baking pan. Bake in 350°F oven 1 hour. Reduce oven temperature to 300°F. Combine barbecue sauce and peach syrup; pour over ribs. Bake 30 to 45 minutes longer or until ribs are tender.   *Makes 8 servings*

Serving Suggestion: Serve with potato salad and lots of napkins.

Italian-Style Meat Loaf

1 egg
1½ pounds lean ground beef or turkey
8 ounces hot or mild Italian sausage, casings removed
1 cup CONTADINA® Seasoned Bread Crumbs

1 can (8 ounces) CONTADINA Tomato Sauce, divided
1 cup finely chopped onion
½ cup finely chopped green bell pepper

1. Beat egg lightly in large bowl. Add beef, sausage, bread crumbs, ¾ cup tomato sauce, onion and bell pepper; mix well.

2. Press into ungreased 9×5-inch loaf pan. Bake, uncovered, in preheated 350°F oven for 60 minutes.

3. Spoon remaining tomato sauce over meat loaf. Bake 15 minutes longer or until no longer pink in center; drain. Let stand for 10 minutes before serving. *Makes 8 servings*

Prep Time: 10 minutes
Cook Time: 75 minutes
Stand Time: 10 minutes

Pork Chops with Apples and Stuffing

4 pork chops, ½ inch thick
Salt and pepper
1 tablespoon oil
2 medium apples, cored, cut into 8 wedges

1 cup apple juice
2 cups STOVE TOP® Cornbread Stuffing Mix in the Canister
¼ cup chopped pecans

SPRINKLE chops with salt and pepper. Heat oil in large skillet on medium-high heat. Add chops and apples; cook until chops are browned on both sides.

STIR in apple juice. Bring to a boil. Reduce heat to low; cover and simmer 8 minutes or until chops are cooked through. Remove chops from skillet.

STIR stuffing mix and pecans into skillet. Return chops to skillet; cover. Remove from heat. Let stand 5 minutes. *Makes 4 servings*

Prep Time: 10 minutes
Cook Time: 20 minutes

Italian-Style Meat Loaf

Fabulous Fajitas

½ cup (1 stick) unsalted butter, melted, divided
4 cups julienned onions
2 cups julienned red, green or yellow bell peppers
4 boneless beef sirloin strip steaks (10½ ounces each), trimmed and cut into julienned strips

2 tablespoons Chef Paul Prudhomme's Meat Magic®, divided
½ cup freshly squeezed lime juice
Flour tortillas, warmed
Sour cream
Guacamole
Tomato salsa
Shredded lettuce

In 12-inch heavy skillet, heat 4 tablespoons butter over high heat; add onions and sauté until onions are clear and turning brown on edges, about 3 minutes, stirring or shaking skillet occasionally. Add bell peppers; toss or stir to combine with onions. Sauté until onions are soft and bell peppers are still crispy, about 3 minutes more, continuing to stir or shake pan (reduce heat, if necessary, to avoid burning vegetables). Transfer vegetables to plate to stop cooking process; without wiping it, set skillet aside to use later for sautéing meat.

Heat several sizzle platters or large cast-iron skillet in 400°F oven.

Meanwhile, place meat strips in large bowl and sprinkle with 1 tablespoon plus 1 teaspoon Meat Magic®, tossing to coat well. Pour lime juice over meat and toss again. Let marinate at least 10 minutes, tossing occasionally. (After 15 minutes, meat strips will break apart when pulled between your fingers.)

Heat reserved unwiped skillet over high heat, 40 to 45 seconds; add remaining butter (it will sizzle), then pick up meat with your fingers, let it drain slightly and add to skillet, reserving marinade. Cook about 45 seconds, turning meat frequently to coat with butter. Add reserved vegetables to meat and sauté about 15 seconds, tossing constantly to combine. Add reserved marinade; sprinkle remaining 2 teaspoons Meat Magic® over all; cook about 1 minute more, tossing or stirring well to combine. Remove from heat and pour onto heated sizzle platters or into heated cast-iron skillet. Serve while still sizzling.

Let everyone prepare his/her own serving or plate using the traditional condiments.

Makes 6 extremely generous servings

Fabulous Fajitas

Campbell's® Garlic Mashed Potatoes & Beef Bake

1 pound ground beef
1 can (10¾ ounces) CAMPBELL'S®
    Condensed Cream of Mushroom with
    Roasted Garlic Soup
1 tablespoon Worcestershire sauce

1 bag (16 ounces) frozen vegetable
    combination (broccoli, cauliflower,
    carrots), thawed
3 cups hot mashed potatoes

1. In medium skillet over medium-high heat, cook beef until browned, stirring to separate meat. Pour off fat.

2. In 2-quart shallow baking dish mix beef, ½ **can** soup, Worcestershire and vegetables.

3. Stir remaining soup into potatoes. Spoon potato mixture over beef mixture. Bake at 400°F. for 20 minutes or until hot.

Makes 4 servings

Prep Time: 10 minutes
Cook Time: 20 minutes

Cure 81® Ham with Honey Mustard Glaze

1 CURE 81® half ham
1 cup packed brown sugar

½ cup honey
2 tablespoons prepared mustard

Bake ham according to package directions. Meanwhile, combine brown sugar, honey and mustard. Thirty minutes before ham is done, remove from oven. Score surface; spoon on glaze. Continue basting with glaze during last 30 minutes of baking.

Makes 8 to 10 servings

Campbell's® Garlic Mashed Potatoes & Beef Bake

Beefy Cabbage Rolls

1 head green cabbage
1½ cups sliced fresh mushrooms
1 can (16 ounces) tomatoes, drained and
    chopped
2 cups shredded cooked beef
1 cup shredded carrots
⅔ cup chopped onion, divided
1 teaspoon dried basil, divided
1 clove garlic, minced

½ teaspoon salt
¼ teaspoon dried rosemary
¼ teaspoon grated lemon peel
⅛ teaspoon black pepper
2 tablespoons olive oil
1 can (15 ounces) tomato sauce
2 tablespoons packed light brown sugar
1 tablespoon cider vinegar
1 teaspoon instant beef bouillon granules

Microwave Directions

1. Cut center core from cabbage; discard. Wrap cabbage in plastic wrap; microwave at HIGH just until outer leaves can be separated from head, 1½ to 3½ minutes.

2. Remove 8 cabbage leaves; cut out hard center rib at base of each leaf and discard. Spread leaves on microwavable baking sheet. Microwave, covered with plastic wrap, at HIGH until pliable 1 to 2½ minutes. Set aside.

3. Shred enough of remaining cabbage to make 1½ cups. (Refrigerate any remaining cabbage, wrapped in plastic, for other use.) Combine shredded cabbage and mushrooms in 2-quart microwavable casserole. Microwave, covered with lid, at HIGH until cabbage is tender, 3 to 6 minutes; stir twice during cooking. Drain well.

4. Add tomatoes, beef, carrots, ⅓ cup onion, ½ teaspoon basil, garlic, salt, rosemary, lemon peel and pepper to mushroom mixture; mix well.

5. Spoon ⅛ of beef filling onto center of each cabbage leaf. Fold sides of each leaf over filling; roll up securely and fasten at seam with wooden pick. Place rolls seam-side-down in 12×8-inch baking dish.

6. For sauce, combine remaining ⅓ cup onion and oil in medium microwavable bowl. Microwave, uncovered, at HIGH until onion is tender, 2 to 3 minutes. Stir in remaining ½ teaspoon basil and remaining ingredients. Microwave, uncovered, at HIGH until sauce is thickened, 8 to 12 minutes; stir 2 to 3 times during cooking.

7. Remove wooden picks from cabbage rolls. Pour sauce over cabbage rolls. Microwave, covered with plastic wrap, at HIGH until heated through, 6 to 10 minutes; rotate dish ½ turn twice during cooking. Let stand 5 minutes before serving.

Makes 4 servings

Beefy Cabbage Rolls

Peppered Steak with Dijon Sauce

4 boneless beef top loin or New York strip
    steaks, cut 1 inch thick (about
    1½ pounds)
1 tablespoon *French's*® Worcestershire
    Sauce
    Crushed black pepper
⅓ cup mayonnaise

⅓ cup *French's*® Napa Valley Style Dijon
    Mustard
3 tablespoons dry red wine
2 tablespoons minced red or green onion
2 tablespoons minced fresh parsley
1 clove garlic, minced

1. Brush steaks with Worcestershire and sprinkle with pepper to taste; set aside. To prepare Dijon sauce, combine mayonnaise, mustard, wine, onion, parsley and garlic in medium bowl.

2. Place steaks on grid. Grill steaks over high heat 15 minutes for medium rare or to desired doneness, turning often. Serve with Dijon sauce. Garnish as desired. *Makes 4 servings*

Prep Time: 10 minutes
Cook Time: 15 minutes

Tip: Dijon sauce is also great served with grilled salmon and swordfish. To serve with fish, substitute white wine for red wine and minced dill for fresh parsley.

Pork Piccata

1 pork tenderloin, about 1 pound
3 tablespoons all-purpose flour
2 teaspoons lemon pepper
2 teaspoons butter

¼ cup dry sherry or white wine
¼ cup lemon juice
4 to 6 thick lemon slices
4 tablespoons capers

Slice tenderloin into 8 equal pieces; flatten each piece gently to a scallop with thickness of ⅛ inch. Dredge scallops lightly with flour; sprinkle with lemon pepper. Melt butter in nonstick pan over medium-high heat. Quickly sauté scallops, turning once, until golden brown, about 4 to 5 minutes. Add sherry and lemon juice to skillet; shake pan gently and cook 2 minutes, until sauce is slightly thickened. Serve garnished with lemon slices and capers. *Makes 4 servings*

Prep Time: 15 minutes

Favorite recipe from **National Pork Board**

Peppered Steak with Dijon Sauce

Super Veg•All® Tacos

1 can (15 ounces) VEG•ALL® Mixed
   Vegetables, drained
1 pound lean ground beef, cooked and
   drained
1 jar (16 ounces) chunky style salsa
½ can (4 ounces) diced jalapeño peppers

1 package (6.6 ounces) taco shells
2 cups shredded Monterey Jack cheese
   Chopped tomatoes
   Lettuce
   Sour cream

Preheat oven to 350°F. In medium mixing bowl, combine Veg•All, ground beef, salsa, and peppers; mix well. Divide mixture among taco shells. Divide cheese and sprinkle over meat mixture in taco shells. Bake for 10 to 15 minutes or until cheese has melted and tacos are hot. Serve with tomatoes, lettuce, and sour cream.

Makes 5 servings

Stuffed Peppers

6 medium green peppers
   Boiling salted water
1 pound ground beef
1 small onion, chopped
1 can (8 ounces) kidney beans, drained
1 can (6 ounces) tomato paste
2½ cups water, divided
1½ teaspoons salt, divided

1 teaspoon sugar
¾ teaspoon chili powder
¼ teaspoon garlic salt
⅓ cup shredded cheddar cheese (optional)
1 tablespoon butter or margarine
   (optional)
2¼ cups uncooked MINUTE® Original Rice

CUT slice from tops of peppers; remove seeds. Cook, uncovered, in enough salted water to cover peppers about 5 minutes; drain.

BROWN beef and onion in large skillet; drain. Add beans, tomato paste, ¼ cup water, ¾ teaspoon salt, sugar, chili powder and garlic salt; mix well. Spoon into peppers and place in 13×9-inch baking dish. Add small amount of water to cover bottom of dish. Bake at 375°F for 25 minutes or until peppers are tender. Sprinkle with cheese.

MEANWHILE, bring remaining 2¼ cups water, ¾ teaspoon salt and butter to a full boil in medium saucepan. Stir in rice. Cover; remove from heat. Let stand 5 minutes. Fluff with fork. Serve with peppers.

Makes 6 servings

Super Veg•All® Tacos

Sweet and Sour Meatballs

1 pound lean ground beef	½ teaspoon pepper
½ cup dry unseasoned bread crumbs	¼ teaspoon dried thyme leaves
¼ cup reduced-sodium beef broth	4 dashes hot pepper sauce
1 egg	Sweet and Sour Sauce (recipe follows)
2 teaspoons reduced-sodium soy sauce	Finely chopped parsley
1 teaspoon minced garlic	
½ teaspoon salt	

• Mix all ingredients except Sweet and Sour Sauce and parsley; shape into 20 meatballs and place in baking pan. Bake meatballs in preheated 350°F oven until browned and no longer pink in center, about 20 minutes.

• Arrange meatballs in serving dish; pour hot Sweet and Sour Sauce over meatballs and sprinkle with parsley. Serve over noodles or rice.   *Makes 4 servings*

Sweet and Sour Sauce

1 cup reduced-sodium beef broth	1 tablespoon reduced-sodium soy sauce
3½ teaspoons EQUAL® FOR RECIPES *or*	1 tablespoon Dijon-style mustard
12 packets EQUAL® sweetener *or*	2 teaspoons tomato paste
½ cup EQUAL® SPOONFUL™	½ teaspoon grated orange peel
1 tablespoon cornstarch	2 to 3 dashes red pepper sauce
1 tablespoon lemon juice	Salt and pepper

• Mix beef broth, Equal® and cornstarch in small saucepan; stir in remaining ingredients except salt and pepper and heat to boiling.

• Boil, stirring constantly, until thickened, about 1 minute. Season to taste with salt and pepper.

Sweet and Sour Meatballs

Fresh Herb Lasagna

1 pound lean ground beef (85% lean)
1 teaspoon olive oil
1 small red onion, finely chopped
3 cloves garlic, minced
2 jars (26 ounces each) BARILLA®
    Lasagna & Casserole Sauce or
    Marinara Pasta Sauce, divided
½ cup Merlot or other dry red wine
2 tablespoons fresh basil, chopped
1 tablespoon fresh parsley, chopped
1 tablespoon fresh cilantro, chopped

2 teaspoons fresh oregano, chopped
1 teaspoon fresh thyme, chopped
2 eggs
2 containers (15 ounces each) ricotta
    cheese, drained
2 cups (8 ounces) shredded mozzarella
    cheese, divided
1 cup (4 ounces) grated Parmesan cheese
1 package (16 sheets) BARILLA® Oven
    Ready Lasagna Noodles (do not boil)

1. Preheat oven to 375°F. Spray 13½×9½×3-inch foil pan or equivalent 3-inch deep lasagna baking dish with nonstick cooking spray.

2. Brown meat in olive oil in large skillet, stirring to break up meat. Drain excess fat. Add onion and garlic; cook over medium-high heat 3 to 4 minutes or until onion is tender, stirring occasionally. Add 1 jar lasagna sauce, wine and all herbs. Heat to boiling; reduce heat to medium and cook 15 minutes.

3. Beat eggs in medium bowl. Stir in ricotta, 1⅓ cups mozzarella and Parmesan.

4. To assemble, spread ½ jar lasagna sauce on bottom of prepared pan. Layer 4 uncooked lasagna noodles, ⅓ of meat mixture (about 1¾ cups) and ⅓ of ricotta mixture (about 2 cups) over lasagna sauce. Repeat layers once. Top with 4 uncooked lasagna noodles, remaining meat mixture and remaining ricotta mixture. Top with remaining 4 uncooked lasagna noodles, remaining ½ jar lasagna sauce and remaining ⅔ cup mozzarella.

5. Cover with foil and bake 60 minutes. Uncover and continue baking about 5 minutes or until center is hot (160°F). Let stand 15 minutes before cutting. *Makes 12 servings*

Note: Both sauce and ricotta mixture can be prepared one day ahead, covered and refrigerated. Let stand at room temperature 30 minutes before assembling lasagna.

Tip: When layering, slightly overlap lasagna sheets. Lasagna sheets will expand to the edges of the pan during cooking. Spread sauce and filling to edges of lasagna sheets.

Savory Pot Roast

⅔ cup A.1.® Original or A.1.® BOLD
  & SPICY Steak Sauce
1 (0.9-ounce) envelope dry onion-
  mushroom soup mix
1 cup water, divided

1 (2½-pound) boneless beef chuck roast
6 medium potatoes, quartered
6 medium carrots, peeled, cut into 1-inch
  pieces
2 tablespoons all-purpose flour

Blend steak sauce, soup mix and ¾ cup water; set aside.

Line shallow baking pan or dish with heavy-duty foil, overlapping edges. Place roast in center of foil; place potatoes and carrots around roast. Pour steak sauce mixture evenly over beef and vegetables. Seal foil loosely over top of beef; secure side edges tightly.

Bake at 350°F 2 hours or until beef is tender. Remove beef to heated serving platter. Using slotted spoon, remove vegetables to same platter; keep warm. Remove and discard foil, pouring liquid into saucepan. Remove excess fat from liquid if necessary.

Dissolve flour in remaining ¼ cup water. Stir into liquid in pan; cook until thickened, stirring occasionally. Slice beef; serve with vegetables and gravy. *Makes 8 servings*

Veal with Mushrooms

¼ cup all-purpose flour
  Salt and freshly ground black pepper
6 veal cutlets, ½ inch thick (about
  2 pounds)
¼ cup FILIPPO BERIO® Olive Oil

½ cup beef broth
8 ounces fresh mushrooms, cleaned and
  quartered *or* 1 (4-ounce) can whole
  mushrooms, drained and quartered
5 tablespoons dry white wine

In small shallow bowl, combine flour with salt and pepper to taste. Lightly coat cutlets in flour mixture. In large skillet, heat olive oil over medium-high heat until hot. Add cutlets; cook 5 minutes or until brown, turning occasionally. Add beef broth. Cover; reduce heat to low and cook 10 minutes. Add mushrooms and wine. Cover; cook an additional 10 minutes or until veal is cooked through and tender. Uncover; simmer 5 minutes. *Makes 6 servings*

Poultry Pleasers ❧

Apricot Glazed Chicken

1 roasting chicken (4 to 5 pounds)
1 cup seedless red or green grapes
4 tablespoons honey, divided
1 can (16 ounces) apricot halves, divided
¼ cup butter or margarine, melted

2 teaspoons seasoned salt
¼ teaspoon pepper
½ cup dry white wine or chicken broth
Grape clusters and fresh herbs for garnish (optional)

Rinse chicken in cold water and pat dry with paper towels. Toss 1 cup grapes with 2 tablespoons honey in small bowl. Place grapes in body cavity. Tie legs close to body and fold wing tips back or secure with skewers or cotton string. Place chicken, breast side up, on rack in roasting pan.

Drain apricot halves, reserving syrup. Set aside 6 halves for garnish. Purée remaining apricots in blender or food processor with melted butter, seasoned salt, pepper and remaining 2 tablespoons honey. Brush over chicken. Pour wine and ¼ cup apricot syrup in bottom of pan. Cover chicken loosely with tented foil.

Roast at 350°F 1¾ to 2 hours or until chicken is tender and thermometer inserted in thigh registers 180°F. Baste occasionally with pan drippings to glaze. Remove foil during last 30 minutes of roasting. Bring apricot mixture to a boil in small saucepan over medium heat. Boil 1 to 2 minutes. Serve chicken on platter with apricot sauce, garnished with clusters of grapes, apricot halves and fresh herbs, if desired.

Makes 6 to 8 servings

Favorite recipe from **National Honey Board**

Apricot Glazed Chicken

Bistro Chicken Skillet

1 (2- to 2½-pound) whole chicken, cut
    into 8 pieces
2 teaspoons dried thyme
1 teaspoon paprika
1 teaspoon salt
½ teaspoon ground black pepper
2 tablespoons olive oil
8 large whole cloves garlic, peeled

¼ cup dry vermouth or water
2 tablespoons margarine or butter
1 (4.6-ounce) package PASTA RONI®
    Garlic & Olive Oil with Vermicelli
1½ cups fresh asparagus, cut into 1½-inch
    pieces or broccoli florets
1 cup sliced carrots

1. Sprinkle meaty side of chicken with thyme, paprika, salt and pepper. In large skillet over medium-high heat, heat oil. Add chicken, seasoned-side down. Cook 5 minutes. Reduce heat to medium-low; turn chicken over. Add garlic. Cover; cook 20 to 25 minutes or until chicken is no longer pink inside.

2. Meanwhile, in medium saucepan, bring 1½ cups water, vermouth and margarine just to a boil. Stir in pasta, asparagus, carrots and Special Seasonings. Reduce heat to medium. Gently boil uncovered, 10 minutes or until pasta is tender, stirring occasionally.

3. Remove chicken and garlic from skillet with slotted spoon. Skim off and discard fat from skillet juices. Serve chicken, garlic and reserved juices over pasta. *Makes 4 servings*

Baked Barbecue Chicken

1 (3-pound) broiler-fryer, cut up
1 small onion, cut into slices
1½ cups ketchup
½ cup firmly packed light brown sugar

¼ cup Worcestershire sauce
2 tablespoons lemon juice
1 tablespoon liquid smoke

Preheat oven to 375°F. Place chicken in 13×9-inch baking dish coated with nonstick cooking spray. Arrange onion slices over chicken.

Combine ketchup, brown sugar, Worcestershire sauce, lemon juice and liquid smoke in small saucepan. Heat over medium heat 2 to 3 minutes or until sugar dissolves. Pour over chicken.

Bake chicken 1 hour or until juices run clear. Discard onion slices. Let stand 10 minutes before serving. *Makes 6 servings*

Serving Suggestion: Serve with baked potatoes, crusty French bread and tossed green salad.

Bistro Chicken Skillet

Chicken Jambalaya

2 tablespoons vegetable oil
¾ pound boneless chicken thighs or breasts, cut into cubes
1 cup ham cut into very thin strips (about 5 ounces)
1 can (14½ to 16 ounces) seasoned diced tomatoes in juice, undrained

1½ cups water
1 can (4 ounces) diced green chilies, undrained
1 package KNORR® Recipe Classics™ Vegetable Soup, Dip and Recipe Mix
1 cup uncooked rice

• In large skillet, heat oil over medium-high heat and brown chicken and ham.

• Stir in tomatoes, water, chilies and recipe mix. Bring to a boil over high heat. Stir in rice.

• Reduce heat to low and simmer covered, stirring occasionally, 20 minutes or until rice is tender.

Makes 4 servings

Prep Time: 15 minutes
Cook Time: 25 minutes

Yummy Weeknight Chicken

1 pound boneless skinless chicken breast, pounded thin
1 small onion, sliced
1 package (10 ounces) mushrooms, sliced

⅓ cup barbecue sauce
¼ cup honey
2 tablespoons *French's®* Worcestershire Sauce

1. Heat *1 tablespoon oil* in large nonstick skillet over medium-high heat. Cook chicken 5 minutes or until chicken is no longer pink in center. Remove chicken to serving platter; keep warm.

2. In same skillet, sauté onion and mushrooms for 5 minutes until mushrooms are golden brown and no liquid remains. Return chicken to skillet.

3. Combine remaining ingredients. Pour into skillet. Bring to a full boil. Reduce heat and cook 2 to 3 minutes or until sauce thickens slightly, stirring occasionally. Serve with hot cooked rice, if desired.

Makes 4 servings

Prep Time: 10 minutes
Cook Time: 12 minutes

Chicken Jambalaya

Grilled Chicken Stix

1 pound thin sliced chicken breast cutlets	½ cup honey
12 to 14 wooden skewers, soaked in water	3 tablespoons *Frank's® RedHot®* Cayenne Pepper Sauce
2 oranges, cut into eighths	Spicy Cucumber Salsa (recipe follows)
½ cup barbecue sauce	

1. Slice cutlets into ½-inch-wide long strips. Weave strips onto upper half of 8 to 10 skewers. Place skewers into large baking dish. Thread 4 orange pieces each onto remaining 4 skewers. Set aside.

2. Combine barbecue sauce, honey and **Frank's RedHot** Sauce in measuring cup. Reserve ¼ cup sauce for Spicy Cucumber Salsa. Pour ½ cup of remaining mixture over chicken, turning skewers to coat.

3. Grill or broil chicken and orange skewers 5 minutes or until chicken is no longer pink in center and oranges are heated through. Turn and baste often with remaining sauce. Serve with Spicy Cucumber Salsa.

Makes 4 servings

Prep Time: 10 minutes
Cook Time: 5 minutes

Spicy Cucumber Salsa

1 large cucumber, peeled, seeded and chopped	2 tablespoons finely chopped fresh cilantro or parsley
1 small red bell pepper, finely chopped	Reserved ¼ cup barbecue sauce mixture
¼ cup finely chopped red onion	

1. Combine all ingredients in large bowl; chill. Serve with Grilled Chicken Stix or your favorite grilled chicken or steak recipe.

Makes 4 to 6 servings (about 2 cups)

Prep Time: 10 minutes

Grilled Chicken Stix

Chicken Marsala

1 tablespoon butter
2 boneless skinless chicken breasts, halved
1 cup sliced carrots
1 cup sliced fresh mushrooms

⅓ cup chicken broth
⅓ cup HOLLAND HOUSE® Marsala Cooking Wine

Melt butter in skillet over medium-high heat. Add chicken; cook 5 minutes. Turn chicken over, add remaining ingredients. Bring to a boil; simmer 15 to 20 minutes until juices run clear. Serve over cooked fettuccine, if desired.

Makes 4 servings

Italian Rotini Bake

8 ounces dry rotini pasta, uncooked
1 tablespoon olive or vegetable oil
1½ cups chopped onions
2 small zucchini, quartered, sliced
3 cloves garlic, minced
1 pound ground turkey
2 cans (14.5 ounces each) CONTADINA® Recipe Ready Diced Tomatoes, undrained

1 can (6 ounces) CONTADINA Tomato Paste
1 cup water
1 tablespoon Italian herb seasoning
1 teaspoon salt
1 egg
1 container (15 ounces) ricotta cheese
3 cups (12 ounces) shredded mozzarella cheese, divided

1. Cook pasta according to package directions; drain.

2. Meanwhile, heat oil over medium-high heat in large skillet. Add onions, zucchini and garlic; sauté for 2 to 3 minutes or until vegetables are tender.

3. Add turkey; cook for 4 to 5 minutes or until turkey is no longer pink. Drain. Add tomatoes and juice, tomato paste, water, Italian seasoning and salt.

4. Bring to a boil. Reduce heat to low; simmer, uncovered, for 5 minutes.

5. Beat egg lightly in small bowl. Add ricotta cheese and 1 cup mozzarella cheese.

6. Layer half of pasta and half of tomato mixture in ungreased 13×9-inch baking dish. Cover with ricotta cheese mixture and 1 cup mozzarella cheese. Top with remaining pasta, tomato mixture and mozzarella cheese.

7. Bake in preheated 350°F oven for 15 to 20 minutes or until heated through.

Makes 8 to 10 servings

Chicken Marsala

Chicken Pot Pie

2 cups cut-up cooked chicken
1 package (10 ounces) frozen mixed
    vegetables, thawed
1¼ cups milk

1 envelope LIPTON® RECIPE SECRETS®
    Garlic Mushroom Soup Mix
1 pie crust or pastry for single-crust pie

1. Preheat oven to 400°F. In large bowl, combine chicken and vegetables; set aside.

2. In small saucepan, bring milk and soup mix to a boil over medium heat, stirring occasionally. Cook 1 minute. Stir into chicken mixture.

3. Pour into 9-inch pie plate. Top with pie crust. Press pastry around edge of pie plate to seal; trim excess pastry, then flute edges. With tip of knife, make small slits in pastry.

4. Bake uncovered 35 minutes or until crust is golden. *Makes 4 servings*

Peanut Chicken

4 boneless, skinless chicken breast halves
2 tablespoons vegetable oil
1 can (14½ ounces) DEL MONTE® Diced
    Tomatoes with Garlic & Onion
2 cloves garlic, minced, *or* ¼ teaspoon
    garlic powder

¼ teaspoon ground ginger *or* 1 teaspoon
    grated ginger root
⅛ to ¼ teaspoon crushed red pepper flakes
3 tablespoons chunky peanut butter

1. Cook chicken in hot oil in large skillet over medium-high heat about 4 minutes on each side or until chicken is no longer pink in center. Remove chicken from skillet.

2. Add tomatoes, garlic, ginger and red pepper flakes to skillet; cook 2 minutes. Stir in peanut butter.

3. Return chicken to skillet; heat through. Garnish with chopped cilantro and peanuts, if desired.
Makes 4 servings

Prep Time: 4 minutes
Cook Time: 12 minutes

Chicken Pot Pie

Chicken and Black Bean Chili

1 tablespoon vegetable oil
1 medium onion, chopped
4 boneless, skinless chicken breast halves (about 1 pound), cooked and cut into strips
2 cans (14½ ounces each) diced tomatoes, undrained
1 can (15 ounces) black beans, rinsed and drained

1 can (4 ounces) diced green chilies
½ cup water
½ teaspoon LAWRY'S® Garlic Powder with Parsley
1 package (1.48 ounces) LAWRY'S® Spices & Seasonings for Chili
½ teaspoon hot pepper sauce (optional)
1 tablespoon chopped fresh cilantro

In large, deep skillet, heat oil. Add onion and cook until tender and translucent. Add all remaining ingredients except cilantro. Bring to a boil over medium-high heat; reduce heat to low and simmer, uncovered, 20 minutes, stirring occasionally. Stir in cilantro. *Makes 5½ cups chili*

Serving Suggestion: Serve with dairy sour cream and tortilla chips. Chopped avocados make a great garnish, too.

Variation: Substitute 1½ pounds ground turkey or chicken, browned in 1 tablespoon oil, for chicken.

Turkey Green Bean Casserole

1 package (6 ounces) STOVE TOP® Traditional Sage Stuffing Mix
1 can (10¾ ounces) condensed cream of mushroom soup

¾ cup milk
3 cups cubed cooked turkey
1 package (10 ounces) frozen French-cut green beans, cooked, drained

PREPARE stuffing mix as directed on package.

MIX soup and milk in 12×8-inch baking dish until smooth. Stir in turkey and green beans. Spoon stuffing evenly over top.

BAKE at 375°F for 30 minutes or until thoroughly heated. *Makes 4 to 6 servings*

Chicken and Black Bean Chili

Oriental Chicken & Asparagus

6 TYSON® Fresh Boneless, Skinless
    Chicken Thighs
2 tablespoons cornstarch, divided
½ teaspoon salt
¼ pound fresh asparagus spears, trimmed
    and chopped
1 small red bell pepper, cut into thin
    strips

1 medium onion, sliced
2 tablespoons oyster sauce
1 clove garlic, minced
½ teaspoon sesame oil
1 can (14½ ounces) chicken broth
1 can (8 ounces) sliced water chestnuts,
    drained

PREP: CLEAN: Wash hands. Cut chicken into strips. CLEAN: Wash hands. Combine 1 tablespoon cornstarch and salt in medium bowl. Add chicken and stir to coat. Refrigerate.

COOK: Spray large nonstick skillet with nonstick cooking spray. Heat over medium-high heat. Cook and stir asparagus, bell pepper, onion, oyster sauce, garlic and oil about 3 minutes. Remove from pan. Cook and stir chicken about 5 minutes or until internal juices of chicken run clear. (Or insert instant-read meat thermometer in thickest part of chicken. Temperature should read 180°F.) Add broth and water chestnuts to skillet. Combine remaining 1 tablespoon cornstarch and ¼ cup water; add to skillet. Cook and stir until sauce is thickened. Return vegetables to skillet and heat through.

SERVE: Serve with cooked rice, if desired.

CHILL: Refrigerate leftovers immediately.

Makes 4 servings

Prep Time: 10 minutes
Cook Time: 20 minutes

Oriental Chicken & Asparagus

Mustard Crusted Chicken & Rice

1 (6.5-ounce) package RICE-A-RONI®
    Broccoli Au Gratin
2½ tablespoons margarine or butter
1½ cups baby carrots, cut crosswise into
    halves
½ cup sliced green onions

¼ cup brown mustard
1 tablespoon honey
2 cloves garlic, minced
4 bone-in, skin-on chicken breasts (1 to
    1½ pounds)

1. Preheat broiler. In large skillet over medium heat, sauté rice-pasta mix with margarine until pasta is light golden brown. Slowly stir in 2¼ cups water, carrots and Special Seasonings; bring to a boil. Reduce heat to low. Cover; simmer 15 to 20 minutes or until rice is tender. Stir in green onions; let stand 5 minutes.

2. Meanwhile, combine mustard, honey and garlic; set aside. Place chicken, meaty-side down, on broiler pan. Broil chicken for 10 minutes. Turn chicken over and brush with half of mustard mixture. Broil 10 to 15 minutes or until chicken is no longer pink inside, brushing chicken once more with remaining mustard mixture. Serve chicken over rice. *Makes 4 servings*

Prep Time: 5 minutes
Cook Time: 35 minutes

Chicken Tostadas

3 cups shredded cooked chicken
1½ cups TACO BELL® HOME
    ORIGINALS®* Thick 'N Chunky
    Salsa
8 tostada shells
1 tub (8 ounces) PHILADELPHIA® Light
    Cream Cheese Spread

1½ cups shredded lettuce
1 tomato, chopped
1 package (8 ounces) KRAFT® 2% Milk
    Shredded Reduced Fat Mild Cheddar
    Cheese

TACO BELL and HOME ORIGINALS are registered trademarks owned and licensed by Taco Bell Corp.

TOSS chicken with salsa.

SPREAD tostada shells with cream cheese spread; top with chicken mixture, lettuce, tomato and cheese. Serve with additional salsa and jalapeño pepper slices, if desired. *Makes 8 servings*

Prep Time: 20 minutes

Stuffed Chicken Breasts

6 boneless skinless chicken breast halves
    (about 1 ½ pounds)
5 ounces goat cheese
2 tablespoons chopped fresh tarragon *or*
    2 teaspoons dried tarragon leaves
Salt and freshly ground black pepper, to
    taste

2 tablespoons all-purpose flour
¼ cup EGG BEATERS® Healthy Real Egg
    Product
1½ cups fresh bread crumbs
¼ cup FLEISCHMANN'S® Original
    Margarine, divided

1. Cut horizontal slit in thickest part of each chicken breast to form pocket; set aside.

2. Blend goat cheese and tarragon; season with salt and pepper to taste.

3. Spoon cheese mixture into chicken breast pockets; secure opening with toothpick.

4. Mix flour with salt and pepper to taste; lightly dust chicken breasts with flour mixture.

5. Dip chicken breasts in Egg Beaters®; coat with bread crumbs, firmly pressing crumbs onto chicken.

6. Heat 2 tablespoons margarine in large nonstick skillet over medium-high heat. Cook 3 chicken breasts at a time for 3 to 5 minutes on each side or until browned and cooked through, using additional margarine as needed.

7. Season with salt and pepper; remove toothpicks and serve. *Makes 6 servings*

Turkey à la King

2 cups cubed BUTTERBALL® Fat Free
    Slice 'N Serve Oven Roasted Breast of
    Turkey, cubed
⅓ cup butter
4 ounces fresh mushrooms, sliced
4 tablespoons flour

½ teaspoon salt
⅛ teaspoon black pepper
1 can (14½ ounces) chicken broth
½ cup light cream
1 cup frozen peas and carrots
Chopped fresh parsley

Melt butter in large saucepan over medium heat; add mushrooms. Cook and stir 5 minutes. Stir in flour, salt and pepper. Slowly blend in chicken broth and cream. Cook, stirring constantly, until thickened. Add turkey and peas and carrots. Heat well. Serve on toasted thick bread slices or pastry shells, if desired. Sprinkle with chopped parsley. *Makes 4 servings*

Salsa Chicken Fajitas

2 tablespoons vegetable oil
1 medium onion, sliced
1 medium red bell pepper, cut into ¼-inch
   strips
1 medium green bell pepper, cut into
   ¼-inch strips
1 clove garlic, minced
4 boneless skinless chicken breast halves
   (about 1 pound), cut into ¼-inch
   strips

½ cup chunky salsa
1 tablespoon minced jalapeño pepper*
8 (8-inch) flour tortillas
   Guacamole
   Shredded mozzarella or Monterey Jack
   cheese
   Additional chunky salsa

Jalapeño peppers can sting and irritate the skin; wear rubber gloves when handling peppers and do not touch eyes. Wash hands after handling peppers.

Heat oil in large skillet over medium-high heat. Add onion, bell peppers and garlic. Cook and stir 3 to 4 minutes or until crisp-tender. Remove vegetables with slotted spoon; set aside. Add chicken to skillet. Cook and stir 4 minutes or until chicken is no longer pink in center. Return vegetables to skillet. Add salsa and jalapeño pepper. Season with salt and black pepper to taste; cover. Continue cooking 2 minutes or until thoroughly heated.

Meanwhile, stack tortillas and wrap in foil. Heat tortillas in 350°F oven 10 minutes or until warm. Fill tortillas with guacamole, chicken mixture and cheese; top with additional salsa.

Makes 4 servings

VELVEETA® Cheesy Chicken & Rice Skillet

1 tablespoon oil
4 small boneless skinless chicken breast
   halves (about 1 pound)
1 can (10¾ ounces) condensed cream of
   chicken soup

1 soup can (1⅓ cups) water
2 cups MINUTE® White Rice, uncooked
1 package (8 ounces) VELVEETA®
   Shredded Pasteurized Process Cheese
   Food, divided

1. Heat oil in large nonstick skillet on medium-high heat. Add chicken; cover. Cook 4 minutes on each side or until cooked through. Remove chicken from skillet.

2. Add soup and water to skillet; stir. Bring to boil.

3. Stir in rice and 1 cup of the Velveeta. Top with chicken. Sprinkle with remaining Velveeta; cover. Cook on low heat 5 minutes.

Makes 4 servings

Salsa Chicken Fajitas

Guinness Chicken

2 tablespoons vegetable oil
1 medium onion, chopped
2 large cloves garlic, minced
1 whole chicken (3 to 4 pounds), cut into
    serving pieces
5 carrots, peeled and chopped
2 parsnips, peeled and chopped

1 teaspoon dried thyme leaves
¾ teaspoon salt
½ teaspoon black pepper
¾ cup Guinness Stout
½ pound fresh button mushrooms
¾ cup frozen peas

1. Heat oil in large skillet over medium heat until hot. Add onion and garlic; cook and stir 3 minutes or until tender. Remove vegetables with slotted spoon to small bowl.

2. Arrange chicken in single layer in skillet. Cook over medium-high heat 5 minutes per side or until lightly browned.

3. Add onion, garlic, carrots, parsnips, thyme, salt and pepper to skillet. Pour stout over chicken and vegetables. Bring to a boil over high heat. Reduce heat to low. Cover and simmer 35 minutes.

4. Add mushrooms and peas to skillet. Cover; cook 10 minutes.

5. Uncover skillet; increase heat to medium. Cook 10 minutes or until sauce is slightly reduced and chicken is no longer pink in center. *Makes 4 servings*

Chicken Stir-Fry

4 boneless skinless chicken breast halves
    (about 1½ pounds)
2 tablespoons vegetable oil
2 tablespoons orange juice
2 tablespoons light soy sauce

1 tablespoon cornstarch
1 bag (16 ounces) BIRDS EYE® frozen
    Farm Fresh Mixtures Broccoli, Carrots
    & Water Chestnuts

• Cut chicken into ½-inch-thick long strips.

• In wok or large skillet, heat oil over medium-high heat. Add chicken; cook 5 minutes, stirring occasionally.

• Meanwhile, in small bowl, combine orange juice, soy sauce and cornstarch; blend well and set aside.

• Add vegetables to chicken; cook 5 minutes more or until chicken is no longer pink in center, stirring occasionally.

• Stir in soy sauce mixture; cook 1 minute or until heated through. *Makes 4 servings*

Guinness Chicken

Monterey Chicken and Rice Quiche

4 boneless, skinless chicken tenderloins,
    cut into 1-inch pieces
1¾ cups water
1 box UNCLE BEN'S® COUNTRY INN®
    Chicken & Vegetable Rice
1 cup frozen mixed vegetables

1 (9-inch) deep-dish ready-to-use frozen
    pie crust
3 eggs
½ cup milk
½ cup (2 ounces) shredded Monterey Jack
    cheese

1. Heat oven to 400°F.

2. In large skillet, combine chicken, water, rice, contents of seasoning packet and frozen vegetables. Bring to a boil. Cover; reduce heat and simmer 10 minutes. Spoon mixture into pie crust.

3. In small bowl, beat eggs and milk. Pour over rice mixture in pie crust; top with cheese. Bake 30 to 35 minutes or until knife inserted in center comes out clean. *Makes 6 servings*

Serving Suggestion: A fresh fruit compote of orange sections and green grapes or blueberries is the perfect accompaniment to this delicious quiche.

Chicken and Vegetable Ragoût

2 tablespoons olive or vegetable oil
½ cup chopped onion
3 cloves garlic, minced
1 pound (about 4) boneless, skinless
    chicken breast halves, cut into ½-inch
    pieces
1 cup water or chicken broth
1 can (14.5 ounces) CONTADINA®
    Recipe Ready Diced Tomatoes,
    undrained

1 can (6 ounces) CONTADINA Italian
    Paste with Italian Seasonings
1 cup sliced peeled carrots
1 cup halved zucchini slices
1 cup red or green bell pepper strips
1 teaspoon Italian herb seasoning
½ teaspoon salt
⅛ teaspoon ground black pepper

1. Heat oil in large skillet. Add onion and garlic; sauté until tender. Add chicken; cook until browned, stirring frequently.

2. Add water, undrained tomatoes, tomato paste and carrots; cover. Simmer for 10 minutes.

3. Add zucchini, bell pepper, Italian seasoning, salt and pepper; cover.

4. Simmer for 15 to 20 minutes or until chicken is no longer pink in center and vegetables are tender. Serve over hot cooked rice or pasta, if desired. *Makes 6 servings*

Monterey Chicken and Rice Quiche

Olive Sauce Pasta Shells with Chicken

1 jar (26 ounces) BARILLA® Green and
    Black Olive Pasta Sauce
2 cups chopped cooked chicken
½ cup (2 ounces) grated Parmesan cheese,
    divided

2 tablespoons capers, drained
1 package (16 ounces) BARILLA® Medium
    Shells

1. Combine pasta sauce, chicken, ¼ cup cheese and capers in large saucepan. Cook over medium heat 10 minutes, stirring occasionally.

2. Meanwhile, cook shells according to package directions; drain. Transfer to large platter.

3. Pour pasta sauce mixture over hot drained shells; sprinkle with remaining ¼ cup cheese.

Makes 8 to 10 servings

Tip: ¾ pound boneless, skinless chicken breasts will yield about 2 cups chopped cooked chicken. To save time, purchase a rotisserie chicken or packaged (frozen) cooked chicken from the supermarket.

Mediterranean Game Hens

1 cup UNCLE BEN'S® Instant Rice
2 TYSON® Rock Cornish Game Hens
    (fresh or frozen, thawed)
¾ cup chopped fresh spinach

¼ cup chopped sun-dried tomatoes packed
    in oil
1 tablespoon butter or margarine, melted
1 clove garlic, minced

COOK: Preheat oven to 425°F. Prepare rice according to package directions. Stir in spinach and tomatoes; cool. Spoon half of rice mixture into cavity of each hen. Tie drumsticks together with string; place hens on rack in shallow roasting pan. Combine butter and garlic; brush each hen with mixture. Roast, basting occasionally with garlic butter, 45 to 50 minutes* or until internal juices of hens run clear. (Or insert instant-read meat thermometer in thickest part of hen. Temperature should read 180°F.)

SERVE: Serve with a spinach salad sprinkled with feta cheese, if desired.

CHILL: Refrigerate leftovers immediately.

Makes 2 servings

Note: If hen weighs over 1 pound 2 ounces, roast 60 to 70 minutes.

Olive Sauce Pasta Shells with Chicken

Phoenix & Dragon

1 boneless, skinless chicken breast half
1 teaspoon cornstarch
2 teaspoons KIKKOMAN® Soy Sauce
½ teaspoon minced fresh ginger root
¼ teaspoon sugar
⅔ cup bottled clam broth
1 tablespoon cornstarch
2 tablespoons KIKKOMAN® Soy Sauce
4 teaspoons water
1 teaspoon distilled white vinegar

2 tablespoons vegetable oil, divided
½ pound medium-size raw shrimp, peeled and deveined
1 large carrot, thinly sliced
1 medium-size green bell pepper, cut into ¾-inch squares
6 ounces fresh mushrooms, sliced
2 large stalks celery, cut diagonally into thin slices

Cut chicken into 1-inch-square pieces. Combine 1 teaspoon cornstarch, 2 teaspoons soy sauce, ginger and sugar in small bowl; stir in chicken. Let stand 15 minutes. Meanwhile, combine clam broth, 1 tablespoon cornstarch, 2 tablespoons soy sauce, water and vinegar in small bowl; set aside. Heat 1 tablespoon oil in hot wok or large skillet over high heat. Add chicken; stir-fry 2 minutes. Add shrimp and stir-fry 2 minutes longer; remove chicken and shrimp. Heat remaining 1 tablespoon oil in same pan. Add carrot and bell pepper; stir-fry 2 minutes. Add mushrooms and celery; stir-fry 2 minutes longer. Stir in chicken, shrimp and soy sauce mixture; cook and stir until sauce boils and thickens. Serve immediately over hot cooked rice. *Makes 4 servings*

Turkey Chili

1 tablespoon vegetable oil
1 pound ground turkey
1 large onion, chopped
1 large green pepper, chopped
1 can (14 ounces) chunky tomatoes, salsa style
1 can (8 ounces) no-salt-added tomato sauce

¾ cup HOLLAND HOUSE® Red Cooking Wine
1 package (1¼ ounces) chili seasoning mix
1 can (15 ounces) kidney beans, drained (optional)

In large saucepan, heat oil. Add turkey, onion and green pepper. Cook until onion is tender. Stir in tomatoes, tomato sauce, Holland House® Red Cooking Wine and chili seasoning mix. Bring to a boil and simmer, partially covered, 10 minutes. Stir in beans and heat through.

Serve, if desired, with rice, shredded cheese and chopped onion. *Makes about 4 servings*

Note: Serve this healthy chili with a crisp green salad and cornbread for a delicious meal.

Roasted Chicken au Jus

1 envelope LIPTON® RECIPE SECRETS®
   Garlic Mushroom Soup Mix*
2 tablespoons olive or vegetable oil

1 (2½- to 3-pound) chicken, cut into
   serving pieces
½ cup hot water

Also terrific with LIPTON® RECIPE SECRETS® Savory Herb with Garlic Soup Mix.

1. Preheat oven to 425°F. In large bowl, combine soup mix and oil; add chicken and toss until evenly coated.

2. In bottom of broiler pan without rack, arrange chicken. Roast chicken, basting occasionally, 40 minutes or until chicken is no longer pink.

3. Remove chicken to serving platter. Add hot water to pan and stir, scraping brown bits from bottom of pan. Serve sauce over chicken.
Makes 4 servings

Dilled Turkey Noodle Bake

1 cup chopped celery
½ cup chopped onion
⅓ cup chopped green bell pepper
1 tablespoon margarine
2 tablespoons all-purpose flour
1¾ cups skim milk
2 teaspoons dried parsley flakes
1 teaspoon dried dill

¾ teaspoon salt
½ teaspoon pepper
4 cups egg noodles, cooked according to
   package directions
2 cups ½-inch cubed cooked turkey
1 cup non-fat sour cream
¼ cup seasoned dry bread crumbs

1. In large nonstick skillet over medium heat, sauté celery, onion and green pepper in margarine 5 minutes or until vegetables are tender. Reduce heat to low; stir in flour. Cook 1 minute, stirring constantly. Gradually add milk, stirring constantly. Stir in parsley, dill, salt and pepper; cook 1 to 2 minutes or until sauce is thickened. Remove from heat.

2. Add noodles, turkey and sour cream to ingredients in skillet; mix well. Spray 11×7-inch baking dish with vegetable cooking spray. Add noodle mixture; sprinkle with bread crumbs. Bake at 350°F 30 minutes or until hot and bubbly.
Makes 4 servings

Favorite recipe from **National Turkey Federation**

Roasted Chicken au Jus

Sonoma® Pot Pie

2 cans (10½ ounces each) chicken gravy
3 cups cooked chicken or turkey chunks
1 package (10 ounces) frozen mixed
  vegetables
⅔ cup SONOMA® Dried Tomato Bits
1 can (3 ounces drained weight) sliced
  mushrooms

¼ cup water
1½ teaspoons dried thyme leaves, divided
2¼ cups reduced-fat buttermilk baking mix
¾ cup plus 2 tablespoons lowfat milk

Preheat oven to 450°F. In 3-quart saucepan combine gravy, chicken, vegetables, tomato bits, mushrooms, water and ½ teaspoon thyme. Stir occasionally over medium-low heat until mixture comes to a boil. Meanwhile, in large bowl combine baking mix, milk and remaining 1 teaspoon thyme; mix just to blend thoroughly. Pour chicken mixture into shallow 2-quart casserole or 9-inch square baking dish. Top with large spoonfuls baking mix mixture, making equal-size mounds. Place casserole on baking sheet and bake about 20 minutes or until chicken mixture is bubbly and topping is golden brown. *Makes 4 to 6 servings*

Classic Chicken Parmesan

6 boneless, skinless chicken breast halves,
  pounded thin (about 1½ pounds)
2 eggs, slightly beaten
1 cup Italian seasoned dry bread crumbs
2 tablespoons BERTOLLI® Olive Oil

1 jar (1 pound 10 ounces) RAGÚ® Old
  World Style® Pasta Sauce
1 cup shredded mozzarella cheese (about
  4 ounces)

Preheat oven to 375°F. Dip chicken in eggs, then bread crumbs, coating well.

In 12-inch skillet, heat oil over medium-high heat and brown chicken; drain on paper towels.

In 11×7-inch baking dish, evenly spread 1 cup Ragú® Pasta Sauce. Arrange chicken in dish, then top with remaining sauce. Sprinkle with mozzarella cheese and, if desired, grated Parmesan cheese. Bake uncovered 25 minutes or until chicken is no longer pink. *Makes 6 servings*

Recipe Tip: To pound chicken, place a boneless, skinless breast between two sheets of waxed paper. Use a rolling pin to press down and out from the center to flatten.

Sonoma® Pot Pie

No-Fuss Roast Turkey & Fixings

1 PERDUE® Fresh Young Turkey (12 to 16 pounds)
  Salt and ground black pepper to taste
1 onion, peeled and quartered
1 small bunch fresh celery leaves (tops)
2 tablespoons butter or margarine, melted
2 packages (about ¾ ounce each) turkey gravy mix
2 packages (6 ounces each) turkey stuffing mix
1 large apple, cored and diced
1 cup chopped toasted walnuts
½ cup raisins

Preheat oven to 325°F. Remove giblets from turkey and reserve for another use. Rinse inside of turkey with cold water; drain and pat dry. Rub inside and out with salt and pepper. Place onion and celery leaves in neck and body cavities. Secure drumsticks with lock provided; fold neck skin back and under body and twist wing tips back to hold skin in place. (Securing legs and wings against body helps turkey cook evenly.)

Place turkey in uncovered roasting pan; brush with melted butter and tent loosely with foil. Roast 3½ to 4½ hours, until BIRD-WATCHER Thermometer pops up and meat thermometer inserted in thigh registers 180°F; baste occasionally. During last hour of roasting time, remove foil tent.

Transfer turkey to serving platter; cover lightly with clean dish towel or foil and let rest 15 to 20 minutes before carving. Remove and discard BIRD-WATCHER Thermometer and drumstick lock; reserve any pan juices for gravy. While turkey is roasting, prepare gravy mix in small saucepan following package directions. Pour juices from roasting pan into large, heatproof measuring cup or small bowl. Skim off clear drippings with large spoon and discard. Stir ½ cup reserved juices into gravy in saucepan; heat until smooth and thickened.

Prepare stuffing mix following package directions, adding diced apple, walnuts and raisins.

Makes 10 to 15 servings

Campbell's® Chicken Florentine Lasagna

2 cans (10¾ ounces each) CAMPBELL'S®
   Condensed Cream of Chicken with
   Herbs Soup
2 cups milk
1 egg
1 container (15 ounces) ricotta cheese
6 *uncooked* lasagna noodles

1 package (about 10 ounces) frozen
   chopped spinach, thawed and well
   drained
2 cups cubed cooked chicken *or* turkey
2 cups shredded Cheddar cheese
   (8 ounces)

1. Mix soup and milk until smooth. Set aside.

2. Mix egg and ricotta. Set aside.

3. In 3-quart shallow baking dish, spread **1 cup** soup mixture. Top with **3 uncooked** lasagna noodles, ricotta mixture, spinach, chicken, **1 cup** Cheddar cheese and **1 cup** soup mixture. Top with remaining **3 uncooked** lasagna noodles and remaining soup mixture. **Cover.**

4. Bake at 375°F. for 1 hour. Uncover and top with remaining Cheddar cheese. Let stand 5 minutes.

Makes 6 servings

Prep Time: 10 minutes
Cook/Stand Time: 1 hour 5 minutes

Tip: To thaw spinach, microwave on HIGH 3 minutes, breaking apart with a fork halfway through heating.

Chicken Fried Rice

½ cup sliced green onions
¼ cup sliced celery
¼ cup chopped red bell pepper
 1 clove garlic, crushed
½ teaspoon grated gingerroot
¼ teaspoon crushed red pepper flakes
2 teaspoons PLANTERS® Peanut Oil

⅓ cup egg substitute
3 cups cooked regular long-grain rice,
   prepared in unsalted water
2 cups cooked diced chicken
2 tablespoons reduced-sodium soy sauce
1 teaspoon sugar

In large nonstick skillet, over high heat, sauté green onions, celery, bell pepper, garlic, ginger and crushed red pepper in oil until tender-crisp. Pour egg substitute into skillet; cook, stirring occasionally until mixture is set. Stir in rice, chicken, soy sauce and sugar; cook until heated through.

Makes 6 servings

❊ *Seafood Treasures* ❊

Champagne Scallops & Asparagus

10 large cloves garlic, peeled and halved
2 tablespoons I CAN'T BELIEVE IT'S
   NOT BUTTER!® Spread
20 large sea scallops, rinsed and dried
¼ cup apple juice or cider
¼ cup chopped shallots or onion
¼ cup dry champagne or white wine

1 tablespoon pure maple syrup or pancake
   syrup
4 tablespoons finely chopped chives,
   divided
   Hot cooked rice
1 pound asparagus, cooked
1 tablespoon lemon juice

In small saucepan, cover garlic with water and bring to a boil over high heat. Boil 5 minutes. Drain garlic and set aside.

In 12-inch skillet, melt I Can't Believe It's Not Butter! Spread over medium heat and cook 1 minute or until lightly golden. Add scallops and cook, stirring occasionally, 4 minutes or until scallops are golden. Remove scallops and set aside.

In same skillet, stir in juice, shallots, champagne, maple syrup, garlic and 2 tablespoons chives. Bring to a boil over high heat. Continue boiling, scraping up any brown bits from bottom of skillet, until slightly thickened, about 2 minutes. On serving platter, arrange scallops over hot rice. Top with sauce and remaining chives. Serve with asparagus tossed with lemon juice and, if desired, salt and ground black pepper to taste.

Makes 4 servings

Champagne Scallops & Asparagus

California-Style Tuna Melts

4 slices bread, cut in half, *or* 8 thin slices
    French bread *or* 4 (8-inch) flour
    tortillas, cut into halves
¼ cup reduced-calorie mayonnaise or salad
    dressing
8 thin slices tomato
1 can (9¼ ounces) STARKIST® Tuna,
    drained and flaked

½ cup chopped red onion
    Alfalfa sprouts
1 cup shredded low-fat Cheddar cheese
½ ripe avocado, peeled, pitted and thinly
    sliced

Microwave Directions

Toast bread, if desired. Arrange bread on flat microwavable plate or tray. Spread with mayonnaise. Place 1 tomato slice on each bread half. Top with tuna, onion and alfalfa sprouts, dividing evenly. Sprinkle cheese over tops. Cover with waxed paper. Microwave on HIGH (100% power) for 2 to 4 minutes, or until sandwiches are heated through and cheese is melted, rotating dish once during cooking. Serve topped with avocado slices. Garnish as desired.   *Makes 8 sandwiches, 4 servings*

Spicy Fish Fillets with Lemon

Grated peel of ½ SUNKIST® lemon
1 teaspoon toasted sesame seeds
¼ teaspoon onion salt
⅛ teaspoon *each* ground cumin, white
    pepper and paprika

⅛ teaspoon red pepper flakes (optional)
4 tilapia or sole fillets (¾ pound)
1 tablespoon vegetable oil
    Fresh SUNKIST® lemon wedges

In small bowl, combine lemon peel, sesame seeds, onion salt and spices. Sprinkle over and rub into both sides of fish fillets. Heat oil in large non-stick skillet sprayed with non-stick cooking spray. Sauté fish over medium-high heat 3 minutes; turn fish and cook 2 to 3 minutes longer or until fish is opaque and just flakes easily with fork. Serve with lemon wedges and garnish with parsley sprigs, if desired.   *Makes 2 to 4 servings*

California-Style Tuna Melts

Quick Cajun Jambalaya

3 tablespoons butter
1 onion, diced
1 *each* red and green bell pepper, diced
12 slices HILLSHIRE FARM® Ham, cut into ½-inch strips
12 large raw shrimp, peeled and deveined
1 can (28 ounces) crushed tomatoes, undrained

2 teaspoons salt
¼ teaspoon garlic powder
¼ teaspoon red pepper flakes
¼ teaspoon black pepper
¼ teaspoon hot pepper sauce
6 cups cooked white rice
    Cajun Garlic Bread (recipe follows)

Heat butter in large saucepan over medium-high heat; cook onion and bell peppers until soft, about 5 minutes. Add Ham and shrimp; cook until shrimp turn pink, about 3 minutes. Add tomatoes with liquid, seasonings and rice; cook 5 minutes or until heated through. Serve with Cajun Garlic Bread.

Makes 6 servings

Cajun Garlic Bread

¼ teaspoon garlic powder
⅛ teaspoon ground red pepper
⅛ teaspoon dried oregano or basil leaves

2 tablespoons butter, melted
1 loaf French bread, cut lengthwise into halves

Preheat oven to 350°F. Stir garlic powder, pepper and oregano into butter in small bowl. Drizzle butter mixture over cut sides of bread. Reassemble loaf; wrap in foil. Bake 10 minutes.

Makes 6 servings

Quick Cajun Jambalaya

Cioppino

1 quart plus 2 tablespoons water, divided
1 cup dry white wine
2 onions, thinly sliced
1 rib celery, chopped
3 sprigs parsley
1 bay leaf
¾ pound ocean perch or snapper fillets
1 can (14½ ounces) whole peeled tomatoes, undrained
1 tablespoon tomato paste
1 clove garlic, minced
1 teaspoon dried oregano leaves

1 teaspoon salt
½ teaspoon sugar
⅛ teaspoon black pepper
6 to 8 hard-shell clams, scrubbed and soaked
1 pound fresh halibut or haddock fillets, skinned and cut into 1-inch pieces
2 large potatoes, peeled and chopped
2 large ripe tomatoes, seeded and chopped
½ pound fresh medium shrimp, peeled and deveined
2 tablespoons chopped fresh parsley

1. To make fish stock, combine 1 quart water, wine, onions, celery, parsley sprigs and bay leaf in 6-quart stockpot or Dutch oven. Bring to a boil over high heat; reduce heat to low. Add perch; uncover and gently simmer 20 minutes.

2. Strain fish stock through sieve into large bowl. Remove perch to plate with slotted spatula; set aside. Discard onions, celery, parsley sprigs and bay leaf.

3. Return stock to stockpot; press canned tomatoes with juice through sieve into stockpot. Discard seeds. Stir in tomato paste, garlic, oregano, salt, sugar and pepper. Simmer, uncovered, over medium-low heat 20 minutes.

4. Combine clams and remaining 2 tablespoons water in large saucepan. Cover and cook over medium heat 5 to 10 minutes or until clams open; remove clams immediately as they open. Discard any clams with unopened shells. Rinse clams; set aside.

5. Add halibut, potatoes and fresh tomatoes to soup mixture in stockpot. Bring to a boil over high heat; reduce heat to medium-low. Cover and cook 12 to 15 minutes or until potatoes are fork-tender. Add shrimp to soup mixture in stockpot.

6. Cook over medium heat 1 to 2 minutes or just until shrimp turn opaque and are cooked through. Flake reserved perch with fork; stir perch, reserved clams and chopped parsley into soup. Garnish, if desired. Serve immediately.
Makes 6 to 8 servings (about 10 cups)

Cioppino

Tuna Tacos

1 pouch (3 ounces) of STARKIST® Tuna,
   drained and flaked
⅓ cup chopped green onions
¼ cup bottled salsa
2 cups shredded lettuce
8 corn taco shells*

1 cup garbanzo beans
1 cup chopped tomato
⅓ cup sliced pitted ripe olives
Salsa, shredded low-fat cheese, diced
   avocado, chopped green chilies for
   toppings (optional)

Substitute 8 (6-inch) flour tortillas for the taco shells if soft tacos are preferred.

In medium bowl toss together tuna, onions and salsa until combined. To assemble tacos, sprinkle lettuce into each taco shell. Divide tuna mixture among tacos, along with garbanzo beans, tomato and olives. Garnish as desired with toppings.

Makes 4 servings

Seafood Marinara with Linguine

1 pound dry linguine
2 tablespoons olive or vegetable oil,
   divided
1 cup chopped onion
3 large cloves garlic, minced
1 can (14.5 ounces) CONTADINA®
   Recipe Ready Diced Tomatoes,
   undrained
1 can (14.5 ounces) chicken broth
1 can (12 ounces) CONTADINA Tomato
   Paste

½ cup dry red wine or water
1 tablespoon chopped fresh basil *or*
   2 teaspoons dried basil leaves, crushed
2 teaspoons chopped fresh oregano *or*
   ½ teaspoon dried oregano leaves,
   crushed
1 teaspoon salt
8 ounces fresh or frozen medium shrimp,
   peeled, deveined
8 ounces fresh or frozen bay scallops

1. Cook pasta according to package directions; drain and keep warm.

2. Meanwhile, heat 1 tablespoon oil in large skillet. Add onion and garlic; sauté for 2 minutes.

3. Add tomatoes and juice, broth, tomato paste, wine, basil, oregano and salt. Bring to a boil. Reduce heat to low; simmer, uncovered, for 10 minutes.

4. Heat remaining oil in small skillet. Add shrimp and scallops; sauté for 3 to 4 minutes or until shrimp turn pink.

5. Add to sauce; simmer for 2 to 3 minutes or until heated through. Serve over pasta.

Makes 6 servings

Tuna Tacos

Sassy Shrimp & Black Bean Pilaf

1 (5.9-ounce) package RICE-A-RONI®
    Low Fat Chicken Flavor
½ tablespoon margarine or butter
2 cloves garlic, minced
¾ to 1 teaspoon Cajun or Creole seasoning
8 ounces uncooked medium shrimp,
    peeled and deveined

1 (15-ounce) can black beans, rinsed and
    drained
1 cup frozen or canned corn, drained
½ cup chopped green bell pepper

1. In large skillet over medium heat, sauté rice-vermicelli mix with margarine until vermicelli is golden brown. Add garlic; sauté 30 seconds. Slowly stir in 2 cups water, Cajun seasoning and Special Seasonings; bring to a boil. Reduce heat to low. Cover; simmer 10 minutes.

2. Stir in shrimp, beans, corn and bell pepper; bring back to a simmer. Cover; simmer 5 to 7 minutes or until rice is tender and shrimp turn pink.

Makes 4 servings

Prep Time: 5 minutes
Cook Time: 25 minutes

Mushroom and Tuna Bake

1 can (10¾ ounces) cream of celery soup
1 cup milk
1 jar (4 ounces) sliced mushrooms,
    drained
½ cup grated Parmesan cheese, divided
1 teaspoon dried Italian herb blend
½ teaspoon seasoned salt

⅛ to ¼ teaspoon garlic powder
1 can (12 ounces) STARKIST® Solid
    White or Chunk Light Tuna, drained
    and chunked
3 cups cooked egg noodles
1 cup crispy rice cereal

In medium saucepan, combine soup and milk; blend well. Add mushrooms, ¼ cup Parmesan cheese, Italian herb blend, seasoned salt, garlic powder and tuna; cook over low heat until heated through. Remove from heat; stir in egg noodles. Transfer mixture to lightly greased 11×7-inch baking dish. Top with remaining ¼ cup Parmesan cheese and cereal. Bake in 350°F oven 30 minutes.

Makes 6 servings

Prep Time: 40 minutes

Sassy Shrimp & Black Bean Pilaf

Maryland Crab Cakes

1 pound fresh backfin crabmeat, cartilage removed
10 low-salt crackers (2 inches each), crushed to equal ½ cup crumbs
1 rib celery, finely chopped
1 green onion, finely chopped
¼ cup cholesterol-free egg substitute
3 tablespoons nonfat tartar sauce
1 teaspoon seafood seasoning
2 teaspoons vegetable oil

1. Combine crabmeat, cracker crumbs, celery and onion in medium bowl; set aside.

2. Mix egg substitute, tartar sauce and seafood seasoning in small bowl; pour over crabmeat mixture. Gently mix so large lumps will not be broken. Shape into six ¾-inch-thick patties. Cover; refrigerate 30 minutes.

3. Spray skillet with nonstick cooking spray. Add oil; heat over medium-high heat. Place crab cakes in skillet; cook 3 to 4 minutes each side or until cakes are lightly browned. Garnish with lemon wedges or twists, if desired.

Makes 6 servings

Halibut Kabobs

1 cup LAWRY'S® Lemon Pepper Marinade with Lemon Juice, divided
1 pound halibut steaks, cut into 1-inch cubes
1 green bell pepper, cut into chunks
12 cherry tomatoes
12 mushrooms, stems removed
Skewers

In large resealable plastic food storage bag, combine ¾ cup Lemon Pepper Marinade and halibut; seal bag. Marinate in refrigerator at least 30 minutes. Remove halibut; discard used marinade. Alternately thread halibut, bell pepper, tomatoes and mushrooms onto skewers. Grill or broil skewers 8 to 10 minutes or until fish flakes easily when tested with fork, turning once and basting often with additional ¼ cup Lemon Pepper Marinade. Do not baste during last 5 minutes of cooking. Discard remaining marinade.

Makes 4 servings

Serving Suggestion: Serve with hot cooked orzo pasta or rice pilaf.

Variation: Lawry's® Herb & Garlic Marinade with Lemon Juice can be substituted for Lemon Pepper Marinade with Lemon Juice.

Hint: If using wooden skewers, soak in water overnight before using to prevent scorching.

Maryland Crab Cakes

Seafood Crêpes

Basic Crêpes (recipe follows)
3 tablespoons butter or margarine
⅓ cup finely chopped shallots or onion
2 tablespoons dry vermouth
3 tablespoons all-purpose flour
1½ cups plus 2 tablespoons milk, divided
¼ to ½ teaspoon hot pepper sauce
(optional)

8 ounces cooked peeled and deveined
shrimp, coarsely chopped (1½ cups)
8 ounces lump crabmeat or imitation
crabmeat, shredded (1½ cups)
2 tablespoons snipped fresh chives
3 tablespoons freshly grated Parmesan
cheese
Fresh chives and red onion for garnish

1. Prepare Basic Crêpes. Preheat oven to 350°F.

2. Melt butter over medium heat in medium saucepan. Add shallots; cook and stir 5 minutes or until shallots are tender. Add vermouth; cook 1 minute. Add flour; cook and stir 1 minute. Gradually stir in 1½ cups milk and hot pepper sauce, if desired. Bring to a boil, stirring frequently. Reduce heat to low; cook and stir 1 minute or until mixture thickens. Remove from heat; stir in shrimp and crabmeat. Reserve ½ cup seafood mixture; set aside.

3. To assemble crêpes, spoon about ¼ cup seafood mixture down center of each crêpe. Roll up crêpes jelly-roll style. Place seam side down in well-greased 13×9-inch baking dish.

4. Stir chives and remaining 2 tablespoons milk into reserved seafood mixture. Spoon seafood mixture down center of crêpes; sprinkle cheese evenly over top. Bake uncovered 15 to 20 minutes or until heated through. Serve immediately. Garnish, if desired. *Makes 6 servings*

Basic Crêpes

1½ cups milk
1 cup all-purpose flour
2 eggs

¼ cup butter or margarine, melted, cooled
and divided
¼ teaspoon salt

1. Combine milk, flour, eggs, 2 tablespoons butter and salt in food processor; process using on/off pulsing action until smooth. Let stand at room temperature 30 minutes.

2. Heat ½ teaspoon butter in 7- or 8-inch crêpe pan or skillet over medium heat. Pour ¼ cup batter into hot pan. Immediately rotate pan to coat entire surface. Cook 1 to 2 minutes or until edges are brown and top is dry. Carefully turn crêpe with spatula; cook 30 seconds. Transfer crêpe to waxed paper. Repeat with remaining batter, adding remaining butter only as needed to prevent sticking.

3. Separate each crêpe with sheet of waxed paper. Cover and refrigerate up to 1 day or freeze up to 1 month before serving. *Makes about 1 dozen crêpes*

Seafood Crêpes

Tuna Potpies

Filling
- 2 tablespoons CRISCO® Oil*
- 3 medium carrots, thinly sliced
- 1 small onion, finely chopped
- 2 tablespoons all-purpose flour
- 1 can (12 ounces) evaporated skimmed milk
- 1 cup water
- 1 package (9 ounces) frozen cut green beans or peas
- 1 can (16 ounces) whole potatoes, drained and chopped
- 1 can (12½ to 13 ounces) solid white tuna in water, drained and flaked
- 1 tablespoon minced fresh dill *or* ¼ teaspoon dried dill weed
- ¼ teaspoon salt

Crust
- 1¼ cups all-purpose flour
- 1 teaspoon baking powder
- ¼ cup cold water
- 3 tablespoons CRISCO® Oil

Use your favorite Crisco Oil product.

1. *For filling,* heat oil in large saucepan on medium heat. Add carrots and onion. Cook and stir until tender. Stir in flour. Cook one minute. Stir in milk and water gradually. Cook and stir until mixture thickens slightly.

2. Add beans, stirring to separate. Remove saucepan from heat. Stir in potatoes, tuna, dill and salt. Spoon into 4 (14 ounces *each*) ramekins.*

3. Heat oven to 400°F. Place cooling rack on countertop.

4. *For crust,* combine flour and baking powder in medium bowl.

5. Combine water and oil in small bowl. Add to flour mixture. Stir with fork until mixture forms large clumps. Press with fingers to form ball. Divide into 4 sections. Flatten between hands to form 4 "pancakes."

6. Roll each "pancake" between two sheets of waxed paper (or plastic wrap) on dampened countertop. Peel off top sheet.

7. Trim dough 1 inch larger than top of ramekin. Moisten outside edge of ramekin with water. Flip dough over onto ramekin. Fold edge under; flute. Cut decorative shapes or slits in dough for steam to escape. Place ramekins on baking sheet.

8. Bake at 400°F for 25 to 30 minutes or until filling is bubbly and crust is golden brown. *Do not overbake.* Remove sheet to cooling rack. *Makes 4 servings*

Substitute one 2-quart casserole for 4 ramekins. Roll dough to fit top of casserole. Bake at 400°F for 30 to 35 minutes.

Tuna Potpies

Easy Salmon Burgers with Honey Barbecue Sauce

⅓ cup honey
⅓ cup ketchup
1½ teaspoons cider vinegar
1 teaspoon prepared horseradish
¼ teaspoon minced garlic
⅛ teaspoon crushed red pepper flakes
  (optional)

1 can (7½ ounces) salmon, drained
½ cup dried bread crumbs
¼ cup chopped onion
3 tablespoons chopped green bell pepper
1 egg white
2 hamburger buns, toasted

In small bowl, combine honey, ketchup, vinegar, horseradish, garlic and red pepper flakes until well blended. Set aside half of sauce. In separate bowl, mix together salmon, bread crumbs, onion, green pepper and egg white. Blend in 2 tablespoons remaining sauce. Divide salmon mixture into 2 patties, ½ to ¾ inch thick. Place patties on well-oiled grill, 4 to 6 inches from hot coals. Grill, turning 2 to 3 times and basting with remaining sauce, until burgers are browned and cooked through. Or place patties on lightly greased baking sheet. Broil 4 to 6 inches from heat source, turning 2 to 3 times and basting with remaining sauce, until cooked through. Place on hamburger buns and serve with reserved sauce.

Makes 2 servings

Favorite recipe from **National Honey Board**

Gemelli with Baby Shrimp and Sweet Peas

1 package (16 ounces) BARILLA® Gemelli
2 tablespoons unsalted butter
2 tablespoons thinly sliced green onion
1 cup heavy cream

Salt and pepper
1½ cups (about 8 ounces) small frozen
  shelled and deveined shrimp, thawed
1 cup frozen baby peas, thawed

1. Cook gemelli according to package directions; drain.

2. Meanwhile, melt butter in large broad saucepan or deep skillet. Add green onion; cook and stir about 2 minutes or until wilted. Add cream and heat to boiling. Boil about 5 minutes or until slightly thickened and reduced to about ¾ cup. Add salt and pepper to taste.

3. Add hot drained gemelli to saucepan with shrimp and peas; cook and stir over low heat until heated through.

Makes 6 to 8 servings

Easy Salmon Burgers with Honey Barbecue Sauce

Oriental Baked Seafood

¼ cup chopped California Almonds
2 cups water
½ teaspoon salt
1 cup long-grain white rice
1 tablespoon grated fresh ginger
1 tablespoon sesame oil
1 teaspoon grated lemon peel

1 pound halibut
½ pound large scallops
¼ pound medium shrimp, shelled and
   deveined
1 clove garlic, minced
1 tablespoon light soy sauce
½ cup slivered green onions

Preheat oven to 350°F. Spread almonds in shallow baking pan. Toast in oven 5 to 8 minutes or until lightly browned, stirring occasionally; cool. Bring water and salt to a boil in medium saucepan. Stir in rice, ginger, sesame oil and lemon peel. Bring to a boil; cover and reduce heat to low. Simmer 20 to 25 minutes or until water is absorbed. Meanwhile, preheat oven to 400°F or preheat broiler or grill. Remove skin and bones from halibut; cut into large pieces. Cut 4 (12-inch) squares of foil. Divide halibut, scallops and shrimp among foil. Sprinkle seafood with garlic and soy sauce; seal squares tightly. Bake 12 minutes or broil or grill 4 inches from heat 15 minutes, turning once. Stir almonds into rice. Pour seafood mixture and juices over rice. Sprinkle with green onions.

Makes 4 servings

Microwave Directions: Spread almonds in shallow pan. Cook at HIGH (100% power) 2 minutes, stirring often; cool. Combine water, salt, rice, ginger, sesame oil and lemon peel in 3-quart microwave-safe dish. Cover with plastic wrap. Cook at HIGH (100% power) 12 minutes, stirring halfway through cooking time. Let stand 10 minutes. Prepare fish packets as above using parchment paper instead of foil. Bring edges up and seal with rubber band. Place packets in microwave-safe baking dish. Cook at HIGH (100% power) 5 minutes, rotating dish. Serve as directed.

*Favorite recipe from **Almond Board of California***

Oriental Baked Seafood

Steamed Sole & Vegetables

4 tablespoons KIKKOMAN® Soy Sauce,
divided
3 tablespoons dry white wine
1½ teaspoons minced fresh ginger root
1 teaspoon onion powder
½ teaspoon sugar

4 fresh sole fillets (about 4 ounces each)
1 large carrot, cut into julienne strips
1 medium zucchini, cut into julienne
strips
3 tablespoons minced green onions and
tops, divided

Combine 3 tablespoons soy sauce, wine, ginger, onion powder and sugar in shallow dish. Add fillets, turning over to coat both sides well. Let stand 10 minutes, turning over once. Meanwhile, toss carrot and zucchini together with remaining 1 tablespoon soy sauce in small bowl; pour off excess sauce. Transfer vegetables to 8-inch round heatproof plate. Remove fillets from marinade; spread out flat. Sprinkle 2 tablespoons green onions evenly over fillets. Starting at thin end, roll up fillets, jelly-roll fashion. Arrange, seam side down, on vegetables. Place plate on large steamer rack set in large pot or wok of boiling water. (Do not allow water level to reach plate.) Cover and steam 12 minutes, or until fish flakes easily when tested with fork. Sprinkle remaining 1 tablespoon green onion evenly over fish.

Makes 4 servings

Catch of the Day Stew

1 can (14½ ounces) reduced-sodium
chicken broth
1 can (10½ ounces) French onion soup,
undiluted
1 cup peeled and cubed potatoes
1 cup baby carrots
½ cup sliced celery

1 pound fish fillets, cut into 1-inch pieces
1 cup zucchini, thinly sliced
1 cup mushrooms, sliced
1 can (14½ ounces) diced tomatoes,
undrained
½ teaspoon *each* dried thyme and
rosemary, crushed

Combine broth, soup, potatoes, carrots and celery in large Dutch oven; bring to a boil over high heat. Reduce heat to medium; cover and cook 5 minutes. Add remaining ingredients; cook 5 to 10 minutes or until fish flakes easily with fork and vegetables are tender.

Makes 4 to 6 servings

Favorite recipe from **National Fisheries Institute**

Steamed Sole & Vegetables

Shrimp Creole

2 tablespoons olive or vegetable oil
1 medium onion, chopped
1 medium green bell pepper, chopped
1 jar (26 to 28 ounces) RAGÚ® Chunky
   Gardenstyle Pasta Sauce

½ cup bottled clam juice
2 to 3 teaspoons hot pepper sauce
1½ pounds medium shrimp, peeled and
   deveined

1. In 12-inch skillet, heat oil over medium-high heat and cook onion and green pepper, stirring frequently, 6 minutes or until tender.

2. Stir in Ragú Pasta Sauce, clam juice and hot pepper sauce. Bring to a boil over high heat. Reduce heat to medium and continue cooking, stirring occasionally, 5 minutes. Stir in shrimp and cook, stirring occasionally, 3 minutes or until shrimp turn pink and opaque.

3. Serve, if desired, over hot cooked rice.

Makes 4 servings

Tip: For a more classic dish, stir in 1 package (9 ounces) chopped frozen okra with Ragú Chunky Gardenstyle Pasta Sauce. Okra is a vegetable native to the Southeastern United States and is used in cooking for thickening and flavor.

Citrus Grove Marinated Salmon

4 salmon fillets or steaks
⅓ cup lemonade concentrate, thawed
¼ cup WESSON® Vegetable Oil
¼ cup orange juice concentrate, thawed

1½ teaspoons fresh dill weed *or* ½ teaspoon
   dried dill weed
WESSON® No-Stick Cooking Spray

1. Rinse salmon and pat dry; set aside.

2. In small bowl, combine *remaining* ingredients *except* Wesson Cooking Spray.

3. Place salmon in large resealable plastic food storage bag; pour ¾ marinade over fish; set *remaining* marinade aside. Seal bag and gently turn to coat; refrigerate 2 hours, turning fish several times during marinating.

4. Preheat broiler. Foil-line jelly-roll pan; spray with Wesson Cooking Spray.

5. Place fish on pan; discard used marinade. Broil fish until it flakes easily with fork, basting frequently with *remaining* marinade.

Makes 4 (6-ounce) servings

Shrimp Creole

Tuna-Stuffed Bakers

4 large baking potatoes or sweet potatoes,
  scrubbed
2 cups chopped or sliced, fresh or frozen
  vegetables*
¼ cup chopped green onions
1 can (12 ounces) STARKIST® Tuna,
  drained and flaked
⅓ cup low-fat ricotta cheese

2 tablespoons drained pimiento strips
1 tablespoon chopped fresh parsley
  (optional)
¼ teaspoon dry mustard
⅛ teaspoon pepper
4 slices (1 ounce each) reduced-calorie
  American cheese, cut into ¼-inch
  strips

Suggested vegetables are: broccoli or cauliflower florets, mushrooms, carrots, pea pods, peas, asparagus or corn.

Pierce potatoes twice with fork. Arrange potatoes 1 inch apart on paper towel in microwave oven. Micro-cook on HIGH power for 10½ to 12½ minutes, turning and rearranging potatoes halfway through cooking time. Wrap potatoes in foil; let stand for 5 minutes to finish cooking while preparing filling.

For filling, in 2-quart microwavable casserole place desired vegetables and onions. Cover with waxed paper; micro-cook on HIGH power for 3 to 5 minutes, or until vegetables are crisp-tender, stirring twice. Drain. Stir in tuna, ricotta cheese, pimiento, parsley, mustard and pepper until well combined. Cover; micro-cook on HIGH power for 2 minutes, or until mixture is heated through, stirring once.

Unwrap potatoes; cut lengthwise into halves. Flake interior with fork. Spoon vegetable filling mixture over potatoes, mounding filling on top. Place potatoes in shallow microwavable dish. Place strips of cheese diagonally over filling. Micro-cook on HIGH power for 1 to 2 minutes, or until cheese is melted.

Makes 4 servings

Tuna-Stuffed Bakers

❊ *Incredible Cakes* ❊

Velvet Chocolate Cheesecake

30 CHIPS AHOY!® Chocolate Chip
    Cookies, divided
¼ cup margarine or butter, melted
1⅓ cups sugar, divided
2 (8-ounce) packages PHILADELPHIA®
    Cream Cheese, softened
⅓ cup unsweetened cocoa

2 eggs
1½ teaspoons vanilla extract, divided
1 cup BREAKSTONE'S® or KNUDSEN®
    Sour Cream
COOL WHIP® Whipped Topping and
    maraschino cherries, for garnish

1. Finely crush 20 cookies. Mix cookie crumbs and margarine or butter; press onto bottom of 8-inch springform pan. Stand remaining cookies around side of pan; set aside.

2. Reserve 2 tablespoons sugar. Beat cream cheese in medium bowl with electric mixer at medium speed until creamy; beat in remaining sugar, cocoa, eggs and 1 teaspoon vanilla until fluffy. Pour into prepared crust. Cover tops of cookies with band of aluminum foil before baking to avoid overbrowning.

3. Bake at 375°F for 50 minutes or until cheesecake is puffed and toothpick inserted ½ inch from edge comes out clean; remove from oven.

4. Blend reserved sugar, sour cream and remaining vanilla; spread evenly over cheesecake. Return to oven; bake 10 minutes more. Cool completely at room temperature. Refrigerate for 3 hours or overnight. Remove side of pan. Garnish with whipped topping and maraschino cherries if desired.

Makes 10 servings

Velvet Chocolate Cheesecake

Ginger Pear Upside-Down Cake

**8 tablespoons (1 stick) softened
    margarine, divided**
¾ cup KARO® Dark Corn Syrup, divided
**½ cup plus 2 tablespoons packed brown
    sugar, divided**
**1 can (16 ounces) pear halves, well
    drained**
½ cup walnut halves

1⅓ cups flour
1 teaspoon ground ginger
½ teaspoon baking soda
½ teaspoon cinnamon
¼ teaspoon salt
1 egg
½ cup buttermilk

1. Preheat oven to 350°F. In small saucepan melt 2 tablespoons margarine. Stir in ¼ cup corn syrup and 2 tablespoons brown sugar. Spread evenly in ungreased 9-inch round cake pan. Arrange pear halves and walnuts, rounded sides down, over corn syrup mixture.

2. In medium bowl combine flour, ginger, baking soda, cinnamon and salt; set aside.

3. In large bowl with mixer at medium speed, beat remaining 6 tablespoons margarine, ½ cup corn syrup and ½ cup brown sugar. Add egg and buttermilk; beat until well blended. Add flour mixture; beat 1 minute or until thoroughly combined. Carefully spoon batter over pears and walnuts, smoothing top.

4. Bake 55 to 60 minutes or until toothpick inserted into center comes out clean. Immediately run spatula around edge of pan and invert cake onto serving plate.   *Makes 8 servings*

Prep Time: 25 minutes
Bake Time: 55 to 60 minutes

Note: Well-drained canned peaches, pineapple or apricots are an excellent substitute for pears. They all complement the spicy flavor of this tender cake.

Ginger Pear Upside-Down Cake

Elegant Chocolate Cake Roll

3 large eggs, separated
½ cup plus 2 tablespoons granulated sugar, divided
5 ounces semisweet chocolate, melted
⅓ cup water
1 teaspoon vanilla
¾ cup all-purpose flour
1 teaspoon baking powder
½ teaspoon baking soda
¼ teaspoon salt
Unsweetened cocoa powder
1 (1-ounce) square unsweetened chocolate
1 cup whipping cream
¾ cup miniature marshmallows
1½ cups powdered sugar
3 to 4 tablespoons light cream
¼ cup chopped pecans

1. Preheat oven to 350°F. Line 15×10-inch jelly-roll pan with foil, extending foil 1 inch over edges of pan. Grease and flour foil.

2. Beat egg yolks and ½ cup granulated sugar in medium bowl until light and fluffy. Beat in melted semisweet chocolate. Add water and vanilla. Mix until smooth. Sift flour, baking powder, baking soda and salt together. Add to chocolate mixture.

3. Using clean beaters and large bowl, beat egg whites until soft peaks form. Gently fold in chocolate mixture. Pour into prepared pan.

4. Bake 8 to 9 minutes or until wooden toothpick inserted into center comes out clean. Carefully loosen sides of cake from foil. Invert cake onto towel sprinkled with cocoa. Peel off foil. Starting at short end, roll up warm cake jelly-roll fashion with towel inside. Cool cake completely.

5. Meanwhile, place unsweetened chocolate in small microwavable bowl. Microwave on HIGH 1 to 2 minutes or until almost melted, stirring after each minute. Stir until smooth. Set aside to cool.

6. Beat whipping cream in separate small bowl at high speed with electric mixer until thickened. Gradually add remaining 2 tablespoons granulated sugar, beating until soft peaks form. Fold in marshmallows.

7. Unroll cake; remove towel. Spread cake with whipped cream mixture; reroll cake without towel.

8. Combine melted unsweetened chocolate and powdered sugar in small bowl. Stir in light cream, 1 tablespoonful at a time, until frosting is of spreading consistency. Spread over cake roll. Sprinkle cake with pecans. Refrigerate until serving time.
Makes 8 to 12 servings

Elegant Chocolate Cake Roll

Creamy Baked Cheesecake

1¼ cups graham cracker crumbs
¼ cup sugar
⅓ cup (⅔ stick) butter, melted
2 (8-ounce) packages cream cheese, softened
1 (14-ounce) can EAGLE® BRAND Sweetened Condensed Milk (NOT evaporated milk)

3 eggs
¼ cup lemon juice from concentrate
1 (8-ounce) container sour cream, at room temperature
Raspberry Topping (recipe follows, optional)

1. Preheat oven to 300°F. Combine crumbs, sugar and butter; press firmly onto bottom of ungreased 9-inch springform pan.

2. In large bowl, beat cream cheese until fluffy.

3. Gradually beat in Eagle Brand until smooth. Add eggs and lemon juice; mix well. Pour into prepared pan.

4. Bake 50 to 55 minutes or until set.

5. Remove from oven; top with sour cream. Bake 5 minutes longer. Cool. Chill. Prepare Raspberry Topping and serve with cheesecake. Store covered in refrigerator.   *Makes 1 (9-inch) cheesecake*

Raspberry Topping

1 (10-ounce) package thawed frozen red raspberries in syrup

¼ cup red currant jelly or red raspberry jam
1 tablespoon cornstarch

1. Drain ⅔ cup syrup from raspberries.

2. In small saucepan over medium heat, combine syrup, jelly and cornstarch. Cook and stir until slightly thickened and clear. Cool. Stir in raspberries.

Creamy Baked Cheesecake

Cranapple Pan-Fried Skillet Cake

Cake

    WESSON® No-Stick Cooking Spray
2½ cups peeled, cored and sliced apples
  1 (16-ounce) can whole cranberry sauce,
    divided
  3 tablespoons melted butter
¾ cup firmly packed light brown sugar
½ cup walnut pieces
  2 cups all-purpose flour
1⅓ cups granulated sugar
  2 teaspoons baking powder
½ teaspoon salt
½ cup WESSON® Vegetable Oil

¼ cup milk
  1 egg
  3 tablespoons fresh orange juice
1½ tablespoons grated fresh orange peel
    (2 oranges)
  1 teaspoon vanilla

Topping

    Remaining ½ can whole cranberry sauce
  2 tablespoons fresh orange juice
  1 tablespoon WESSON® Vegetable Oil
    Walnut pieces for garnish

Cake

Generously spray an 11-inch skillet with straight sides with Wesson® Cooking Spray. Place apples in pan in a single layer. Spoon half the can of cranberry sauce evenly on and around apples; reserve *remaining* cranberry sauce. Drizzle apples with butter and sprinkle with brown sugar and walnuts. Set aside. In a large bowl, combine flour, sugar, baking powder and salt; blend well. Add *next* 6 ingredients, ending with vanilla. With an electric mixer, on LOW speed, beat 2 minutes until moistened and then an additional 2 minutes on HIGH, scraping bowl often. Carefully pour batter evenly over fruit mixture in skillet. Cover skillet and place on range top over LOW heat for 1 hour or until wooden pick inserted into center comes out clean. Cut around edges of skillet to loosen cake and invert onto serving plate. (Leave any fruit that sticks to the skillet; it may be combined with the topping ingredients.)

Topping

Add topping ingredients except walnuts to skillet; heat through. Spread quickly over warm cake and top with walnuts, if desired.

Makes 8 servings

Cranapple Pan-Fried Skillet Cake

Chocolate Orange Marble Chiffon Cake

⅓ cup HERSHEY'S Cocoa
¼ cup hot water
3 tablespoons plus 1½ cups sugar, divided
2 tablespoons plus ½ cup vegetable oil, divided
2¼ cups all-purpose flour
1 tablespoon baking powder

1 teaspoon salt
¾ cup cold water
7 egg yolks
1 cup egg whites (about 8)
½ teaspoon cream of tartar
1 tablespoon freshly grated orange peel
Orange Glaze (recipe follows)

1. Remove top oven rack; move other rack to lowest position. Heat oven to 325°F.

2. Stir together cocoa and hot water in medium bowl. Stir in 3 tablespoons sugar and 2 tablespoons oil; set aside. Stir together flour, remaining 1½ cups sugar, baking powder and salt in large bowl. Add cold water, remaining ½ cup oil and egg yolks; beat with spoon until smooth.

3. Beat egg whites and cream of tartar in another large bowl on high speed of mixer until stiff peaks form. Pour egg yolk mixture in a thin stream over egg white mixture, gently folding just until blended. Remove 2 cups batter; add to chocolate mixture, gently folding until well blended. Fold orange peel into remaining batter.

4. Spoon half the orange batter into ungreased 10-inch tube pan; drop half the chocolate batter on top by spoonfuls. Repeat layers of orange and chocolate batters. Gently swirl with knife for marbled effect, leaving definite orange and chocolate areas.

5. Bake 1 hour and 15 to 20 minutes or until top springs back when lightly touched. Immediately invert cake onto heatproof funnel; cool cake completely. Remove cake from pan; invert onto serving plate. Prepare Orange Glaze; spread over top of cake, allowing glaze to run down sides. Garnish as desired. *Makes 12 to 16 servings*

Orange Glaze

⅓ cup butter or margarine
2 cups powdered sugar

2 tablespoons orange juice
½ teaspoon freshly grated orange peel

Melt butter in medium saucepan over low heat. Remove from heat; gradually stir in powdered sugar, orange juice and orange peel, beating until smooth and of desired consistency. Add additional orange juice, 1 teaspoon at a time, if needed. *Makes about 1½ cups glaze*

Chocolate Orange Marble Chiffon Cake

Cappuccino Cheesecake

14 squares Low Fat HONEY MAID® Honey
    Grahams, finely crushed (about 1 cup
    crumbs)
2 tablespoons margarine, melted
1¼ cups sugar, divided

2 (8-ounce) packages low-fat cream cheese
1 cup egg substitute
1 tablespoon instant espresso powder
1 teaspoon vanilla extract

1. Mix graham crumbs, melted margarine and ¼ cup sugar in medium bowl. Press crumbs onto bottom and 1 inch up side of lightly greased 9-inch springform pan.

2. Blend cream cheese and remaining 1 cup sugar in large bowl with mixer; beat in egg substitute, espresso powder and vanilla until well blended. Pour batter into prepared crust.

3. Bake in preheated 325°F oven for 55 to 60 minutes or until firm to touch. Turn oven off; cool in oven for 1 hour, leaving door ajar. Refrigerate at least 4 hours before serving.   *Makes 12 servings*

Luscious Spring Poke Cake

2 baked 8- or 9-inch round white cake
    layers, cooled completely
2 cups boiling water
1 package (8-serving size) *or* 2 packages
    (4-serving size each) JELL-O® Brand
    Gelatin, any flavor

1 tub (8 or 12 ounces) COOL WHIP®
    Whipped Topping, thawed, divided

PLACE cake layers, top sides up, in 2 clean 8- or 9-inch round cake pans. Pierce cake with large fork at ½-inch intervals.

STIR boiling water into gelatin in medium bowl at least 2 minutes or until completely dissolved. Carefully pour 1 cup of the gelatin over 1 cake layer. Pour remaining gelatin over second cake layer. Refrigerate 3 hours.

DIP 1 cake pan in warm water 10 seconds; unmold onto serving platter. Spread with about 1 cup of whipped topping. Unmold second cake layer; carefully place on first cake layer. Frost top and side of cake with remaining whipped topping.

REFRIGERATE at least 1 hour or until ready to serve. Decorate as desired. Store leftover cake in refrigerator.   *Makes 12 servings*

Cappuccino Cheesecake

Brownie Apple Sauce Cake

½ cup butter
3 squares (1 ounce each) unsweetened
    chocolate
1½ cups MOTT'S® Apple Sauce
1 cup sugar
3 eggs, well beaten
1 teaspoon vanilla extract

1½ cups all-purpose flour
1 teaspoon baking soda
½ teaspoon salt
½ cup chopped walnuts
Apple Cream Cheese Frosting (recipe
    follows)

1. Heat oven to 350°F. In large heavy saucepan, over low heat, melt butter and chocolate, stirring constantly. Remove from heat and cool. Blend apple sauce, sugar, eggs and vanilla into chocolate mixture. In large bowl, mix flour, baking soda and salt. With wooden spoon, stir in chocolate mixture until blended. Stir in walnuts.

2. Pour batter into 2 greased and floured 8-inch round cake pans. Bake 35 to 40 minutes or until toothpick inserted in center comes out clean. Cool in pans 10 minutes. Prepare Apple Cream Cheese Frosting. Remove cakes from pans; cool completely on wire racks. Fill and frost with Apple Cream Cheese Frosting. Garnish as desired. *Makes 12 servings*

Apple Cream Cheese Frosting: In large bowl, beat 2 packages (8 ounces each) softened cream cheese and ½ cup softened butter until light and fluffy. Blend in 1 cup confectioners' sugar, ½ cup MOTT'S® Apple Sauce, ½ cup melted and cooled caramels and 1 teaspoon vanilla extract.

Tropical Snack Cake

1½ cups all-purpose flour
1 cup QUAKER® Oats (quick or old
    fashioned, uncooked)
¼ cup granulated sugar *or* 2 tablespoons
    fructose
2 teaspoons baking powder
½ teaspoon baking soda
¼ teaspoon salt (optional)

1 can (8 ounces) crushed pineapple in
    juice, undrained
½ cup fat-free milk
⅓ cup mashed ripe banana
¼ cup egg substitute *or* 2 egg whites
2 tablespoons vegetable oil
2 teaspoons vanilla

Heat oven to 350°F. Grease and flour 8×8-inch square baking pan. Combine first 6 ingredients; mix well. Set aside. Blend pineapple, milk, banana, egg substitute, oil and vanilla until mixed thoroughly. Add to dry ingredients, mixing just until moistened. Pour into prepared pan. Bake 45 to 50 minutes or until golden brown and wooden pick inserted in center comes out clean. Cool slightly before serving. *Makes 12 servings*

Brownie Apple Sauce Cake

Maple Praline Cheesecake

1 package (11.1 ounces) JELL-O® Brand
    No Bake Real Cheesecake
2 tablespoons sugar
6 tablespoons butter or margarine, melted
1 tablespoon water

1⅓ cups cold milk
½ cup maple syrup
1 cup PLANTERS® Pecan Halves or Pieces
1 cup firmly packed brown sugar
1 egg, beaten

HEAT oven to 350°F.

STIR Crust Mix, sugar, butter and water thoroughly in 8- or 9-inch square baking pan until crumbs are well moistened. Firmly press crumbs onto bottom of pan, using small measuring cup.

POUR milk into large bowl. Add Filling Mix and syrup. Beat with electric mixer on lowest speed until blended. Beat on medium speed 3 minutes. (Filling will be thick.) Spoon over crust.

REFRIGERATE at least 1 hour or until set.

MIX pecans, brown sugar and beaten egg, stirring until well combined. Pour into greased 13×9-inch baking pan. Bake 10 to 12 minutes or until browned and crunchy; cool. Using spatula, loosen nut mixture from pan and chop into small pieces. Just before serving, sprinkle over cheesecake. Cut cheesecake into squares.   *Makes 8 servings*

How To Serve: To make cheesecake easier to serve, line 8- or 9-inch square pan with foil extending over edges to form handles. To serve, run knife around edges of pan to loosen cheesecake from sides. Lift cheesecake, using foil as handles, onto cutting board.

Maple Praline Cheesecake

Chocolate Lava Cakes

6 tablespoons I CAN'T BELIEVE IT'S
   NOT BUTTER!® Spread
3 squares (1 ounce each) bittersweet or
   semi-sweet chocolate, cut into pieces
½ cup granulated sugar
6 tablespoons all-purpose flour

Pinch salt
2 large eggs
2 large egg yolks
¼ teaspoon vanilla extract
Confectioners' sugar

Preheat oven to 425°F. Line bottom of four (4-ounce) ramekins* or custard cups with waxed paper, then grease; set aside.

In medium microwave-safe bowl, microwave I Can't Believe It's Not Butter! Spread and chocolate at HIGH (Full Power) 45 seconds or until chocolate is melted; stir until smooth. With wire whisk, beat in granulated sugar, flour and salt until blended. Beat in eggs, egg yolks and vanilla. Evenly spoon into prepared ramekins. Refrigerate 1 hour or until ready to bake.

Bake 13 minutes or until edges are firm but centers are still slightly soft. Do not overbake. On wire rack, cool 5 minutes. To serve, carefully run sharp knife around cake edges. Unmold onto serving plates, then remove waxed paper. Sprinkle with confectioners' sugar and serve immediately.

Makes 4 servings

*Tip: To bake in 12-cup muffin pan, line bottoms of 8 muffin cups with waxed paper; grease. Spoon in batter. Refrigerate as above. Bake at 425°F for 9 minutes or until edges are firm but centers are still slightly soft. Do not overbake. On wire rack, cool 5 minutes. To serve, carefully run sharp knife around cake edges and gently lift out of pan. (Do not turn pan upside-down to unmold.) Arrange cakes, bottom sides up, on serving plates, 2 cakes per serving. Remove waxed paper and sprinkle as above.

Lemon Blueberry Layer Cake

1 (10.75-ounce) pound cake, sliced into
   10 slices
2 (10-ounce) jars KNOTT'S® Blueberry
   Preserves
2 (4-cup packs) HUNT'S® Snack Pack
   Lemon Pudding

Grated peel from 1 lemon
1 (8-ounce) tub frozen whipped topping,
   thawed

Arrange cake slices on bottom of 13×9×2-inch pan. Reserve 3 tablespoons preserves. Spread remaining preserves over cake slices. In small bowl, combine pudding with lemon peel (for a tarter lemon flavor, add 2 tablespoons lemon juice to filling); mix well. Spread filling over preserves; top with whipped topping. Cover and refrigerate until ready to serve. Just before serving, randomly swirl in remaining preserves.

Makes 10 to 12 servings

Chocolate Lava Cake

Spice Cake with Fresh Peach Sauce

Cake
1 package DUNCAN HINES® Moist
    Deluxe® Spice Cake Mix
3 egg whites
1¼ cups water
⅓ cup vegetable oil

Sauce
6 cups sliced fresh peaches
1 cup water
⅓ cup sugar
⅛ teaspoon ground cinnamon

1. Preheat oven to 350°F. Grease and flour 10-inch Bundt or tube pan.

2. For Cake, place cake mix, egg whites, water and oil in large bowl. Beat at low speed with electric mixer until blended. Beat at medium speed 2 minutes. Pour into pan. Bake at 350°F for 42 to 47 minutes or until toothpick inserted in center comes out clean. Cool in pan 25 minutes. Invert onto serving plate. Cool completely. Dust with confectioners' sugar, if desired.

3. For Sauce, combine peaches and water in large saucepan. Cook over medium heat 5 minutes. Reduce heat to low. Cover and simmer 10 minutes. Cool. Reserve ½ cup peach slices. Combine remaining peaches with any cooking liquid, sugar and cinnamon in blender or food processor. Process until smooth. Stir in reserved peach slices. To serve, spoon peach sauce over cake slices.

Makes 12 to 16 servings

Tip: Fresh peach sauce can be served either warm or chilled.

Note: Use ¾ cup egg substitute in place of egg whites, if desired.

Spice Cake with Fresh Peach Sauce

Triple Chocolate Cake

¾ cup butter, softened
1½ cups sugar
1 egg
1 teaspoon vanilla
2 cups all-purpose flour
⅔ cup unsweetened cocoa powder
2 teaspoons baking soda

¼ teaspoon salt
1 cup buttermilk
¾ cup sour cream
Chocolate Ganache Filling (recipe follows)
Easy Chocolate Frosting (recipe follows)

Preheat oven to 350°F. Grease and flour two 9-inch round cake pans. Beat butter and sugar in large bowl with electric mixer at medium speed until light and fluffy. Beat in egg and vanilla until blended. Combine flour, cocoa, baking soda and salt in medium bowl. Add flour mixture to butter mixture alternately with buttermilk and sour cream, beginning and ending with flour mixture. Beat well after each addition. Divide batter evenly between prepared pans.

Bake 30 to 35 minutes or until wooden toothpick inserted in centers comes out clean. Cool in pans 10 minutes. Remove from pans to wire racks; cool completely. Cut each cake layer in half horizontally.

Meanwhile, prepare Chocolate Ganache Filling. Place one cake layer on serving plate. Spread with ⅓ of filling. Repeat layers two more times. Top with remaining cake layer. Prepare Easy Chocolate Frosting; spread over cake. Garnish as desired.

Makes 1 (9-inch) layer cake

Chocolate Ganache Filling: Heat ¾ cup heavy cream, 1 tablespoon butter and 1 tablespoon granulated sugar to a boil; stir until sugar is dissolved. Place 1½ cups semisweet chocolate chips in medium bowl; pour cream mixture over chocolate and let stand 5 minutes. Stir until smooth; let stand 15 minutes or until filling reaches desired consistency. (Filling will thicken as it cools.) Makes about 1½ cups.

Easy Chocolate Frosting: Beat ½ cup softened butter in large bowl with electric mixer at medium speed until creamy. Add 4 cups powdered sugar and ¾ cup cocoa alternately with ½ cup milk; beat until smooth. Stir in 1½ teaspoons vanilla. Makes about 3 cups.

Banana Gingerbread Upside Down Cake

¾ cup margarine, divided
1 cup packed brown sugar, divided
1 firm, large DOLE® Banana
¼ cup DOLE® Chopped Dates
1 egg
2 extra-ripe, medium DOLE® Bananas
¼ cup molasses

1⅔ cups all-purpose flour
1½ teaspoons ground ginger
1 teaspoon baking soda
¾ teaspoon ground allspice
½ teaspoon baking powder
½ teaspoon salt

• Melt ¼ cup margarine in 9- or 10-inch cast iron skillet. Stir in ½ cup brown sugar. Slice firm banana; arrange in single layer in brown sugar mixture. Press dates in spaces between bananas.

• Beat remaining ½ cup margarine and ½ cup brown sugar until light and fluffy. Beat in egg.

• Purée ripe bananas in blender; blend ¾ cup banana purée with molasses.

• Combine dry ingredients in bowl; stir into beaten mixture alternately with molasses mixture until smooth. Spread batter over bananas in skillet. Bake in 350°F oven 30 minutes or until wooden pick inserted in center comes out clean. Cool in pan on wire rack 10 minutes. Invert onto serving plate.

Makes 9 servings

Fresh Apple Cake

3 cups flour, divided
3 cups finely chopped apples
1 cup finely chopped pecans or walnuts
3 eggs *or* ¾ cup egg substitute
2 cups sugar
1 cup vegetable oil

2 teaspoons ground cinnamon
2 teaspoons vanilla
1 teaspoon ARM & HAMMER® Baking Soda
1 teaspoon nutmeg
½ teaspoon salt

Toss ¼ cup flour with apples and nuts. Beat eggs thoroughly in large bowl; blend in sugar. Alternately add remaining 2¾ cups flour and oil. Stir in cinnamon, vanilla, Baking Soda, nutmeg and salt; mix well. Fold in apple mixture. Pour batter into greased and floured 10-inch tube pan. Bake at 350°F 1 hour.

Makes 16 servings

Glazed Chocolate Pound Cake

Cake
1¾ cups Butter Flavor CRISCO®
    all-vegetable shortening or 1¾ Butter
    Flavor CRISCO® Stick
3 cups granulated sugar
5 eggs
1 teaspoon vanilla
3¼ cups all-purpose flour
½ cup unsweetened cocoa powder
1 teaspoon baking powder
½ teaspoon salt

1⅓ cups milk
1 cup miniature semi-sweet chocolate
    chips

Glaze
1 cup miniature semi-sweet chocolate
    chips
¼ cup Butter Flavor CRISCO®
    all-vegetable shortening or ¼ Butter
    Flavor CRISCO® Stick
1 tablespoon light corn syrup

1. For cake, heat oven to 325°F. Grease and flour 10-inch tube pan.

2. Combine 1¾ cups shortening, sugar, eggs and vanilla in large bowl. Beat at low speed of electric mixer until blended, scraping bowl constantly. Beat on high speed 6 minutes, scraping bowl occasionally. Combine flour, cocoa, baking powder and salt in medium bowl. Mix in dry ingredients alternately with milk, beating after each addition until batter is smooth. Stir in 1 cup chocolate chips. Spoon into pan.

3. Bake at 325°F for 75 to 85 minutes or until wooden pick inserted in center comes out clean. Cool on cooling rack 20 minutes. Invert onto serving dish. Cool completely.

4. For glaze, combine 1 cup chocolate chips, ¼ cup shortening and corn syrup in top part of double boiler over hot, not boiling water. Stir until just melted and smooth. Cool slightly. (Or place mixture in microwave-safe bowl. Microwave at 50% (Medium) for 1 minute and 15 seconds. Stir. Repeat at 15 second intervals, if necessary, until just melted and smooth. Cool slightly.) Spoon glaze over cake. Let stand until glaze is firm.

Makes 1 (10-inch) tube cake

Prep Time: about 30 minutes
Bake Time: 75 to 85 minutes

Glazed Chocolate Pound Cake

Classic New York Cheesecake

Crust
1 cup HONEY MAID® Graham Cracker
    Crumbs
3 tablespoons sugar
3 tablespoons butter or margarine, melted

Filling
4 packages (8 ounces each)
    PHILADELPHIA® Cream Cheese,
    softened

1 cup sugar
3 tablespoons flour
1 tablespoon vanilla
1 cup BREAKSTONE'S® or KNUDSEN®
    Sour Cream
4 eggs

Crust
MIX crumbs, 3 tablespoons sugar and butter; press onto bottom of 9-inch springform pan. Bake at 325°F for 10 minutes if using a silver springform pan. (Bake at 300°F for 10 minutes if using a dark nonstick springform pan.)

Filling
BEAT cream cheese, 1 cup sugar, flour and vanilla with electric mixer on medium speed until well blended. Blend in sour cream. Add eggs, 1 at a time, mixing on low speed after each addition just until blended. Pour over crust.

BAKE at 325°F for 1 hour to 1 hour 5 minutes or until center is almost set if using a silver springform pan. (Bake at 300°F for 1 hour to 1 hour 5 minutes or until center is almost set if using a dark nonstick springform pan.) Run knife or metal spatula around rim of pan to loosen cake; cool before removing rim of pan. Refrigerate 4 hours or overnight. *Makes 12 servings*

Prep Time: 15 minutes plus refrigerating
Bake Time: 1 hour 10 minutes

Classic New York Cheesecake

Peanut Butter Surprise

2 cups all-purpose flour
2 teaspoons baking powder
¼ teaspoon salt
1¾ cups sugar
½ cup (1 stick) butter, softened
¾ cup reduced-fat (2%) or whole milk
1 teaspoon vanilla

3 large egg whites
2 (3-ounce) bittersweet chocolate candy
  bars, melted and cooled
30 mini peanut butter cups
1 container prepared chocolate frosting
3 ounces white chocolate candy bar,
  broken into chunks

1. Preheat oven to 350°F. Line 30 regular-size (2½-inch) muffin cups with paper muffin cup liners.

2. For cupcakes, combine flour, baking powder and salt in medium bowl; mix well and set aside. Beat sugar and butter with electric mixer at medium speed 1 minute. Add milk and vanilla. Beat with electric mixer at low speed 30 seconds. Gradually beat in flour mixture; beat at medium speed 2 minutes. Add egg whites; beat 1 minute. Stir in melted chocolate.

3. Spoon 1 heaping tablespoon batter into each prepared muffin cup; use back of spoon to slightly spread batter over bottom. Place one mini peanut butter cup in center of each cupcake. Spoon 1 heaping tablespoon batter over peanut butter cup; use back of spoon to smooth out batter. (Do not fill cups more than ¾ full.)

4. Bake 24 to 26 minutes or until puffed and golden brown. Cool in pans on wire racks 10 minutes. (Center of cupcakes will sink slightly upon cooling.) Remove cupcakes to racks; cool completely. (At this point, cupcakes may be frozen up to 3 months). Spread frosting over cooled cupcakes.

5. For white drizzle, place white chocolate in small resealable plastic food storage bag. Microwave at HIGH 30 to 40 seconds. Turn bag over; microwave additional 30 seconds or until chocolate is melted. Cut off tiny corner of bag; pipe chocolate decoratively over frosted cupcakes. Store at room temperature up to 24 hours, or cover and refrigerate up to 3 days before serving.

Makes 30 cupcakes

Peanut Butter Surprise

Sweet and Spicy Fruitcake

3 cups chopped walnuts
2 cups chopped dried figs
1 cup chopped dried apricots
1 cup chocolate chips
1½ cups flour, divided
¾ cup granulated sugar
4 large eggs
¼ cup butter or margarine, softened

⅓ cup apple jelly
2 tablespoons orange-flavor liqueur
1 tablespoon grated orange peel
1 tablespoon vanilla extract
2 teaspoons TABASCO® brand Pepper Sauce
1 teaspoon baking powder

Preheat oven to 325°F. Grease two 3-cup heat-safe bowls. Line bottoms and sides with foil; grease foil. Combine walnuts, figs, apricots, chocolate chips and ¼ cup flour in large bowl; mix well.

Beat sugar, eggs and butter in small bowl with mixer at low speed until well blended. Add jelly, remaining 1¼ cups flour and remaining ingredients. Beat at low speed until blended. Toss mixture with dried fruit in large bowl. Spoon into prepared bowls. Cover bowls with greased foil. Bake 40 minutes; uncover and bake 40 minutes or until toothpicks inserted in centers come out clean. Remove to wire racks to cool.

If desired, brush cooled fruitcakes with 1 tablespoon melted apple jelly and sprinkle each with 2 tablespoons finely chopped dried apricots. Store in cool place for up to 3 weeks.

Makes 2 small fruitcakes

Oreo® White Chocolate Mousse Cake

1 (1-pound 4-ounce) package Holiday
   OREO® Chocolate Sandwich Cookies,
   divided
6 tablespoons margarine or butter, melted
1 envelope KNOX® Unflavored Gelatine
1¼ cups milk

1 (11-ounce) package white chocolate
   chips
1 pint heavy cream, whipped *or* 4 cups
   COOL WHIP® Whipped Topping,
   thawed
Fresh raspberries, for garnish

1. Finely crush 24 cookies. Mix crushed cookies and margarine or butter; press onto bottom and 1 inch up side of 9-inch springform pan. Set aside.

2. Sprinkle gelatine over milk in large saucepan; let stand 1 minute. Stir over low heat about 3 minutes or until gelatine completely dissolves. Add white chocolate chips to gelatine mixture; continue heating until chocolate chips are melted and smooth. Refrigerate 30 minutes or until slightly thickened.

3. Coarsely chop 24 cookies. Gently fold chopped cookies and whipped cream into cooled chocolate mixture. Spoon into prepared crust. Refrigerate 6 hours or overnight.

4. Halve remaining cookies; garnish with cookie halves and raspberries if desired.

Makes 16 servings

Peanut Butter Pudding Cake

1 cup roasted peanuts, chopped, divided
1 cup all-purpose flour
½ cup butter, softened
1 package (8 ounces) cream cheese
⅓ cup creamy peanut butter
1 cup confectioners' sugar
1 container (4½ ounces) frozen whipped
   topping, thawed

1 package (3 ounces) instant vanilla
   pudding
1 package (3 ounces) instant chocolate
   pudding
2¾ cups milk
1 container (9 ounces) frozen whipped
   topping, thawed
1 square (1 ounce) chocolate, grated

In small bowl, mix ⅔ cup peanuts, flour and butter. Press onto bottom of 8×12-inch baking dish. Bake 20 minutes at 350°F. Cool. Beat cream cheese and peanut butter until smooth. Add sugar; mix well. Fold in 4½ ounces whipped topping. Spread over cooled peanut layer. Mix puddings with milk until thickened. Spread over peanut butter layer. Top with 9 ounces whipped topping. Sprinkle with chocolate and remaining ⅓ cup peanuts. Chill 2 to 3 hours.

Makes 12 servings

Favorite recipe from **Peanut Advisory Council**

✳ *Sensational Pies* ✳

Candy Bar Pie

4 ounces cream cheese, softened
1¾ cups plus 1 tablespoon cold milk, divided
1 (12-ounce) tub COOL WHIP® Whipped Topping, thawed, divided
2 packages (2.07 ounces each) chocolate-covered caramel peanut nougat bars, chopped

1 (4-serving size) package JELL-O® Chocolate Flavor Instant Pudding & Pie Filling
1 (6-ounce) READY CRUST® Chocolate Pie Crust

1. Mix cream cheese and 1 tablespoon milk in medium bowl with wire whisk until smooth. Gently stir in 2 cups whipped topping and chopped candy bars; set aside.

2. Pour remaining 1¾ cups milk into another medium bowl. Add pudding mix. Beat with wire whisk 1 minute. Gently stir in ½ cup whipped topping. Spread half of pudding mixture over bottom of crust. Spread cream cheese mixture over pudding mixture. Top with remaining pudding mixture.

3. Refrigerate 4 hours or until set. Garnish with remaining whipped topping. Refrigerate leftovers.

Makes 8 servings

Prep Time: 15 minutes
Chill Time: 4 hours

Candy Bar Pie

Crisco's® Door County Cherry Pie

Filling
- 2 cans (16 ounces each) pitted red tart cherries in water
- 1 cup sugar
- ¼ cup cornstarch
- 1 cup reserved cherry liquid

Crust
- Classic CRISCO® Single Crust (page 306)

Cream Cheese Layer
- 1 package (8 ounces) cream cheese, softened
- ½ cup sugar
- ½ teaspoon vanilla
- 2 eggs

Topping
- 1½ cups dairy sour cream

1. For filling, drain cherries, reserving 1 cup liquid. Combine 1 cup sugar and cornstarch in medium saucepan. Stir in 3 cups cherries and 1 cup reserved liquid. Set aside remaining cherries and liquid for another use. Cook and stir on medium-high heat until mixture comes to a boil. Boil 1 minute. Cool while preparing crust.

2. For crust, prepare as directed. Do not bake. Heat oven to 425°F.

3. Spoon half of cherry filling into unbaked pie crust.

4. Bake at 425°F for 15 minutes.

5. For cream cheese layer, beat cream cheese, ½ cup sugar and vanilla in small bowl at medium speed of electric mixer until smooth. Beat in eggs until blended.

6. Spoon cream cheese mixture over cherry filling.

7. Reduce oven temperature to 350°F. Return pie to oven. Bake 25 minutes. *Do not overbake.* Cool to room temperature. Top with remaining cherry mixture.

8. For topping, place spoonfuls of sour cream around edge of pie. Refrigerate leftover pie.

Makes 1 (9-inch) pie

Crisco's® Door County Cherry Pie

Confetti Pie

1 cup boiling water
1 package (4-serving size) JELL-O® Brand Lemon Flavor Gelatin
½ cup cold water
1 cup boiling water
1 package (4-serving size) JELL-O® Brand Orange Flavor Gelatin
½ cup cold orange juice
2 cups thawed COOL WHIP® Whipped Topping
⅓ cup multi-colored sprinkles
1 HONEY MAID® Honey Graham Pie Crust (9 inch)

STIR 1 cup boiling water into lemon gelatin in medium bowl at least 2 minutes or until completely dissolved. Stir in cold water. Pour into 8-inch square pan. Refrigerate 4 hours or until firm. Cut into ½-inch cubes.

STIR 1 cup boiling water into orange gelatin in large bowl at least 2 minutes or until completely dissolved. Stir in orange juice. Refrigerate about 20 minutes or until slightly thickened (consistency of unbeaten egg whites). Gently stir in whipped topping. Gently stir in gelatin cubes and sprinkles. Refrigerate until mixture will mound. Pour into crust.

REFRIGERATE at least 4 hours or until firm. Garnish with additional whipped topping and sprinkles, if desired.

Makes 8 servings

Great Substitutes: Try Berry Blue or Lime Flavor Gelatin instead of Lemon Flavor when making the gelatin cubes.

Brownie Pie à la Mode

1 pint vanilla ice cream, slightly softened
1 (15½-ounce) package brownie mix
½ cup chopped walnuts
½ cup SMUCKER'S® Chocolate Fudge Topping
2 tablespoons flaked coconut

Spoon ice cream into chilled 2-cup bowl or mold, packing it firmly with back of spoon. Cover with plastic wrap or aluminum foil; freeze at least 1 hour or until firm.

Prepare brownie mix according to package directions; stir in walnuts. Pour into greased 9-inch pie plate. Bake as directed on package. Cool completely on wire rack.

To serve, remove ice cream from freezer. Dip bowl in lukewarm water for 5 seconds. Cut around edge of ice cream with knife and invert onto center of brownie pie. Pour fudge topping over ice cream; sprinkle with coconut. Let stand 5 to 10 minutes at room temperature for easier slicing.

Makes 8 servings

Confetti Pie

Chocolate Fudge Pie

¼ cup CRISCO® all-vegetable shortening
  or ¼ CRISCO® Stick
1 bar (4 ounces) sweet baking chocolate
1 can (14 ounces) sweetened condensed
  milk
2 eggs, beaten
½ cup all-purpose flour
1 teaspoon vanilla

¼ teaspoon salt
1 cup flaked coconut
1 cup chopped pecans
1 unbaked Classic CRISCO® Single Crust
  (page 306)
Unsweetened whipped cream or ice
  cream

1. Heat oven to 350°F.

2. Melt shortening and chocolate in heavy saucepan over low heat. Remove from heat. Stir in sweetened condensed milk, eggs, flour, vanilla and salt; mix well. Stir in coconut and nuts. Pour into unbaked pie crust.

3. Bake at 350°F for 40 minutes or until wooden pick inserted into center comes out clean. Cool completely on cooling rack before cutting.

4. Serve with unsweetened whipped cream or ice cream, if desired. Refrigerate leftover pie.

Makes 1 (9-inch) pie (8 servings)

Frozen Pumpkin Cream Pie

1 cup canned solid pack pumpkin
⅔ cup KARO® Dark Corn Syrup
½ cup coarsely chopped walnuts
1 teaspoon cinnamon

¼ teaspoon nutmeg
2 cups frozen whipped topping, thawed
1 prepared (9-inch) graham cracker crust
Additional whipped topping for garnish

1. In medium bowl combine pumpkin, corn syrup, walnuts, cinnamon and nutmeg.

2. Fold in whipped topping. Spoon into crust.

3. Cover; freeze 3 to 4 hours or until firm.

4. Let stand 15 minutes before serving. If desired, garnish with additional whipped topping.

Makes 8 servings

Prep Time: 10 minutes, plus freezing

Cheesecake Garden Tarts

¼ cup strawberry or apricot preserves
10 prepared graham cracker crumb tart shells
1 package (8 ounces) PHILADELPHIA® Cream Cheese, softened
⅓ cup sugar
1 teaspoon vanilla

1 tub (8 ounces) COOL WHIP® Whipped Topping, thawed
Sliced almonds
Assorted berries and sliced fresh fruits
Hot fudge topping
Fresh mint leaves

SPREAD preserves onto bottom of tart shells. Beat cream cheese, sugar and vanilla in large bowl with wire whisk until smooth. Gently stir in whipped topping. Spoon evenly into tart shells.

REFRIGERATE 2 hours or until set. Decorate with almonds, fruits and topping to resemble flowers. Arrange on serving plate. Garnish with mint leaves. *Makes 10 tarts*

Oreo® Black Forest Pie

1 package (8 ounces) PHILADELPHIA® Cream Cheese, softened
2½ cups cold milk
2 packages (4-serving size each) JELL-O® Chocolate Flavor Instant Pudding & Pie Filling

1 OREO® Pie Crust (9 inch)
1 cup cherry pie filling
1 cup thawed COOL WHIP® Whipped Topping
OREO® Crunchies for garnish

BEAT cream cheese in large bowl with electric mixer on medium speed. Gradually beat in milk. Add pudding mixes. Beat on low speed 1 minute. Beat on medium speed 1 minute or until well blended. Spoon into crust.

REFRIGERATE 2 hours or until set. Just before serving, spoon cherry pie filling over pudding. Garnish with whipped topping and crunchies. *Makes 8 servings*

Prep Time: 20 minutes plus refrigerating

Helpful Hint: Soften cream cheese in microwave on HIGH 15 to 20 seconds.

Cheesecake Garden Tarts

Key Lime Pie

1 cup graham cracker crumbs
3 tablespoons melted margarine
1 teaspoon EQUAL® FOR RECIPES *or*
   3 packets EQUAL® sweetener *or*
   2 tablespoons EQUAL® SPOONFUL™
1 envelope (¼ ounce) unflavored gelatin
1¾ cups skim milk, divided
1 package (8 ounces) reduced-fat cream
   cheese, softened

⅓ to ½ cup fresh lime juice
3½ teaspoons EQUAL® FOR RECIPES *or*
   12 packets EQUAL® sweetener *or*
   ½ cup EQUAL® SPOONFUL™
Lime slices, raspberries and fresh mint
   sprigs, for garnish (optional)

• Combine graham cracker crumbs, margarine and 1 teaspoon Equal® For Recipes *or* 3 packets Equal® sweetener *or* 2 tablespoons Equal® Spoonful™ in bottom of 7-inch springform pan; pat evenly onto bottom and ½ inch up side of pan.

• Sprinkle gelatin over ½ cup milk in small saucepan; let stand 2 to 3 minutes. Cook over low heat, stirring constantly, until gelatin is dissolved. Beat cream cheese in small bowl until fluffy; beat in remaining 1¼ cups milk and gelatin mixture. Mix in lime juice and 3½ teaspoons Equal® For Recipes *or* 12 packets Equal® sweetener *or* ½ cup Equal® Spoonful™. Refrigerate pie until set, about 2 hours.

• To serve, loosen side of pie from pan with small spatula and remove side of pan. Place pie on serving plate; garnish with lime slices, raspberries and mint, if desired.   *Makes 8 servings*

Black and White Almond Pie

2 tablespoons margarine or butter
2 ounces white chocolate, chopped
1 (6-ounce) HONEY MAID® Honey
   Graham Pie Crust
3 tablespoons PLANTERS® Slivered Almonds,
   toasted, chopped and divided

1 (4-serving size) package instant
   chocolate pudding & pie filling
2 cups cold milk
¼ teaspoon almond extract
   Prepared whipped topping, for garnish

1. Melt margarine or butter and white chocolate in top of double boiler over hot water, stirring until blended. Pour into pie crust; sprinkle with 2 tablespoons almonds.

2. Prepare pudding mix according to package directions for pie using milk and almond extract; pour into crust. Refrigerate at least 1 hour.

3. Garnish with whipped topping and remaining almonds.   *Makes 8 servings*

Key Lime Pie

Apple Custard Tart

1 folded refrigerated unbaked pastry crust
    (one-half of 15-ounce package)
1½ cups sour cream
1 (14-ounce) can EAGLE® BRAND
    Sweetened Condensed Milk (NOT
    evaporated milk)
¼ cup thawed frozen apple juice
    concentrate

1 egg
1½ teaspoons vanilla extract
¼ teaspoon ground cinnamon
    Apple Cinnamon Glaze (recipe follows)
2 medium all-purpose apples, cored, pared
    and thinly sliced
1 tablespoon butter or margarine

1. Let refrigerated pastry crust stand at room temperature according to package directions. Preheat oven to 375°F. On floured surface, roll pastry crust from center to edge, forming circle about 13 inches in diameter. Ease pastry into 11-inch tart pan with removable bottom. Trim pastry even with rim of pan. Place pan on baking sheet. Bake crust 15 minutes or until lightly golden.

2. Meanwhile with mixer, beat sour cream, Eagle Brand, apple juice concentrate, egg, vanilla and cinnamon in small bowl until smooth. Pour into prebaked pie crust. Bake 25 minutes or until center appears set when shaken. Cool 1 hour on wire rack. Prepare Apple Cinnamon Glaze.

3. In large skillet, cook apples in butter until tender-crisp. Arrange apples on top of tart; drizzle with Apple Cinnamon Glaze. Chill in refrigerator at least 4 hours.   *Makes 1 tart*

Apple Cinnamon Glaze: In small saucepan, mix ⅓ cup thawed frozen apple juice concentrate, 1 teaspoon cornstarch and ½ teaspoon cinnamon. Cook and stir over low heat until thick and bubbly.

Pungent Pumpkin Pie

Prepared pie crust for one 9-inch pie
1 (16-ounce) can pumpkin
1 (12-ounce) can evaporated milk
2 eggs
¾ cup packed brown sugar
2 teaspoons TABASCO® brand Pepper
    Sauce

1½ teaspoons ground cinnamon
½ teaspoon ground ginger
½ teaspoon ground nutmeg
    Whipped cream
¼ cup chopped pecans

Preheat oven to 400°F. Place pie crust in 9-inch pie plate; flute edge. Combine pumpkin, milk, eggs, sugar, TABASCO® Sauce, cinnamon, ginger and nutmeg in bowl; beat until well blended. Pour into prepared crust. Bake 40 to 45 minutes or until knife inserted 1 inch from edge comes out clean. Cool on wire rack. Top with large dollop of whipped cream; garnish with pecans.   *Makes 8 servings*

Apple Custard Tart

No Bake Frozen Chocolate Indulgence

1 package (11.4 ounces) JELL-O® No
    Bake Chocolate Lover's Dessert
6 tablespoons butter or margarine, melted
1⅓ cups cold milk
¾ cup raspberry preserves

1 tub (8 ounces) EXTRA CREAMY
    COOL WHIP® Whipped Topping or
    COOL WHIP® Whipped Topping

STIR Crust Mix and butter thoroughly in 9-inch pie plate until crumbs are well moistened. First, firmly press crumbs against side of pie plate, using measuring cup or large spoon to shape edge. Next, firmly press remaining crumbs onto bottom.

POUR milk into large bowl. Add Filling Mix. Beat with electric mixer on lowest speed until blended. Beat on medium speed 3 minutes. (Filling will be thick.) Spoon into crust. Spread raspberry preserves evenly over filling. Top with whipped topping and drizzle with Topping.

FREEZE at least 4 hours or until firm. To serve, dip bottom of pan in hot water 30 seconds for easy cutting and serving.

Makes 8 servings

Lemon Meringue Pie

1⅓ cups sugar, divided
¼ cup ARGO® or KINGSFORD'S® Corn
    Starch
1½ cups cold water
3 egg yolks, slightly beaten

Grated peel of 1 lemon
¼ cup lemon juice
1 tablespoon margarine or butter
1 baked (9-inch) pie crust
3 egg whites

1. Preheat oven to 350°F.

2. In medium saucepan combine 1 cup sugar and corn starch. Gradually stir in water until smooth. Stir in egg yolks. Stirring constantly, bring to a boil over medium heat; boil 1 minute. Remove from heat.

3. Stir in lemon peel, lemon juice and margarine. Spoon hot filling into pie crust.

4. In small bowl with mixer at high speed beat egg whites until foamy. Gradually beat in remaining ⅓ cup sugar; continue beating until stiff peaks form. Spread meringue evenly over hot filling, sealing to edge of crust.

5. Bake 15 to 20 minutes or until golden. Cool on wire rack; refrigerate.

Makes one 9-inch pie

No Bake Frozen Chocolate Indulgence

Fluffy Lemon Berry Pie

4 ounces cream cheese, softened
1½ cups cold milk
2 (4-serving size) packages JELL-O®
    Lemon Flavor Instant Pudding & Pie
    Filling
1 (8-ounce) tub COOL WHIP® Whipped
    Topping, thawed

1 (6-ounce) READY CRUST® Shortbread
    or Graham Cracker Pie Crust
1 cup blueberries, raspberries or sliced
    strawberries

1. Beat cream cheese in large bowl with wire whisk until smooth. Gradually beat in milk until well blended. Add pudding mixes. Beat 2 minutes or until smooth. Immediately stir in half of whipped topping.

2. Spoon into crust. Top with remaining whipped topping.

3. Refrigerate 3 hours or until set. Garnish with berries. Refrigerate leftovers.   *Makes 8 servings*

Apple Butterscotch Tart

Pastry for single-crust pie
5 cups (about 5 medium) peeled and
    thinly sliced tart green apples
1 cup (6 ounces) NESTLÉ® TOLL
    HOUSE® Butterscotch Flavored
    Morsels

¾ cup all-purpose flour
½ cup packed brown sugar
½ teaspoon ground cinnamon
¼ cup (½ stick) chilled butter or
    margarine
Ice cream or sweetened whipped cream

PREHEAT oven to 375°F.

LINE 9-inch tart pan with removable bottom with pastry; trim away excess pastry. Arrange apples in pastry shell; sprinkle morsels over apples. Combine flour, sugar and cinnamon in medium bowl. Cut in butter with pastry blender or two knives until mixture resembles coarse crumbs. Sprinkle mixture over filling.

BAKE for 40 to 45 minutes or until apples are tender when pierced with sharp knife. Remove side of tart pan. Serve warm with ice cream.   *Makes 8 servings*

Fluffy Lemon Berry Pie

Frozen Peanut Butter Pie

Chocolate Crunch Crust (recipe follows)
1 (8-ounce) package cream cheese, softened
1 (14-ounce) can EAGLE® BRAND Sweetened Condensed Milk (NOT evaporated milk)

¾ cup peanut butter
2 tablespoons lemon juice from concentrate
1 teaspoon vanilla extract
1 cup (½ pint) whipping cream, whipped
Chocolate fudge ice cream topping

1. Prepare Chocolate Crunch Crust. In large mixing bowl, beat cream cheese until fluffy; gradually beat in Eagle Brand and peanut butter until smooth. Stir in lemon juice and vanilla.

2. Fold in whipped cream. Turn into prepared crust. Drizzle topping over pie. Freeze 4 hours or until firm. Return leftovers to freezer.   *Makes 1 (9-inch) pie*

Chocolate Crunch Crust: In heavy saucepan, over low heat, melt ⅓ cup butter or margarine and 1 (6-ounce) package semi-sweet chocolate chips. Remove from heat; gently stir in 2½ cups oven-toasted rice cereal until completely coated. Press onto bottom and up side to rim of buttered 9-inch pie plate. Chill 30 minutes.

Prep Time: 20 minutes
Freeze Time: 4 hours

Quaker's Best Oatmeal Pie

6 egg whites, lightly beaten *or* ¾ cup egg substitute
⅔ cup firmly packed brown sugar
⅓ cup granulated sugar
¾ cup fat-free milk
1 teaspoon vanilla
1¼ cups QUAKER® Oats (quick or old fashioned, uncooked)

¾ cup raisins or other dried fruit such as cherries, cranberries or chopped apricots
½ cup flaked or shredded coconut
½ cup chopped nuts (optional)
1 prepared 9-inch pie crust, unbaked

Heat oven to 375°F. Beat egg whites and sugars until well blended. Add milk and vanilla; mix well. Stir in oats, raisins, coconut and nuts; mix well. Pour filling into prepared pie crust. Bake 35 to 45 minutes or until center of pie is set. Cool completely on wire rack. Serve with ice cream or whipped cream. Store, covered, in refrigerator.   *Makes 8 servings*

Frozen Peanut Butter Pie

Banana Caramel Spice Pie

1 large ripe banana, sliced
1 (6-ounce) READY CRUST® Shortbread
   Pie Crust
2 cups cold milk
2 (4-serving size) packages white chocolate
   or vanilla flavor instant pudding
   & pie filling

½ teaspoon ground cinnamon
1 (8-ounce) tub whipped topping, thawed
   Caramel ice cream topping

1. Place banana slices in bottom of crust.

2. Pour milk into large bowl. Add pudding mixes and cinnamon. Beat with wire whisk 1 minute. Gently stir in whipped topping. Spoon into crust.

3. Refrigerate 4 hours or until set. Serve with caramel topping. *Makes 8 servings*

Prep Time: 10 minutes
Chill Time: 4 hours

Delicious American Apple Pie

Prepared frozen or refrigerated pastry
   for double-crust 9-inch pie
¾ cup firmly packed DOMINO® Light
   Brown Sugar
1 tablespoon all-purpose flour
½ teaspoon cinnamon
¼ teaspoon nutmeg

⅛ teaspoon salt
1 tablespoon grated lemon peel
6 cups peeled, cored and thickly sliced
   apples
1 tablespoon lemon juice
2 tablespoons butter or margarine

Heat oven to 425°F. Line 9-inch pie pan with one half of pastry. Combine sugar, flour, cinnamon, nutmeg, salt and lemon peel in large bowl. Add apples and toss to coat evenly. Spoon apple mixture into pastry-lined pie pan. Sprinkle with lemon juice and dot with butter. Top with remaining pastry. Trim and flute edges. Cut slits in top crust to allow steam to escape. Bake at 425°F. for 40 to 45 minutes or until golden brown. Serve warm or at room temperature. *Makes 8 servings*

Prep Time: 30 minutes
Bake Time: 45 minutes

Banana Caramel Spice Pie

Double Blueberry Cheese Pie

Crust
Classic CRISCO® Single Crust
(page 306)

Filling
2 packages (8 ounces each) cream cheese, softened
1 cup granulated sugar
2 tablespoons all-purpose flour
2 eggs

2 teaspoons vanilla
½ cup whipping cream
2 cups fresh blueberries

Topping
2 cups whipping cream
2 tablespoons confectioners' sugar
1 teaspoon vanilla
1 cup fresh blueberries

1. For crust, prepare as directed in 9- or 9½-inch deep-dish pie plate. Do not bake. Heat oven to 350°F.

2. For filling, place cream cheese and granulated sugar in food processor bowl. Process, using steel blade, until smooth. Add flour, eggs, 2 teaspoons vanilla and ½ cup whipping cream through feed tube while processor is running. Process until blended. Add 2 cups blueberries. Pulse (quick on and off) twice. Pour into unbaked pie crust.

3. Bake at 350°F for 45 minutes. *Do not overbake.* Turn oven off. Allow pie to remain in oven with door ajar for 1 hour. Cool to room temperature. Refrigerate 6 hours or overnight.

4. For topping, beat 2 cups whipping cream in large bowl at high speed of electric mixer until stiff peaks form. Beat in confectioners' sugar and 1 teaspoon vanilla. Spread over top of pie. Garnish with 1 cup blueberries. Serve immediately. Refrigerate leftover pie.

Makes 1 (9- or 9½-inch deep-dish) pie

continued on page 306

Double Blueberry Cheese Pie

Double Blueberry Cheese Pie, continued

Classic Crisco® Single Crust

1⅓ cups all-purpose flour
½ teaspoon salt
½ CRISCO® Stick or ½ cup CRISCO®
    all-vegetable shortening

3 tablespoons cold water

1. Spoon flour into measuring cup and level. Combine flour and salt in medium bowl.

2. Cut in shortening using pastry blender or 2 knives until all flour is blended to form pea-size chunks.

3. Sprinkle with water, 1 tablespoon at a time. Toss lightly with fork until dough forms a ball.

4. Press dough between hands to form 5- to 6-inch "pancake." Flour rolling surface and rolling pin lightly. Roll dough into circle. Trim circle 1 inch larger than upside-down pie plate. Carefully remove trimmed dough. Set aside to reroll and use for pastry cutout garnish, if desired.

5. Fold dough into quarters. Unfold and press into pie plate. Fold edge under. Flute.

6. For recipes using a baked pie crust, heat oven to 425°F. Prick bottom and side thoroughly with fork (50 times) to prevent shrinkage. Bake at 425°F for 10 to 15 minutes or until lightly browned.

7. For recipes using an unbaked pie crust, follow directions given for that recipe.

Makes 1 (9-inch) single crust

Awesome Sundae Pie

6 squares BAKER'S® Semi-Sweet Baking
    Chocolate
1 tablespoon butter or margarine
¾ cup finely chopped nuts, toasted
¾ cup BAKER'S® ANGEL FLAKE®
    Coconut

2 pints ice cream, any flavor, softened
    Thawed COOL WHIP® Whipped
    Topping, chopped nuts and
    maraschino cherries
Hot Fudge Sauce (recipe follows)

LINE 9-inch pie plate with foil; lightly grease foil.

MICROWAVE chocolate and butter in large microwavable bowl on HIGH 2 minutes or until butter is melted. Stir until chocolate is completely melted. Stir in nuts and coconut. Spread evenly onto bottom and up side of prepared pie plate.

REFRIGERATE 1 hour or until firm. Lift crust out of pie plate. Carefully peel off foil. Return crust to pie plate or place on serving plate. Refrigerate until ready to use. Fill crust with scoops of ice cream and cover.

FREEZE 2 hours or until firm. Garnish with whipped topping, nuts and maraschino cherries. Serve with Hot Fudge Sauce.

Makes 8 servings

Tip: To serve, let stand at room temperature 10 minutes or until pie can be easily cut.

Hot Fudge Sauce

1 package (8 squares) BAKER'S®
    Unsweetened Baking Chocolate
¼ cup (½ stick) butter or margarine
½ cup milk

½ cup whipping (heavy) cream
2 cups sugar
1 tablespoon vanilla

MICROWAVE chocolate and butter in large microwavable bowl on HIGH 2 minutes or until butter is melted. Stir until chocolate is completely melted.

STIR in milk, cream and sugar until well blended. Microwave 5 minutes until mixture is thick and smooth and sugar is completely dissolved, stirring halfway through cooking time. Stir in vanilla. Pour into clean canning jars. Store in refrigerator up to 2 weeks. Before giving, attach warming directions (see below) to jar.

Makes 3½ cups

Warming Directions: Microwave, uncovered, on HIGH 2 minutes or just until heated through.

Dakota "Plain Jane" Green Apple Pie

Crust
Classic CRISCO® Double Crust
(page 310)

Filling
6 cups sliced, peeled tart green cooking
apples (about 2 pounds or 6 medium)
1 cup granulated sugar
⅓ cup firmly packed brown sugar
3 tablespoons all-purpose flour

1 teaspoon cinnamon
3 tablespoons butter or margarine,
softened

Decorations
Reserved dough
2 tablespoons water, divided
2 drops red food color
2 drops green food color

1. For crust, prepare as directed. Roll and press bottom crust into 9-inch pie plate. Do not bake. Reserve dough scraps. Heat oven to 425°F.

2. For filling, combine apples, granulated sugar, brown sugar, flour, cinnamon and butter in large bowl. Toss to coat. Spoon into unbaked pie crust. Moisten pastry edge with water.

3. Roll top crust same as bottom. Lift onto filled pie. Trim ½ inch beyond edge of pie plate. Fold top edge under bottom crust. Flute.

4. For decorations, roll out reserved dough. Divide in half. Pour 1 tablespoon water into each of 2 cake pans or pie plates. Add red food color to one and green food color to the other. Stir until blended. Dip one half of dough in red mixture and other half in green mixture. Place each on separate sheets of waxed paper. Cut out 1-inch circles with floured cutter. Cut vent in top crust to resemble branches of apple tree. Lift red circles with knife and place on branches. Decorate with leaves cut from part of green circles.

5. Bake at 425°F for 10 minutes. Reduce oven temperature to 325°F. Cover edge with foil, if necessary, to prevent overbrowning. Bake 40 minutes or until filling in center is bubbly and crust is golden brown. *Do not overbake.* Cool to room temperature before serving.   *Makes 1 (9-inch) pie*

Note: Use any tart green-skinned apple such as Granny Smith.

continued on page 310

Dakota "Plain Jane" Green Apple Pie

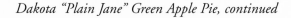

Dakota "Plain Jane" Green Apple Pie, continued

Classic Crisco® Double Crust

2 cups all-purpose flour
1 teaspoon salt
¾ CRISCO® Stick or ¾ cup CRISCO® all-vegetable shortening

5 tablespoons cold water (or more as needed)

1. Spoon flour into measuring cup and level. Combine flour and salt in medium bowl.

2. Cut in ¾ cup shortening using pastry blender or 2 knives until all flour is blended to form pea-size chunks.

3. Sprinkle with water, 1 tablespoon at a time. Toss lightly with fork until dough forms a ball. Divide dough in half.

4. Press dough between hands to form 5- to 6-inch "pancake." Flour rolling surface and rolling pin lightly. Roll both halves of dough into circle. Trim one circle of dough 1 inch larger than upside-down pie plate. Carefully remove trimmed dough. Set aside to reroll and use for pastry cutout garnish, if desired.

5. Fold dough into quarters. Unfold and press into pie plate. Trim edge even with plate. Add desired filling to unbaked crust. Moisten pastry edge with water. Lift top crust onto filled pie. Trim ½ inch beyond edge of pie plate. Fold top edge under bottom crust. Flute. Cut slits in top crust to allow steam to escape. Follow baking directions given for that recipe. _Makes 1 (9-inch) double crust_

Rich Chocolate Cream Pie

9-inch baked pastry shell
1 package (6-serving size, about 4.6 ounces) vanilla cook & serve pudding and pie filling mix*

3 cups milk
2 cups (12-ounce package) HERSHEY¿S Semi-Sweet Chocolate Chips
Whipped topping (optional)

*Do not use instant pudding.

1. Prepare pastry shell as directed on package; cool.

2. Prepare pudding mix with milk in medium saucepan, cooking as directed on package. Remove from heat; immediately add chocolate chips to hot pudding mixture, stirring until chips are melted and mixture is smooth.

3. Pour into prepared pastry shell. Place plastic wrap directly onto surface of filling; refrigerate several hours or overnight. Garnish with whipped topping, if desired. _Makes about 8 servings_

Rice Pudding Tarts

1 cup cooked rice	½ teaspoon vanilla extract
1 cup low-fat milk	¼ teaspoon almond extract
⅓ cup sugar	6 frozen tartlet pastry shells, partially
¼ cup raisins	baked and cooled
⅛ teaspoon salt	⅛ teaspoon ground nutmeg for garnish
2 eggs, beaten	Fresh berries for garnish
¾ cup heavy cream	Fresh mint for garnish

Combine rice, milk, sugar, raisins and salt in medium saucepan. Cook over medium-low heat 30 to 35 minutes or until thick and creamy, stirring frequently. Remove from heat; add ¼ of rice mixture to eggs. Return egg mixture to saucepan; stir in cream and extracts. Spoon equally into pastry shells; sprinkle with nutmeg. Place tarts on baking sheet. Bake at 350°F 20 to 30 minutes or until pudding is set. Cool on wire rack 1 hour. Unmold tarts and garnish with berries and mint. Serve at room temperature. Refrigerate remaining tarts. *Makes 6 servings*

Favorite recipe from **USA Rice Federation**

Ritz® Mock Apple Pie

Pastry for two-crust 9-inch pie	2 teaspoons cream of tartar
36 RITZ® Crackers, coarsely broken (about	2 tablespoons lemon juice
1¾ cups crumbs)	Grated peel of 1 lemon
2 cups sugar	2 tablespoons margarine or butter
1¾ cups water	½ teaspoon ground cinnamon

1. Roll out half the pastry and line 9-inch pie plate. Place cracker crumbs in prepared crust; set aside.

2. Heat sugar, water and cream of tartar to a boil in saucepan over high heat; simmer for 15 minutes. Add lemon juice and peel; cool.

3. Pour syrup over cracker crumbs. Dot with margarine or butter; sprinkle with cinnamon. Roll out remaining pastry; place over pie. Trim, seal and flute edges. Slit top crust to allow steam to escape.

4. Bake at 425°F for 30 to 35 minutes or until crust is crisp and golden. Cool completely.

Makes 10 servings

❧ *Luscious Desserts* ❧

Crunch Peach Cobbler

⅓ cup plus 1 tablespoon granulated sugar, divided
1 tablespoon cornstarch
1 can (29 ounces) *or* 2 cans (16 ounces each) cling peach slices in syrup, drained, reserving ¾ cup syrup
½ teaspoon vanilla
2 cups all-purpose flour, divided
½ cup packed light brown sugar

⅓ cup uncooked old-fashioned or quick oats
¼ cup butter, melted
½ teaspoon ground cinnamon
½ teaspoon salt
½ cup shortening
4 to 5 tablespoons cold water
Whipped cream for garnish

1. Combine ⅓ cup granulated sugar and cornstarch in small saucepan. Slowly add reserved peach syrup. Stir well. Add vanilla. Cook over low heat, stirring constantly, until thickened. Set aside.

2. For crumb topping, combine ½ cup flour, brown sugar, oats, butter and cinnamon in small bowl; stir until mixture forms coarse crumbs. Set aside.

3. Preheat oven to 350°F. Combine remaining 1½ cups flour, remaining 1 tablespoon granulated sugar and salt in small bowl. Cut in shortening with pastry blender or 2 knives until mixture forms pea-sized pieces. Sprinkle water, 1 tablespoon at a time, over flour mixture. Toss lightly with fork until mixture holds together. Press together to form a ball.

4. Roll out dough into 10-inch square, ⅛ inch thick. Fold dough in half, then in half again. Carefully place folded dough in center of 8-inch square baking dish. Unfold and press onto bottom and about 1 inch up sides of dish. Arrange peaches over crust. Pour sauce over peaches. Sprinkle with crumb topping.

5. Bake 45 minutes. Serve warm or at room temperature with whipped cream.

Makes about 6 servings

Crunch Peach Cobbler

Berry Squares

1 package (12 ounces) pound cake, cut
    into 10 slices
3 tablespoons orange juice
2 pints fresh seasonal berries (strawberries,
    raspberries or blueberries)
2 tablespoons sugar

2½ cups cold milk
2 packages (4-serving size each) JELL-O®
    Vanilla or Lemon Flavor Instant
    Pudding & Pie Filling
1 tub (8 ounces) COOL WHIP® Whipped
    Topping, thawed, divided

ARRANGE cake slices in bottom of 13×9-inch pan. Drizzle cake with juice. Top with berries; sprinkle with sugar.

POUR milk into large bowl. Add pudding mixes. Beat with wire whisk 1 minute or until well blended. Gently stir in 1 cup whipped topping. Spoon mixture over berries in pan. Top with remaining whipped topping.

REFRIGERATE until ready to serve or overnight. Garnish as desired.   *Makes 15 servings*

Prep Time: 10 minutes

Deep Dark Chocolate Soufflé

1 tablespoon sugar
½ cup HERSHEY'S Dutch Processed
    Cocoa
¼ cup all-purpose flour
¼ cup (½ stick) butter or margarine,
    softened

1 cup milk
½ cup plus 2 tablespoons sugar, divided
1 teaspoon vanilla extract
4 eggs, separated
Ice cream

1. Heat oven to 350°F. Butter 6-cup soufflé dish; lightly coat with 1 tablespoon sugar.

2. Stir together cocoa and flour in medium bowl. Add butter; blend well. Heat milk in medium saucepan until very hot. *Do not boil.* Reduce heat to low. Add cocoa mixture; beat with whisk until smooth and thick. Remove from heat; stir in ½ cup sugar and vanilla. Cool slightly. Add egg yolks, one at a time, beating well after each addition. Cool to room temperature.

3. Beat egg whites in large bowl until foamy; gradually add remaining 2 tablespoons sugar, beating until stiff peaks form. Stir small amount of beaten whites into chocolate mixture; fold chocolate mixture into remaining whites. Carefully pour into prepared dish.

4. Bake 40 to 45 minutes or until puffed. Serve immediately with ice cream.   *Makes 6 servings*

Berry Square

Rocky Road Icebox Cake

3½ cups JET-PUFFED® Miniature
    Marshmallows, divided
2 tablespoons milk
3 cups half-and-half or milk
2 packages (4-serving size each) JELL-O®
    Chocolate Flavor Instant Pudding
    & Pie Filling

1 tub (8 ounces) COOL WHIP® Whipped
    Topping, thawed, divided
5 or more whole HONEY MAID® Honey
    Grahams, broken into pieces
1 jar (11.75 ounces) hot fudge topping
1 cup PLANTERS COCKTAIL® Peanuts

LINE 9×5-inch loaf pan with foil extending over edges to form handles. Spray foil with no stick cooking spray.

MICROWAVE 3 cups marshmallows in medium microwavable bowl with 2 tablespoons milk 1 to 2 minutes or until almost melted. Stir until completely melted; cool.

POUR half-and-half into large bowl. Add pudding mixes. Beat with wire whisk 2 minutes or until well blended. (Mixture will be thick.) Gently stir in 1 cup whipped topping. Stir remaining whipped topping into cooled marshmallows.

LINE bottom of prepared pan with ⅓ of the honey graham crackers to form crust. Spread with ⅓ jar of hot fudge topping. Sprinkle with ⅓ cup peanuts. Spoon ½ of the pudding mixture over peanuts. Spoon ½ of the marshmallow mixture over pudding. Smooth with spatula. Repeat layers. Freeze at least 4 hours or until firm.

Makes 8 to 10 servings

Prep Time: 15 minutes plus freezing

How To Serve: Lift dessert from pan, using foil as handles, onto cutting board. Remove foil. Let stand at room temperature 10 minutes before slicing. Top dessert with remaining peanuts, marshmallows and honey graham crackers. Drizzle remaining hot fudge sauce on top. Run knife under hot water and dry with towel for easier cutting.

Rocky Road Icebox Cake

Chocolate and Orange Crêpes Sundaes

1 quart vanilla ice cream, softened
8 Hint of Orange Crêpes (recipe follows)
1 package (6 ounces) semi-sweet chocolate
  pieces
½ cup marshmallow creme
¼ cup almond-flavored liqueur or orange
  juice

Grated peel of ½ SUNKIST® orange
2 SUNKIST® oranges, peeled and cut into
  half-cartwheel slices
Sliced almonds (optional)

Spread ice cream on crêpes and roll up. Arrange on serving platter or individual dessert plates
and place in freezer while preparing sauce. To make sauce, in saucepan, over very low heat, melt
chocolate pieces. Stir in marshmallow creme, liqueur, orange peel and heat. To serve, spoon sauce
over crêpes and arrange orange half-cartwheel slices and almonds on top.   *Makes 10 servings*

Hint of Orange Crêpes

1 cup milk
2 eggs
⅔ cup all-purpose flour
1 tablespoon sugar

1 tablespoon fresh-squeezed SUNKIST®
  orange juice
1 tablespoon vegetable oil
½ teaspoon salt

In blender or food processor, combine all ingredients; blend until smooth. In hot, lightly oiled
6-inch skillet, pour about 2 tablespoons of batter, tilting pan slightly to quickly spread batter until
thin and even. Lightly brown first side; turn and cook second side for a few seconds. Place on plate
lined with waxed paper. Repeat with remaining batter, separating cooked crêpes with waxed paper.
                                                                        Makes 12 crêpes

Chocolate and Orange Crêpe Sundae

Cappuccino Cream

1 cup freshly brewed strong MAXWELL HOUSE® Coffee, at room temperature
½ cup milk
1 package (8 ounces) PHILADELPHIA® Cream Cheese, softened
1 package (4-serving size) JELL-O® Brand Vanilla Flavor Instant Pudding & Pie Filling

¼ teaspoon ground cinnamon
1 tub (8 ounces) COOL WHIP® Whipped Topping, thawed, divided
Cookies, such as biscotti or chocolate-laced pirouettes

BEAT coffee and milk gradually into cream cheese in large bowl with electric mixer on medium speed until smooth.

ADD pudding mix and cinnamon. Beat on low speed 2 minutes. Let stand 5 minutes or until thickened. Gently stir in 2 cups of COOL WHIP®. Spoon mixture into 6 dessert glasses or 1-quart serving bowl.

REFRIGERATE until ready to serve. Just before serving, top with remaining COOL WHIP®. Sprinkle with additional ground cinnamon. Serve with cookies.   *Makes 6 servings*

Prep Time: 20 minutes plus refrigerating

English Bread Pudding

2 cups hot milk
½ small loaf of bread, sliced
1 tablespoon butter
1 egg
½ cup GRANDMA'S® Molasses

½ cup sugar
1 teaspoon cinnamon
½ teaspoon nutmeg
1 cup chopped raisins
½ cup chopped nuts

Heat oven to 350°F. In large baking dish, pour milk over bread and butter. In medium bowl, combine egg, molasses, sugar, cinnamon and nutmeg. When bread is cool pour egg mixture, raisins and nuts over it. Bake 2 hours or until mixture is set and tip of knife comes out clean. Serve with whipped cream.   *Makes 4 servings*

Cappuccino Cream

Grandma's Apple Crisp

¾ cup apple juice
3½ teaspoons EQUAL® FOR RECIPES *or*
    12 packets EQUAL® sweetener *or*
    ½ cup EQUAL® SPOONFUL™

1 tablespoon cornstarch
1 teaspoon grated lemon peel
4 cups sliced peeled apples
    Crispy Topping (recipe follows)

• Combine apple juice, Equal®, cornstarch and lemon peel in medium saucepan; add apples and heat to boiling. Reduce heat and simmer, uncovered, until juice is thickened and apples begin to lose their crispness, about 5 minutes.

• Arrange apples in 8-inch square baking pan; sprinkle Crispy Topping over apples. Bake in preheated 400°F oven until topping is browned and apples are tender, about 25 minutes. Serve warm.

Makes 6 servings

Crispy Topping

¼ cup all-purpose flour
2½ teaspoons EQUAL® FOR RECIPES *or*
    8 packets EQUAL® sweetener *or*
    ⅓ cup EQUAL® SPOONFUL™
1 teaspoon ground cinnamon
½ teaspoon ground nutmeg

3 dashes ground allspice
4 tablespoons cold margarine, cut into
    pieces
¼ cup quick-cooking oats
¼ cup unsweetened flaked coconut*

Unsweetened coconut can be purchased in health food stores.

• Combine flour, Equal® and spices in small bowl; cut in margarine with pastry blender until mixture resembles coarse crumbs. Stir in oats and coconut.

Grandma's Apple Crisp

Chocolate Toffee Bar Dessert

1 cup flour
½ cup pecans, toasted and finely chopped
¼ cup sugar
½ cup (1 stick) butter or margarine, melted
1 cup toffee bits, divided

2 cups cold milk
2 packages (4-serving size each) JELL-O® Chocolate Flavor Instant Pudding & Pie Filling
1 tub (8 ounces) COOL WHIP® Whipped Topping, thawed, divided

HEAT oven to 400°F.

MIX flour, pecans, sugar, butter and ½ cup toffee bits in large bowl until well mixed. Press firmly onto bottom of 13×9-inch pan. Bake 10 minutes or until lightly browned. Cool.

POUR milk into large bowl. Add pudding mixes. Beat with wire whisk 1 minute or until well blended. Spread 1½ cups pudding on bottom of crust.

GENTLY stir ½ of the whipped topping into remaining pudding. Spread over pudding in pan. Top with remaining whipped topping. Sprinkle with remaining toffee bits.

REFRIGERATE 3 hours or overnight.

Makes 15 servings

Fresh Cherry Jubilee

½ cup sugar
1 tablespoon cornstarch
¼ cup water
¼ cup orange juice
3 cups pitted Northwest fresh sweet cherries

½ teaspoon grated orange peel
¼ cup brandy (optional)
1 quart vanilla ice cream

Combine sugar and cornstarch in skillet. Blend in water and orange juice. Cook and stir over medium-high heat until thickened and smooth. Add cherries and orange peel; simmer 10 minutes. Gently heat brandy, pour over sauce and flame, if desired. Serve over ice cream.

Makes about 8 servings

Favorite recipe from **Northwest Cherry Growers**

Chocolate Toffee Bar Dessert

Passionate Sorbet

2 cups MAUNA LA'I® Paradise Passion® Juice Drink

¼ cup sugar
½ envelope of unflavored gelatin

1. Combine Mauna La'i Paradise Passion Juice Drink and sugar in medium saucepan. Sprinkle gelatin over juice drink and let sit 1 to 2 minutes to soften. Cook on low heat until gelatin and sugar dissolve, stirring occasionally. Pour into 9×9-inch pan and freeze until just firm.

2. Remove from freezer and cut into small pieces. Place frozen pieces in food processor. Process until light and creamy. Return to pan. Cover and freeze until firm. To serve, scrape off thin layers with spoon.

Makes 6 servings

Kahlúa® Tiramisu for Two

12 small packaged ladyfingers
2 egg yolks*
½ cup powdered sugar
4 ounces softened cream cheese, beaten until fluffy
⅓ cup whipping cream, whipped

½ teaspoon instant espresso powder
1 tablespoon water
¼ cup KAHLÚA®
1 ounce semisweet chocolate, chopped fine
2 teaspoons unsweetened cocoa powder

Use clean, uncracked eggs.

Arrange ladyfingers in single layer on baking sheet. Toast at 325°F for 10 minutes. Set aside. In bowl, whisk yolks with sugar until smooth and thick. Whisk in cream cheese. Fold in whipped cream.

In separate bowl, dissolve espresso powder in water. Stir in KAHLÚA®. In third bowl, combine chopped chocolate and cocoa.

Place 2 tablespoons cream cheese mixture in bottom of each of two (12-ounce) wine goblets or dessert dishes. Top each with three ladyfingers, 3 to 4 teaspoons KAHLÚA® mixture and ⅓ cup cream cheese mixture. Cover each with ¼ of the chocolate mixture, three ladyfingers and 3 to 4 teaspoons KAHLÚA® mixture. Top each dessert with ½ of the remaining cream cheese mixture; smooth top. Sprinkle with remaining chocolate mixture. Cover and chill several hours or overnight before serving.

Makes 2 servings

Variation: For KAHLÚA® Banana-Almond Tiramisu, add 1 medium banana, sliced ¼ inch thick (about twenty slices), and 4 teaspoons toasted slivered or chopped almonds. Layer five banana slices over each layer of ladyfingers and sprinkle 1 teaspoon almonds over second and third layers of cream cheese.

Passionate Sorbet

Chocolate Shortcakes

1¼ cups all-purpose flour
½ cup unsweetened cocoa powder
⅔ cup granulated sugar, divided
1 tablespoon baking powder
⅛ teaspoon salt
½ cup (1 stick) cold butter
½ cup milk
1 teaspoon vanilla extract

1¼ cups "M&M's"® Milk Chocolate Mini
    Baking Bits, divided
1 large egg
1 teaspoon water
½ cup cold whipping cream
2 cups sliced strawberries
⅓ cup chocolate syrup

Preheat oven to 425°F. In medium bowl combine flour, cocoa powder, ⅓ cup sugar, baking powder and salt. Cut in butter with pastry blender or two knives until mixture resembles coarse crumbs. Add milk and vanilla; mix just until dry ingredients are moistened. On lightly floured surface gently knead ¾ cup "M&M's"® Milk Chocolate Mini Baking Bits into dough until evenly dispersed. Roll or pat out to ½-inch thickness. Cut with 3-inch round biscuit cutter; place on ungreased cookie sheet. If necessary, reroll scraps of dough in order to make six shortcakes. In small bowl combine egg and water; brush lightly over dough. Bake 12 to 14 minutes. Cool on pan 1 minute. Remove to wire racks; cool completely. In large bowl beat whipping cream until soft peaks form. Add remaining ⅓ cup sugar; beat until stiff peaks form. Reserve ½ cup whipped cream. Split shortcakes and place bottom of each on plate; divide strawberries evenly among shortcakes. Top with remaining whipped cream; sprinkle with ¼ cup "M&M's"® Milk Chocolate Mini Baking Bits. Replace tops of shortcakes; drizzle with chocolate syrup. Garnish with reserved whipped cream and remaining ¼ cup "M&M's"® Milk Chocolate Mini Baking Bits. Serve immediately. *Makes 6 servings*

Hot Rum-Glazed Bananas over Ice Cream

2 tablespoons butter
2 tablespoons dark brown sugar
2 tablespoons honey
¾ teaspoon TABASCO® brand Pepper
    Sauce

4 bananas, cut into 1-inch slices
3 tablespoons dark rum
4 (¼-cup) scoops vanilla ice cream
    Chocolate syrup

Combine butter, brown sugar, honey and TABASCO® Sauce in large skillet; cook over medium-high heat until mixture sizzles. Add bananas; toss gently until each slice is coated. Increase heat to high; add rum and cook 20 seconds or until mixture has syrupy consistency and bananas are glazed.

Scoop ice cream into bowls; spoon warm bananas on top. Drizzle with chocolate syrup and serve immediately. *Makes 4 servings*

Chocolate Shortcake

The Mega Mint Sundae

Mint chocolate chip ice cream
Crème de menthe syrup
HERSHEY'S Chocolate Shoppe™ Hot
  Fudge Topping

YORK® Peppermint Patties, crumbled
REDDI-WIP® Real Whipped Cream

• Place ice cream in sundae dish.

• Top ice cream with crème de menthe syrup, HERSHEY'S Chocolate Shoppe Hot Fudge Topping and YORK Peppermint Patties.

• Top with lots of REDDI-WIP Real Whipped Cream.

Makes 1 sundae

Walnut Pumpkin Torte

1 cup chopped California walnuts
¾ cup raisins
1 cup flour, divided
½ cup butter or margarine
1½ cups packed brown sugar
1 cup canned pumpkin
1½ teaspoons vanilla
3 eggs
1 teaspoon ground cinnamon

¾ teaspoon baking powder
½ teaspoon baking soda
½ teaspoon ground nutmeg
½ teaspoon ground ginger
  Powdered sugar
  Additional chopped walnuts for garnish
1 cup whipping cream
2 tablespoons brandy
1 tablespoon granulated sugar

Toss 1 cup walnuts and raisins with 2 tablespoons flour to coat; set aside. In medium saucepan melt butter; blend in brown sugar until dissolved. Remove from heat; stir in pumpkin and vanilla. Whisk in eggs, 1 at a time. Combine remaining flour, cinnamon, baking powder, baking soda, nutmeg and ginger; stir into pumpkin mixture. Add walnut-raisin mixture; mix just to blend. Turn into greased and floured 9-inch springform pan. Bake in preheated 350°F oven 50 to 55 minutes or until wooden pick inserted into center comes out clean. Cool on rack 15 to 20 minutes. Remove outer ring from pan. Dust top of torte with powdered sugar; garnish with additional chopped walnuts. Whip cream with brandy to form soft peaks; beat in granulated sugar. Serve torte warm or cooled with brandied whipped cream.

Makes 6 to 8 servings

Favorite recipe from **Walnut Marketing Board**

The Mega Mint Sundae

Peach Melba Bread Pudding

1 (16-ounce) can sliced peaches in their
  own juice
4 cups white bread cubes
½ cup seedless raisins
1¼ cups skim milk
1 cup EGG BEATERS® Healthy Real Egg
  Product

½ cup sugar
2 tablespoons FLEISCHMANN'S®
  Original Margarine, melted
1 teaspoon vanilla extract
¼ teaspoon ground cinnamon
½ cup seedless raspberry preserves, warmed
  or raspberry syrup

1. Drain peaches, reserving ¼ cup juice; chop peaches. Mix bread cubes, chopped peaches and raisins in greased 2-quart shallow casserole; set aside.

2. Blend reserved peach juice, milk, Egg Beaters®, sugar, melted margarine, vanilla and cinnamon; pour over bread mixture.

3. Bake in preheated 350°F oven for 45 to 50 minutes or until knife inserted in center comes out clean. Serve warm topped with preserves or syrup.   *Makes 8 servings*

Prep Time: 20 minutes
Cook Time: 45 minutes
Total Time: 1 hour and 5 minutes

Grandma's Old-Fashioned Rice Pudding

1 bag SUCCESS® Rice
1 can (12 ounces) evaporated skim milk,
  divided
⅓ cup sugar
¼ cup water
¼ teaspoon salt

½ cup raisins
  Boiling water
1 egg
1½ teaspoons vanilla
  Cinnamon or ground nutmeg (optional)

Prepare rice according to package directions.

Combine rice, 1 cup milk, sugar, water and salt in medium saucepan. Cook over medium heat, stirring frequently, until thick and creamy, about 20 minutes.

Meanwhile, place raisins in small bowl. Add enough boiling water to cover raisins; let stand 15 minutes. Beat egg with remaining milk in small bowl. Gradually pour into hot rice mixture, stirring constantly. Remove from heat. Stir in vanilla. Drain raisins well; stir into pudding. Sprinkle lightly with cinnamon. Serve warm or chilled.   *Makes 6 servings*

Peach Melba Bread Pudding

Plum Streusel

Plum Filling
    ½ cup firmly packed light brown sugar
    3 tablespoons cornstarch
    ½ teaspoon ground nutmeg
    2½ pounds ripe plums, pitted and sliced
        ½ inch thick

Streusel
    1 cup all-purpose flour

    ½ cup Butter Flavor CRISCO®
       all-vegetable shortening or ½ Butter
       Flavor CRISCO® Stick
    ½ cup firmly packed light brown sugar
    1 teaspoon ground cinnamon
    1 teaspoon vanilla
    ¼ teaspoon salt

1. Heat oven to 350°F. Spray 3-quart shallow baking dish with CRISCO® No-Stick cooking spray; set aside.

2. For filling, combine brown sugar, cornstarch and nutmeg in large bowl; mix well. Add plums and stir gently to coat evenly. Place in prepared pan.

3. For streusel, combine flour, shortening, brown sugar, cinnamon, vanilla and salt in large bowl. Mix with fork until mixture is combined and just crumbly. *Do not overmix.* Sprinkle over fruit mixture.

4. Bake at 350°F for 45 minutes or until streusel top is crisp. Cool about 10 minutes; serve warm with whipped cream or ice cream. *Makes 6 to 8 servings*

Chocolate-Banana Parfait

    1 (4-serving size) package cook and serve
       chocolate pudding and pie filling
    2 cups milk
    1 banana, chopped

    ½ cup PLANTERS® Pecans, chopped
    1½ cups prepared whipped topping
       PLANTERS® Pecan Halves and banana
       slices, for garnish

1. Prepare pudding according to package directions using milk. Pour into bowl; cover pudding surface directly with plastic wrap and refrigerate 2 hours.

2. Stir banana and pecans into pudding. Alternately spoon pudding and whipped topping in layers into 6-ounce parfait glasses. Garnish with pecan halves and banana slices. *Makes 4 servings*

Plum Streusel

Juicy Berry Sorbet

¾ cup boiling water
1 package (4-serving size) JELL-O® Brand
   Cranberry Flavor Gelatin

½ cup sugar
2 cups cold juice, any flavor

STIR boiling water into gelatin and sugar in large bowl at least 2 minutes or until completely dissolved. Stir in cold juice. Pour into 9-inch square pan.

FREEZE about 1 hour or until ice crystals form 1 inch around edges. Spoon into blender container; cover. Blend on high speed about 30 seconds or until smooth. Return to pan.

FREEZE 6 hours or overnight until firm. Scoop into dessert dishes. Store leftover sorbet in freezer.

Makes 8 to 10 servings

Fruit Dessert Pizza

1 package (18 ounces) refrigerated sugar
   cookie dough
2 DOLE® Bananas, divided
1 package (8 ounces) light cream cheese
¼ cup sugar
2 tablespoons orange juice

1 package (16 ounces) frozen peaches,
   thawed *or* 1 can (15 ounces) sliced
   peaches, drained
2 cups DOLE® Fresh Pineapple Chunks
½ cup orange marmalade preserves
   Mint leaves (optional)

• Press small pieces of cookie dough onto greased 12-inch pizza pan. Bake at 350°F, 10 to 12 minutes or until browned and puffed. Cool completely in pan on wire rack.

• Cut 1 banana into blender container. Cover; blend until smooth (½ cup). Beat cream cheese, sugar, orange juice and blended banana in bowl until smooth. Spread over cooled cookie.

• Slice remaining banana. Arrange banana slices, peaches and pineapple over cream cheese. Brush orange marmalade over fruit. Garnish with mint leaves, if desired. Serve.   *Makes 10 servings*

Prep Time: 15 minutes
Bake Time: 12 minutes

Juicy Berry Sorbet

Passionate Profiteroles

Vanilla Custard Filling (recipe follows)
⅔ cup water
7 tablespoons plus 2 teaspoons I CAN'T
    BELIEVE IT'S NOT BUTTER!®
    Spread, divided

1 tablespoon sugar
¼ teaspoon salt
¾ cup all-purpose flour
4 large eggs
1 square (1 ounce) semi-sweet chocolate

Preheat oven to 400°F. Lightly grease baking sheet; set aside.

In 2½-quart saucepan, bring water, 7 tablespoons I Can't Believe It's Not Butter! Spread, sugar and salt to a boil over high heat. Remove from heat and immediately stir in flour. With wooden spoon, cook flour mixture over medium heat, stirring constantly, 5 minutes or until film forms on bottom of pan. Remove from heat; stir in eggs, one at a time, beating well after each addition. Immediately drop by heaping tablespoonfuls onto prepared baking sheet. Place baking sheet on middle rack in oven.

Bake 20 minutes. Decrease oven temperature to 350°F and bake an additional 20 minutes. Turn off oven without opening door and let profiteroles stand in oven 10 minutes. Cool completely on wire rack. To fill, slice off top ⅓ of profiteroles and set aside. Fill with Vanilla Custard Filling. Replace profiterole tops.

In small microwave-safe bowl, microwave chocolate and remaining 2 teaspoons I Can't Believe It's Not Butter! Spread at HIGH (Full Power) 30 seconds or until chocolate is melted; stir until smooth. Drizzle chocolate mixture over profiteroles, then sprinkle, if desired, with toasted sliced almonds.

Makes 16 servings

Vanilla Custard Filling

1 package (3.4 ounces) instant vanilla
    pudding
1 cup milk
3 to 4 tablespoons hazelnut, coffee,
    almond, orange or cherry liqueur
    (optional)

½ teaspoon vanilla extract
2 cups whipped cream or non-dairy
    whipped topping

In medium bowl, with wire whisk, blend pudding mix, milk, liqueur and vanilla. Fold in whipped cream. Cover with plastic wrap and chill 1 hour or until set.

Passionate Profiteroles

Fudgy Milk Chocolate Fondue

1 (16-ounce) can chocolate-flavored syrup
1 (14-ounce) can EAGLE® BRAND
    Sweetened Condensed Milk (NOT
    evaporated milk)

Dash salt
1½ teaspoons vanilla extract
    Dippers: fresh fruit, cookies, pound cake
    cubes, angel food cake cubes

1. In heavy saucepan over medium heat, combine syrup, Eagle Brand and salt. Cook and stir 12 to 15 minutes or until slightly thickened.

2. Remove from heat; stir in vanilla. Serve warm with Dippers. Store covered in refrigerator.

Makes about 3 cups

Microwave Directions: In 1-quart glass measure, combine syrup, Eagle Brand and salt. Cook on 100% power (HIGH) 3½ to 4 minutes, stirring after 2 minutes. Stir in vanilla.

Tip: Can be served warm or cold over ice cream. Can be made several weeks ahead. Store tightly covered in refrigerator.

Double Apple Turnovers

½ cup SMUCKER'S® Cider Apple Butter
½ cup apple cider or juice
½ teaspoon cinnamon
1 orange peel, grated*
¼ cup golden raisins

4 large firm apples, peeled, cored and
    chopped
1 package frozen filo (phyllo) dough
    Nonstick cooking spray
    Sugar

Grate orange part of peel only, not bitter white part.

In large saucepan, combine apple butter, cider, cinnamon and grated orange peel; simmer for 5 minutes. Add raisins and simmer for 2 minutes more. Add apples and cook over medium heat for about 10 minutes or until apples begin to soften and most of liquid evaporates. Cool in refrigerator.

Unwrap filo dough but keep covered with damp cloth. Remove 1 sheet of dough; spray with nonstick cooking spray. Top with second sheet of dough; spray with nonstick cooking spray. Spoon about ⅓ cup apple filling on lower right corner of dough. Fold dough over filling to form large rectangle. Then fold turnover as if it were a flag, making triangular packet with each turn. Repeat process until all turnovers are made.

Place finished turnovers on baking sheet; sprinkle with sugar. Bake at 375°F for about 25 minutes or until golden brown.

Makes 6 turnovers

JELL-O® Yogurt Parfaits

2 cups boiling water, divided
1 package (4-serving size) JELL-O® Brand
    Gelatin, any red flavor
1 container (8 ounces) BREYERS® Vanilla
    Lowfat Yogurt, divided

1 cup cold water, divided
1 package (4-serving size) JELL-O® Brand
    Orange Flavor Gelatin

STIR 1 cup boiling water into red gelatin in medium bowl at least 2 minutes or until completely dissolved. Remove ½ cup gelatin to small bowl. Stir in ½ of the yogurt. Stir ½ cup cold water into other bowl. Refrigerate both bowls 15 to 20 minutes or until slightly thickened (consistency of unbeaten egg whites).

SPOON creamy red gelatin mixture evenly into 4 dessert glasses. Refrigerate 10 minutes or until thickened (spoon drawn through leaves a definite impression). Top each with clear red gelatin. Refrigerate until thickened.

MEANWHILE, repeat procedure with orange gelatin and remaining ingredients.

REFRIGERATE 3 hours or until firm.
Makes 4 servings

Prep Time: 10 minutes plus refrigerating

Great Substitute: For a fun holiday treat, substitute Lime Flavor Gelatin for the Orange Flavor Gelatin. Garnish each serving with a dollop of thawed COOL WHIP® Whipped Topping.

❊ *Irresistible Treats* ❊

Double Delicious Cookie Bars

½ cup (1 stick) butter or margarine
1½ cups graham cracker crumbs
1 (14-ounce) can EAGLE® BRAND Sweetened Condensed Milk (NOT evaporated milk)

2 cups (12 ounces) semi-sweet chocolate chips*
1 cup (6 ounces) peanut butter-flavored chips*

Butterscotch-flavored chips or white chocolate chips may be substituted for the semi-sweet chocolate chips and/or peanut butter-flavored chips.

1. Preheat oven to 350°F (325°F for glass dish). In 13×9-inch baking pan, melt butter in oven.

2. Sprinkle crumbs evenly over butter; pour Eagle Brand evenly over crumbs. Top with remaining ingredients; press down firmly.

3. Bake 25 to 30 minutes or until lightly browned. Cool. Cut into bars. Store covered at room temperature.

Makes 24 to 36 bars

Prep Time: 10 minutes
Bake Time: 25 to 30 minutes

Double Delicious Cookie Bars

Cinnamon Caramel Corn

8 cups air-popped popcorn (about ⅓ cup
    kernels)
2 tablespoons honey

4 teaspoons margarine
¼ teaspoon ground cinnamon

1. Preheat oven to 350°F. Spray jelly-roll pan with nonstick cooking spray. Place popcorn in large bowl.

2. Stir honey, margarine and cinnamon in small saucepan over low heat until margarine is melted and mixture is smooth; immediately pour over popcorn. Toss with spoon to coat evenly. Pour onto prepared pan; bake 12 to 14 minutes or until coating is golden brown and appears crackled, stirring twice. Let cool on pan 5 minutes. (As popcorn cools, coating becomes crisp. If not crisp enough, or if popcorn softens upon standing, return to oven and heat 5 to 8 minutes.) *Makes 4 servings*

Cajun Popcorn: Preheat oven and prepare jelly-roll pan as directed above. Combine 7 teaspoons honey, 4 teaspoons margarine and 1 teaspoon Cajun or Creole seasoning in small saucepan. Proceed with recipe as directed above. Makes 4 servings.

Italian Popcorn: Spray 8 cups of air-popped popcorn with fat-free butter-flavored spray to coat. Sprinkle with 2 tablespoons finely grated Parmesan cheese, ⅛ teaspoon black pepper and ½ teaspoon dried oregano leaves. Gently toss to coat. Makes 4 servings.

Chocolate & Peanut Butter Truffles

¾ cup (1½ sticks) butter (no substitutes)
1 cup REESE'S® Peanut Butter Chips
½ cup HERSHEY'S Cocoa
1 can (14 ounces) sweetened condensed
    milk (not evaporated milk)

1 tablespoon vanilla extract
HERSHEY'S Cocoa or finely chopped
    nuts or graham cracker crumbs

1. Melt butter and peanut butter chips in saucepan over very low heat. Add cocoa; stir until smooth. Add sweetened condensed milk; stir constantly until mixture is thick and glossy, about 4 minutes. Remove from heat; stir in vanilla.

2. Refrigerate 2 hours or until firm enough to handle. Shape into 1-inch balls; roll in cocoa. Refrigerate until firm, about 1 hour. Store, covered, in refrigerator.

Makes about 3½ dozen candies

Clockwise from top: Italian Popcorn, Cinnamon Caramel Corn and Cajun Popcorn

---

Chocolate Cherry Treats

½ cup (1 stick) butter, softened
¾ cup firmly packed light brown sugar
¼ cup granulated sugar
½ cup sour cream
1 large egg
1 tablespoon maraschino cherry juice
1 teaspoon vanilla extract
2 cups all-purpose flour

½ teaspoon baking soda
¼ teaspoon salt
1¼ cups "M&M's"® Milk Chocolate Mini Baking Bits
½ cup chopped walnuts
⅓ cup well-drained chopped maraschino cherries

Preheat oven to 350°F. In large bowl cream butter and sugars until light and fluffy; beat in sour cream, egg, maraschino cherry juice and vanilla. In medium bowl combine flour, baking soda and salt; add to creamed mixture. Stir in "M&M's"® Milk Chocolate Mini Baking Bits, walnuts and maraschino cherries. Drop by heaping tablespoonfuls about 2 inches apart onto ungreased cookie sheets. Bake about 15 minutes. Cool 1 minute on cookie sheets; cool completely on wire racks. Store in tightly covered container.   *Makes 3 dozen cookies*

Banana Jumbles

2 extra-ripe, medium DOLE® Bananas
¾ cup packed brown sugar
½ cup creamy peanut butter
¼ cup margarine, softened
1 egg

1½ cups old-fashioned oats
1 cup all-purpose flour
1½ teaspoons baking powder
½ teaspoon salt
¾ cup DOLE® Seedless Raisins

• Mash bananas with fork. Measure 1 cup.

• Beat brown sugar, peanut butter and margarine in large bowl. Beat in egg and mashed bananas.

• Combine oats, flour, baking powder and salt. Stir into banana mixture until well combined. Stir in raisins.

• Drop by heaping tablespoonfuls onto cookie sheets coated with nonstick cooking spray. Shape cookies with back of spoon. Bake in 375°F oven 12 to 14 minutes until lightly browned. Cool on wire racks.   *Makes 18 cookies*

Chocolate Cherry Treats

Cashew & Pretzel Toffee Clusters

¾ cup packed brown sugar
¾ cup light corn syrup
½ cup butter
2 teaspoons vanilla
4 cups tiny pretzel twists (not sticks)

4 cups bite-sized toasted wheat squares
  cereal
1 can (10 ounces) salted cashew halves and
  pieces

1. Preheat oven to 300°F. Spray large baking sheet with nonstick cooking spray.

2. Place brown sugar, corn syrup and butter in heavy small saucepan. Heat over medium heat until mixture boils and sugar dissolves, stirring frequently. Remove from heat; stir in vanilla.

3. Combine pretzels, cereal and cashews in large bowl. Pour sugar mixture over pretzel mixture; toss to coat evenly. Spread on prepared baking sheet. Bake 30 minutes, stirring after 15 minutes. Spread onto greased waxed paper. Cool completely; break into clusters. Store in airtight container at room temperature. *Makes about 8 cups clusters*

Chewy Macadamia Nut Blondies

¾ cup Butter Flavor CRISCO®
  all-vegetable shortening or ¾ Butter
  Flavor CRISCO® Stick
1 cup firmly packed light brown sugar
1 large egg
1 teaspoon vanilla

1 teaspoon almond extract
1 cup all-purpose flour
½ teaspoon baking soda
⅛ teaspoon salt
6 ounces white chocolate chips
1 cup chopped macadamia nuts

1. Heat oven to 325°F.

2. Combine shortening and sugar in large bowl. Beat at medium speed with electric mixer until well blended. Beat in egg, vanilla and almond extract until well blended.

3. Combine flour, baking soda and salt in small bowl. Add to creamed mixture until just incorporated. *Do not overmix.* Fold in white chocolate chips and nuts until just blended.

4. Spray 9-inch square baking pan with CRISCO® No-Stick Cooking Spray. Pour batter into prepared pan. Bake at 325°F for 25 to 30 minutes or until a wooden pick inserted in center comes out almost dry and top is golden. *Do not overbake or overbrown.*

5. Place on cooling rack; cool completely. Cut into bars. *Makes about 16 bars*

Cashew & Pretzel Toffee Clusters

Pretty Posies

1 package (20 ounces) refrigerated sugar cookie dough
Orange and purple food colors

1 tablespoon sprinkles
All-purpose flour (optional)

1. Remove dough from wrapper. Reserve ⅙ of dough. Add orange food color and sprinkles to reserved dough until well blended; shape into 7½ inch log. Wrap with plastic wrap and refrigerate 30 minutes or until firm. Add purple food color to remaining dough until well blended. Shape dough into disc. Wrap with plastic wrap and refrigerate 30 minutes or until firm.

2. Roll out purple dough to 6×7½-inch rectangle on sheet of waxed paper. Place orange log in center of rectangle. Bring waxed paper and edges of purple dough up and over top of orange log; press gently. Overlap purple dough edges slightly; press gently. Wrap waxed paper around dough and twist ends to secure. Freeze log 20 minutes.

3. Preheat oven to 350°F. Lightly grease cookie sheets. Remove waxed paper from dough log. Cut log into ¼-inch slices. Place 2 inches apart on prepared cookie sheets. Using 2½-inch flower-shaped cookie cutter, cut slices into flowers; remove and discard dough scraps.

4. Bake 15 to 17 minutes or until edges are lightly browned. Remove to wire racks; cool completely.

Makes about 1½ dozen cookies

Cinnamon & Spice Trail Mix

¼ cup FLEISCHMANN'S® Original Margarine
¼ cup honey
4 cups bite-size crispy rice squares

2 tablespoons sugar
½ teaspoon ground cinnamon
1 cup seedless raisins

1. Mix margarine and honey in large bowl; add cereal, tossing to coat well.

2. Spread mixture on greased 15½×10½×1-inch baking pan. Bake in preheated 350°F oven for 15 minutes, stirring every 5 minutes.

3. Mix sugar and cinnamon; sprinkle over cereal mixture, stirring to coat well. Stir in raisins; cool completely. Store in airtight container.

Makes about 5 cups

Prep Time: 5 minutes
Cook Time: 15 minutes
Cool Time: 30 minutes

Nut Brittle

½ cup peanut butter, toasted cashew butter
    or toasted almond butter
1 teaspoon baking soda
1 teaspoon vanilla
1 cup sugar

1 cup light corn syrup
2 tablespoons water
1½ cups raw peanuts, cashews or
    unblanched almonds
½ cup butter or margarine

1. Melt peanut butter in top of double boiler over medium heat, stirring constantly. Reduce heat to low. Let stand, stirring occasionally.

2. Lightly grease 16×14-inch baking sheet. Set aside. Blend baking soda and vanilla in small bowl until smooth.

3. Combine sugar, corn syrup and water in saucepan. Bring to a boil over medium-high heat, stirring constantly. Add nuts and butter. Return to a boil, stirring constantly. Reduce heat to medium. Boil until temperature registers 280°F on candy thermometer, stirring constantly.

4. Remove saucepan from heat. Stir in peanut butter until well blended. Stir in vanilla mixture until well blended. Immediately pour mixture evenly over prepared baking sheet.

5. Quickly roll out brittle with buttered rolling pin to as thin as possible. Cool completely on baking sheet. Break into pieces. Store tightly covered at room temperature for up to 1 week.

Makes about 1½ pounds

Fudgey Raspberry Brownies

1⅔ cups (10-ounce package) HERSHEY'S
    Raspberry Chips
½ cup (1 stick) butter or margarine
2 eggs
1 teaspoon vanilla extract

1 cup all-purpose flour
½ cup sugar
¼ teaspoon baking soda
½ cup coarsely chopped nuts (optional)

1. Heat oven to 350°F. Grease 8-inch square baking pan.

2. Combine raspberry chips and butter in medium saucepan. Cook over medium heat, stirring constantly, until melted. Remove from heat. Add eggs and vanilla; stir until well blended. Add flour, sugar and baking soda; stir until well blended. Stir in nuts, if desired. Spread batter into prepared pan.

3. Bake 25 to 30 minutes or until wooden pick inserted in center comes out almost clean. Cool completely in pan on wire rack. Cut into squares.

Makes about 20 brownies

Nut Brittle

Chocolate Chunk Caramel Pecan Brownies

4 squares BAKER'S® Unsweetened Baking
    Chocolate
¾ cup (1½ sticks) butter or margarine
2 cups sugar
4 eggs
1 cup flour

1 package (14 ounces) KRAFT® Caramels,
    unwrapped
⅓ cup whipping (heavy) cream
2 cups pecan or walnut halves, divided
1 package (12 ounces) BAKER'S® Semi-
    Sweet Chocolate Chunks, divided

HEAT oven to 350°F. Line 13×9-inch baking pan with foil; grease foil.

MICROWAVE chocolate and butter in large microwavable bowl on HIGH 2 minutes or
until butter is melted. Stir until chocolate is completely melted. Stir sugar into chocolate mixture
until well blended. Mix in eggs. Stir in flour until well blended. Spread ½ of brownie batter in
prepared pan.

BAKE 25 minutes or until brownie is firm to the touch.

MEANWHILE, microwave caramels and cream in microwavable bowl on HIGH 2 minutes or until
caramels begin to melt. Stir until smooth. Stir in 1 cup pecan halves. Gently spread caramel mixture
over baked brownie in pan. Sprinkle with ½ of chocolate chunks. Pour remaining unbaked brownie
batter evenly over top; sprinkle with remaining chocolate chunks and 1 cup pecan halves. (Some
caramel mixture may peak through.)

BAKE an additional 30 minutes or until brownie is firm to the touch. Cool in pan on wire rack.
Lift out of pan onto cutting board.   *Makes 2 dozen brownies*

Prep Time: 20 minutes
Bake Time: 55 minutes

Tip: For 13×9-inch glass baking dish, bake at 325°F.

Chocolate Chunk Caramel Pecan Brownies

Rocky Road Bars

2 cups (12-ounce package) NESTLÉ®
    TOLL HOUSE® Semi-Sweet
    Chocolate Morsels, divided
1½ cups all-purpose flour
1½ teaspoons baking powder
1 cup granulated sugar

6 tablespoons (¾ stick) butter or
    margarine, softened
1½ teaspoons vanilla extract
2 eggs
2 cups (4 ounces) miniature marshmallows
1½ cups coarsely chopped walnuts

MICROWAVE 1 cup morsels in medium, microwave-safe bowl on HIGH (100% power) for 1 minute; stir. Microwave at additional 10- to 20-second intervals; stir until smooth. Cool to room temperature. Combine flour and baking powder in small bowl.

BEAT sugar, butter and vanilla in large mixer bowl until crumbly. Beat in eggs. Add melted chocolate; beat until smooth. Gradually beat in flour mixture. Spread batter into greased 13×9-inch baking pan.

BAKE in preheated 375°F. oven for 16 to 20 minutes or until wooden pick inserted in center comes out still slightly sticky.

REMOVE from oven; sprinkle immediately with marshmallows, nuts and remaining morsels. Return to oven for 2 minutes. Remove from oven; cool in pan on wire rack.

Makes 2½ dozen bars

Lemon Bars

15 whole graham crackers
2 packages (8 ounces each)
    PHILADELPHIA® Cream Cheese,
    softened
3½ cups cold milk

3 packages (4-serving size each) JELL-O®
    Lemon Flavor Instant Pudding & Pie
    Filling
1 tub (8 ounces) COOL WHIP® Whipped
    Topping, thawed, divided

ARRANGE ½ of the crackers in bottom of 13×9-inch pan, cutting crackers to fit, if necessary.

BEAT cream cheese in large bowl with electric mixer on low speed until smooth. Gradually beat in 1 cup milk. Add remaining 2½ cups milk and pudding mixes. Beat 1 to 2 minutes. (Mixture will be thick.) Gently stir in 2 cups whipped topping.

SPREAD ½ of pudding mixture over crackers in pan. Arrange remaining crackers over pudding in pan. Top with remaining pudding mixture. Cover with remaining whipped topping. Refrigerate 4 hours or freeze 3 hours. Cut into bars.

Makes 18 servings

Rocky Road Bars

Cut-Out Sugar Cookies

1¼ cups granulated sugar
1 Butter Flavor CRISCO® Stick or 1 cup
    Butter Flavor CRISCO® all-vegetable
    shortening
2 eggs
¼ cup light corn syrup or regular pancake
    syrup
1 tablespoon vanilla

3 cups all-purpose flour plus
    4 tablespoons, divided
¾ teaspoon baking powder
½ teaspoon baking soda
½ teaspoon salt
    Granulated sugar or colored sugar
    crystals

1. Combine sugar and 1 cup shortening in large bowl. Beat at medium speed of electric mixer until well blended. Add eggs, syrup and vanilla. Beat until well blended and fluffy.

2. Combine 3 cups flour, baking powder, baking soda and salt. Add gradually to shortening mixture at low speed. Mix until well blended.

3. Divide dough into 4 quarters. Wrap each quarter of dough with plastic wrap. Refrigerate at least 1 hour. Keep refrigerated until ready to use.

4. Heat oven to 375°F. Place sheets of foil on countertop for cooling cookies.

5. Spread 1 tablespoon flour on large sheet of waxed paper. Place one quarter of dough on floured paper. Flatten slightly with hands. Turn dough over and cover with another large sheet of waxed paper. Roll dough to ¼-inch thickness. Remove top sheet of waxed paper. Cut out with floured cutters. Place 2 inches apart on ungreased baking sheets. Repeat with remaining dough.

6. Sprinkle with granulated sugar or colored sugar crystals, or leave plain to frost or decorate when cooled.

7. Bake one baking sheet at a time at 375°F for 5 to 9 minutes, depending on size of cookies (bake smaller, thinner cookies closer to 5 minutes; larger cookies closer to 9 minutes). *Do not overbake.* Cool 2 minutes on baking sheets. Remove cookies to foil to cool completely, then frost and decorate, if desired.

Makes about 3 to 4 dozen cookies

Toffee-Top Cheesecake Bars

1¼ cups all-purpose flour
1 cup powdered sugar
½ cup unsweetened cocoa
¼ teaspoon baking soda
¾ cup (1½ sticks) butter or margarine
1 (8-ounce) package cream cheese, softened

1 (14-ounce) can EAGLE® BRAND Sweetened Condensed Milk (NOT evaporated milk)
2 eggs
1 teaspoon vanilla extract
1½ cups (8-ounce package) English toffee bits, divided

1. Preheat oven to 350°F. Combine flour, powdered sugar, cocoa and baking soda in medium bowl; cut in butter until mixture is crumbly. Press onto bottom of ungreased 13×9-inch baking pan. Bake 15 minutes.

2. Beat cream cheese until fluffy. Add Eagle Brand, eggs and vanilla; beat until smooth. Stir in 1 cup English toffee bits. Pour mixture over hot crust. Bake 25 minutes or until set and edges just begin to brown.

3. Remove from oven. Cool 15 minutes. Sprinkle remaining ½ cup English toffee bits evenly over top. Cool completely. Refrigerate several hours or until cold. Store leftovers covered in refrigerator.

Makes about 36 bars

Drop Sugar Cookies

2½ cups sifted all-purpose flour
½ teaspoon ARM & HAMMER® Baking Soda
¼ teaspoon salt
½ cup butter, softened

½ cup butter-flavored shortening
1 cup sugar
1 egg *or* ¼ cup egg substitute
1 teaspoon vanilla extract
2 teaspoons skim milk

Preheat oven to 400°F. Sift together flour, Baking Soda and salt; set aside. Beat butter and shortening in large bowl with electric mixer on medium speed until blended; add sugar gradually and continue beating until light and fluffy. Beat in egg and vanilla. Add flour mixture and beat until smooth; blend in milk. Drop dough by teaspoonfuls about 3 inches apart onto greased cookie sheets. Flatten with bottom of greased glass that has been dipped in sugar.

Bake 12 minutes or until edges are lightly browned. Cool on wire racks.

Makes about 5½ dozen cookies

Toffee-Top Cheesecake Bars

Autumn Leaves

1½ cups unsalted butter, softened	½ teaspoon salt
⅔ cup packed light brown sugar	⅛ teaspoon ground ginger
1 egg	⅛ teaspoon ground cloves
½ teaspoon vanilla	2 tablespoons unsweetened cocoa powder
3 cups all-purpose flour	Yellow, orange and red food colors
1 teaspoon ground cinnamon	¼ cup semisweet chocolate chips

1. Beat butter and brown sugar in large bowl with electric mixer at medium speed until light and fluffy. Beat in egg and vanilla. Add flour, cinnamon, salt, ginger and cloves; beat at low speed until well blended.

2. Divide dough into 5 equal sections; reserve 1 section. Stir cocoa into 1 section until well blended. Stir yellow food color into 1 section until well blended. Repeat with remaining 2 sections and orange and red food colors.

3. Preheat oven to 350°F. Lightly grease cookie sheets. Working with half of each dough color, press colors together lightly. Roll out dough on lightly floured surface to ¼-inch thickness. Cut out dough with leaf-shaped cookie cutters of various shapes and sizes. Place 2 inches apart on prepared cookie sheets. Repeat with remaining dough sections and scraps.

4. Bake 10 to 15 minutes or until edges are lightly browned. Remove to wire racks; cool completely.

5. Place chocolate chips in small resealable plastic food storage bag; seal. Microwave at HIGH 1 minute; knead bag lightly. Microwave at HIGH for additional 30-second intervals until chips are completely melted, kneading bag after each 30-second interval. Cut off very tiny corner of bag. Pipe chocolate onto cookies in vein patterns.   *Makes about 1½ dozen cookies*

Baker's® Premium Chocolate Chunk Cookies

1¾ cups flour
¾ teaspoon baking soda
¼ teaspoon salt
¾ cup (1½ sticks) butter or margarine, softened
½ cup granulated sugar

½ cup firmly packed brown sugar
1 egg
1 teaspoon vanilla
1 package (12 ounces) BAKER'S® Semi-Sweet Chocolate Chunks
1 cup chopped nuts (optional)

HEAT oven to 375°F.

MIX flour, baking soda and salt in medium bowl; set aside.

BEAT butter and sugars in large bowl with electric mixer on medium speed until light and fluffy. Add egg and vanilla; beat well. Gradually beat in flour mixture. Stir in chocolate chunks and nuts. Drop by heaping tablespoonfuls onto ungreased cookie sheets.

BAKE 11 to 13 minutes or just until golden brown. Cool on cookie sheets 1 minute. Remove to wire racks and cool completely.

Makes about 3 dozen cookies

Butterscotch Oat Bars

1¾ cups rolled oats
1½ cups all-purpose flour
¾ cup firmly packed light brown sugar
½ teaspoon baking soda

½ teaspoon salt
¾ cup CRISCO® Canola Oil
1 teaspoon vanilla
11 ounces butterscotch morsels

1. Heat oven to 350°F.

2. Combine oats, flour, sugar, baking soda and salt in large bowl; mix well. Add oil and vanilla; mix until well combined and crumbly. Add butterscotch morsels; mix evenly.

3. Spray 8-inch square baking pan with CRISCO® No-Stick Cooking Spray. Lightly press mixture into baking pan. Bake at 350°F for 17 to 20 minutes or until top is golden. Cool completely on cooling rack. Cut into bars.

Makes about 16 bars

Baker's® Premium Chocolate Chunk Cookies

Chocolate-Dipped Coconut Macaroons

1 package (14 ounces) BAKER'S® ANGEL
    FLAKE® Coconut (5⅓ cups)
⅔ cup sugar
6 tablespoons flour
¼ teaspoon salt

4 egg whites
1 teaspoon almond extract
1 package (8 squares) BAKER'S® Semi-
    Sweet Baking Chocolate, melted

HEAT oven to 325°F.

MIX coconut, sugar, flour and salt in large bowl. Stir in egg whites and almond extract until well blended. Drop by teaspoonfuls onto greased and floured cookie sheets.

BAKE 20 minutes or until edges of cookies are golden brown. Immediately remove from cookie sheets to wire racks and cool completely. Dip cookies halfway into melted chocolate. Let stand at room temperature or refrigerate on wax paper-lined tray 30 minutes or until chocolate is firm.

Makes about 3 dozen cookies

Oatmeal-Raisin Spice Cookies

½ cup granulated sugar
½ cup packed light brown sugar
⅓ cup Dried Plum Purée (recipe follows)
    or prepared dried plum butter *or* 1 jar
    (2½ ounces) first-stage baby food
    dried plums
¼ cup water
2 tablespoons nonfat milk

2 teaspoons vanilla
1 cup all-purpose flour
1½ teaspoons pumpkin pie spice
1 teaspoon baking soda
½ teaspoon salt
1½ cups rolled oats
½ cup golden or dark raisins

Preheat oven to 350°F. Coat baking sheets with vegetable cooking spray. In large bowl, whisk together sugars, Dried Plum Purée, water, milk and vanilla until mixture is creamy, about 1 minute. In medium bowl, combine flour, spice, baking soda and salt; stir into sugar mixture until well blended. Stir in oats and raisins. Spoon twelve mounds of dough onto prepared baking sheets, spacing 2 inches apart. Bake in center of oven 18 to 20 minutes or until set and golden brown. Remove from baking sheets to wire rack to cool completely. *Makes 12 large cookies*

Dried Plum Purée: Mix 1⅓ cups (8 ounces) pitted dried plums and 6 tablespoons hot water in container of food processor or blender. Pulse on and off until dried plums are finely chopped and smooth. Store leftovers in covered container in refrigerator for up to two months. Makes 1 cup.

Favorite recipe from **California Dried Plum Board**

Chocolate-Dipped Coconut Macaroons

Apple Golden Raisin Cheesecake Bars

1½ cups rolled oats
¾ cup all-purpose flour
½ cup firmly packed light brown sugar
¾ cup plus 2 tablespoons granulated sugar, divided
¾ cup Butter Flavor CRISCO® all-vegetable shortening or ¾ Butter Flavor CRISCO® Stick
2 (8-ounce) packages cream cheese, softened

2 large eggs
1 teaspoon vanilla
1 cup chopped Granny Smith apples
½ cup golden raisins
1 teaspoon almond extract
½ teaspoon ground cinnamon
¼ teaspoon ground nutmeg
¼ teaspoon ground allspice

1. Heat oven to 350°F.

2. Combine oats, flour, brown sugar and ¼ cup granulated sugar in large bowl; mix well. Cut in shortening with fork until crumbs form. Reserve 1 cup mixture.

3. Spray 13×9-inch baking pan with CRISCO® No-Stick Cooking Spray. Press remaining mixture onto bottom of prepared pan. Bake at 350°F for 12 to 15 minutes or until mixture is set. *Do not brown.* Place on cooling rack.

4. Combine cream cheese, eggs, ½ cup granulated sugar and vanilla in large bowl. Beat at medium speed with electric mixer until well blended. Spread evenly over crust.

5. Combine apples and raisins in medium bowl. Add almond extract; stir. Add 2 tablespoons sugar, cinnamon, nutmeg and allspice; mix well. Top cream cheese mixture evenly with apple mixture; sprinkle reserved oat mixture evenly over top. Bake at 350°F for 20 to 25 minutes or until top is golden. Place on cooling rack; cool completely. Cut into bars. *Makes 18 bars*

Kitchen Hint: Forgot to take the cream cheese out to soften? Don't worry, simply remove from wrapper and place in medium microwave-safe bowl. Microwave on MEDIUM (50% power) 15 to 20 seconds or until slightly softened.

Apple Golden Raisin Cheesecake Bars

Coconutty "M&M's"® Brownies

6 squares (1 ounce each) semi-sweet
    chocolate
¾ cup granulated sugar
½ cup (1 stick) butter
2 large eggs
1 tablespoon vegetable oil
1 teaspoon vanilla extract

1¼ cups all-purpose flour
3 tablespoons unsweetened cocoa powder
1 teaspoon baking powder
½ teaspoon salt
1½ cups "M&M's"® Chocolate Mini Baking
    Bits, divided
Coconut Topping (recipe follows)

Preheat oven to 350°F. Lightly grease 8×8×2-inch baking pan; set aside. In small saucepan combine chocolate, sugar and butter over low heat; stir constantly until chocolate is melted. Remove from heat; let cool slightly. In large bowl beat eggs, oil and vanilla; stir in chocolate mixture until well blended. In medium bowl combine flour, cocoa powder, baking powder and salt; add to chocolate mixture. Stir in 1 cup "M&M's"® Chocolate Mini Baking Bits. Spread batter evenly in prepared pan. Bake 35 to 40 minutes or until toothpick inserted in center comes out clean. Cool completely on wire rack. Prepare Coconut Topping. Spread over brownies; sprinkle with remaining ½ cup "M&M's"® Chocolate Mini Baking Bits. Cut into bars. Store in tightly covered container.

Makes 16 brownies

Coconut Topping

½ cup (1 stick) butter
⅓ cup firmly packed light brown sugar
⅓ cup light corn syrup
1 cup sweetened shredded coconut,
    toasted*

¾ cup chopped pecans
1 teaspoon vanilla extract

*To toast coconut, spread evenly on cookie sheet. Toast in preheated 350°F oven 7 to 8 minutes or until golden brown, stirring occasionally.

In large saucepan melt butter over medium heat; add brown sugar and corn syrup, stirring constantly until thick and bubbly. Remove from heat and stir in remaining ingredients.

Coconutty "M&M's"® Brownies

Double Almond Butter Cookies

Dough
2 cups butter, softened
2½ cups powdered sugar, divided
4 cups all-purpose flour
2 teaspoons vanilla

¼ cup packed light brown sugar
½ cup BLUE DIAMOND® Chopped
    Natural Almonds, toasted
¼ teaspoon vanilla

Filling
⅔ cup BLUE DIAMOND® Blanched
    Almond Paste

For dough, beat butter and 1 cup powdered sugar until smooth. Gradually beat in flour. Beat in 2 teaspoons vanilla. Chill dough ½ hour.

For filling, combine almond paste, brown sugar, almonds and ¼ teaspoon vanilla.

Preheat oven to 350°F. Shape dough around ½ teaspoon filling mixture to form 1-inch balls. Place on ungreased cookie sheets.

Bake 15 minutes. Cool on wire racks. Roll cookies in remaining 1½ cups powdered sugar or sift over cookies.

Makes about 8 dozen cookies

Maple Walnut Bars

1 package DUNCAN HINES® Moist
    Deluxe® Classic Yellow Cake Mix,
    divided
⅓ cup butter or margarine, melted
4 eggs, divided

1⅓ cups MRS. BUTTERWORTH® Maple
    Syrup
⅓ cup packed light brown sugar
½ teaspoon vanilla extract
1 cup chopped walnuts

Preheat oven to 350°F. Grease 13×9-inch pan.

Reserve ⅔ cup cake mix; set aside. Combine remaining cake mix, melted butter and 1 egg in large bowl. Stir until thoroughly blended. (Mixture will be crumbly.) Press into prepared pan. Bake 15 to 20 minutes or until light golden brown.

Combine reserved cake mix, maple syrup, remaining 3 eggs, sugar and vanilla extract in large mixing bowl. Beat at low speed with electric mixer for 3 minutes. Pour over crust. Sprinkle with walnuts. Bake 30 to 35 minutes or until filling is set. Cool completely in pan. Cut into bars. Store in refrigerator.

Makes 24 bars

Acknowledgments

The publisher would like to thank the companies and organizations listed below for the use of their recipes and photographs in this publication.

A.1.® Steak Sauce
Almond Board of California
American Lamb Council
Arm & Hammer Division, Church
   & Dwight Co., Inc.
Barilla America, Inc.
Birds Eye®
Blue Diamond Growers®
Bob Evans®
Butterball® Turkey Company
California Dried Plum Board
California Tree Fruit Agreement
Campbell Soup Company
Chef Paul Prudhomme's Magic Seasoning Blends®
Cherry Marketing Institute
CHIPS AHOY!® Chocolate Chip Cookies
Colorado Potato Administrative Committee
ConAgra Foods®
Del Monte Corporation
Dole Food Company, Inc.
Domino® Foods, Inc.
Duncan Hines® and Moist Deluxe® are registered
   trademarks of Aurora Foods Inc.
Eagle® Brand
Equal® sweetener
Filippo Berio® Olive Oil
Fleischmann's® Original Spread
Fleischmann's® Yeast
The Fremont Company, Makers of Frank's
   & SnowFloss Kraut and Tomato Products
The Golden Grain Company®
Grandma's® is a registered trademark of Mott's, Inc.
GREY POUPON® Dijon Mustard
Hershey Foods Corporation
The Hidden Valley® Food Products Company
Hillshire Farm®
Holland House® is a registered trademark of
   Mott's, Inc.
HONEY MAID® Honey Grahams
Hormel Foods, LLC
Idaho Potato Commission
Kahlúa® Liqueur
Keebler® Company
Kikkoman International Inc.

Kraft Foods Holdings
Lawry's® Foods, Inc.
© Mars, Incorporated 2003
Mauna La'i® is a registered trademark of Mott's, Inc.
McIlhenny Company (TABASCO® brand
   Pepper Sauce)
Minnesota Cultivated Wild Rice Council
Mott's® is a registered trademark of Mott's, Inc.
Nabisco Biscuit and Snack Division
National Fisheries Institute
National Honey Board
National Onion Association
National Pork Board
National Turkey Federation
Nestlé USA
Newman's Own, Inc.®
North Dakota Beef Commission
North Dakota Wheat Commission
Northwest Cherry Growers
OREO® Chocolate Sandwich Cookies
Peanut Advisory Board
Perdue Farms Incorporated
PLANTERS® Nuts
The Quaker® Oatmeal Kitchens
Reckitt Benckiser
RED STAR® Yeast, a product of
   Lasaffre Yeast Corporation
Reddi-wip® is a registered trademark of
   ConAgra Brands, Inc.
RITZ® Crackers
Riviana Foods Inc.
The J.M. Smucker Company
Sonoma® Dried Tomatoes
StarKist® Seafood Company
The Sugar Association, Inc.
Sunkist Growers, Inc.
Tyson Foods, Inc.
Uncle Ben's Inc.
Unilever Bestfoods North America
USA Rice Federation
Veg-All®
Walnut Marketing Board
Washington Apple Commission
Wisconsin Milk Marketing Board

Index

METRIC CONVERSION CHART

VOLUME MEASUREMENTS (dry)

1/8 teaspoon = 0.5 mL
1/4 teaspoon = 1 mL
1/2 teaspoon = 2 mL
3/4 teaspoon = 4 mL
1 teaspoon = 5 mL
1 tablespoon = 15 mL
2 tablespoons = 30 mL
1/4 cup = 60 mL
1/3 cup = 75 mL
1/2 cup = 125 mL
2/3 cup = 150 mL
3/4 cup = 175 mL
1 cup = 250 mL
2 cups = 1 pint = 500 mL
3 cups = 750 mL
4 cups = 1 quart = 1 L

VOLUME MEASUREMENTS (fluid)

1 fluid ounce (2 tablespoons) = 30 mL
4 fluid ounces (1/2 cup) = 125 mL
8 fluid ounces (1 cup) = 250 mL
12 fluid ounces (1 1/2 cups) = 375 mL
16 fluid ounces (2 cups) = 500 mL

WEIGHTS (mass)

1/2 ounce = 15 g
1 ounce = 30 g
3 ounces = 90 g
4 ounces = 120 g
8 ounces = 225 g
10 ounces = 285 g
12 ounces = 360 g
16 ounces = 1 pound = 450 g

DIMENSIONS

1/16 inch = 2 mm
1/8 inch = 3 mm
1/4 inch = 6 mm
1/2 inch = 1.5 cm
3/4 inch = 2 cm
1 inch = 2.5 cm

OVEN TEMPERATURES

250°F = 120°C
275°F = 140°C
300°F = 150°C
325°F = 160°C
350°F = 180°C
375°F = 190°C
400°F = 200°C
425°F = 220°C
450°F = 230°C

BAKING PAN SIZES

Utensil	Size in Inches/Quarts	Metric Volume	Size in Centimeters
Baking or	8×8×2	2 L	20×20×5
Cake Pan	9×9×2	2.5 L	23×23×5
(square or	12×8×2	3 L	30×20×5
rectangular)	13×9×2	3.5 L	33×23×5
Loaf Pan	8×4×3	1.5 L	20×10×7
	9×5×3	2 L	23×13×7
Round Layer	8×1½	1.2 L	20×4
Cake Pan	9×1½	1.5 L	23×4
Pie Plate	8×1¼	750 mL	20×3
	9×1¼	1 L	23×3
Baking Dish	1 quart	1 L	—
or Casserole	1½ quart	1.5 L	—
	2 quart	2 L	—